THE POET-PHYSICIAN

The Poet-Physician

Keats and Medical Science

DONALD C. GOELLNICHT

UNIVERSITY OF PITTSBURGH PRESS

Published by the University of Pittsburgh Press, Pittsburgh, PA 15260
Copyright 1984, University of Pittsburgh Press
All rights reserved
Feffer and Simons, Inc., London
Manufactured in the United States of America

Library of Congress Cataloging in Publication Data

Goellnicht, Donald C., 1953–
  The poet-physician.

  Bibliography: p. 271.
  Includes index.
  1. Keats, John, 1795–1821—Knowledge—Medicine.
  2. Medicine in literature.   I. Title.
  PR4838.M4G63   1984   821'.7   83–47618
  ISBN 0–8229–3807–3

Cover decoration is from *Pictorial Archive of Printer's Ornaments from the Renaissance to the 20th Century,* selected by Carol Belanger Grafton (New York: Dover Publications, Inc., 1980).

For Susan

"If it please,
Majestic shadow, tell me: sure not all
Those melodies sung into the world's ear
Are useless: sure a poet is a sage;
A humanist, physician to all men."

Contents

Preface

T *his* book examines the influence of Keats's medical training and knowledge on his poems and letters, an influence that has usually been ignored or denied. Although a fair amount of attention has been focused on the immediate biographical facts of Keats's five-year apprenticeship to the surgeon Thomas Hammond and his year of training at Guy's Hospital, very little has been paid to the influence of medical science on his thought; no comprehensive study of such influence has been attempted previously.

Because a certain amount of confusion still surrounds the details of Keats's personal experiences as a medical student, the first chapter examines the biographical facts of his training. In addition, it outlines the state of medical education in the early nineteenth century, generally in England and specifically at Guy's Hospital. The subsequent chapters trace the influence of Keats's medical knowledge on his thought, a single chapter being devoted to each of the subjects Keats studied as a medical student: chemistry, botany, anatomy and physiology, and pathology and medicine. In each case, specific images and metaphors, as well as broader ideas and attitudes, are examined in the poems and letters. Throughout, my purpose has been to enhance our understanding of the poetry and correspondence, to illuminate some of the dark passages of Keats's thought.

During the preparation of this book I have been assisted by a number of individuals and institutions to whom I owe debts of

Preface

gratitude. First, I am happy to acknowledge the generous advice and valuable criticism given by Professor Joan Coldwell at each stage of the project's development, from its original inception as a doctoral dissertation (which she supervised) at McMaster University in 1978 to its final revisions for publication. I am also grateful to those who have taken the time and care to read the manuscript and have offered important suggestions: Professors W. J. B. Owen and Brian John of McMaster University, Professor Walter H. Evert of the University of Pittsburgh, and Professor Stuart M. Sperry of Indiana University.

For assistance in obtaining research material, I am grateful to the staffs of the following libraries: Keats House, Hampstead, in particular Mrs. Christina Gee and Ms. Maggie Van Reenan; the Wellcome Institute for the History of Medicine, London; the Wills Library, Guy's Hospital, London; the Thomas Fisher Rare Book Library and the John Robarts Library, University of Toronto; the Mills Memorial Library and the Health Sciences Library, McMaster University. I am also grateful to the Social Sciences and Humanities Research Council of Canada and to McMaster University, generally for support during my doctoral studies, and specifically for travel and research grants that enabled me to work at libraries in England during the summer of 1979.

On a more personal note, I wish to thank the two teachers who introduced me to the Romantic poets: Brother Lawrence of Presentation College, San Fernando, Trinidad, and Professor F. S. Colwell of Queen's University, Kingston, Ontario. To my parents, who have encouraged me in all my academic endeavors, I owe special thanks.

Finally, my deepest gratitude goes to my wife, Susan Chang-Hong, who not only performed the onerous task of typing the manuscript through various drafts, but also has given constant support and encouragement during its lengthy preparation.

THE POET-PHYSICIAN

Introduction

To undertake a study that involves poetry and science is perhaps daring; to do so with a Romantic poet, and especially with Keats, who is often still acclaimed as preeminently a poet of the senses and of the imagination, is to invite scholarly controversy. After all, Blake's claim that "Art is the Tree of Life . . . Science is the Tree of Death" and Wordsworth's comment about the "contradistinction . . . of Poetry and Science" have helped to define our view of the age.[1] Yet any close and comprehensive reading of Romantic poetry reveals that, in branding the period the era of imagination, of anti-intellectualism and of total revolt against the eighteenth-century Age of Reason, we were seeing Romanticism with tunnel vision. This narrow view has been seriously challenged, although by no means completely overthrown, in the last twenty years as critics have increasingly come to recognize the intellectual significance of Romantic thought.

The temptation still exists, however, to trot out neat little catch phrases as so much fodder for the minds of students; with Keats the ones paraded most frequently remain: "I am certain of nothing but of the holiness of the Heart's affections and the truth of Imagination—What the imagination seizes as Beauty must be truth— . . . I have never yet been able to perceive how any thing can be known for truth by consequitive reasoning— . . . O for a Life of Sensations rather than of Thoughts!" (*Letters* 1:184–85).[2] This, the most famous of Keats's letters, has formulated his thoughts for many readers, and it is much more convenient, much more facile, to accept a neat formula than to discover complexities and contradictions.

3

In addition, distinguished critics have supported the view that the Romantic poets were antirational and antiscientific. Douglas Bush, for example, writes, in his chapter "The Romantic Revolt Against Rationalism":

The romantic theory of poetry enlarged and deepened what seemed to be the narrow and shallow limits of neo-classical and scientific rationality. . . . The rich stream of classical myth and symbol, which had flowed through Spenser and Shakespeare and Milton, had been dried up, or rather driven underground, by the scientific rationalism of the Augustan age, but it emerged, in the benign air of romantic idealism, to inspire nostalgia in Coleridge and more than nostalgia in Wordsworth. . . . [Romantic poetry] does not call imagination to the help of reason, but conceives of imagination as above reason, or as reason in its highest form of intuition. And, since reason is superseded or transcended by the senses and imagination, the poetry of rational statement more or less gives way to the poetry of image, symbol, and suggestion. . . . one main impulse in romanticism is the conscious and subconscious revolt against the Newtonian universe and the spirit of science.[3]

Of Keats, Bush says, "The only one of the romantic poets who had a scientific training was Keats, but his poetic themes and creed rarely admitted the medical, and in fact most of the images that might be called scientific are astronomical."[4]

Bush's view is one-sided and narrow, yet for years it remained the dominant approach to the relationship between Romanticism and science. Even M. H. Abrams, whose chapter "Science and Poetry in Romantic Criticism" is much more comprehensive in elucidating the subtle and complex relationship between these two fields of endeavor, states: "Keats was one among the lovers of poetry to whom it seemed that matter of fact of science is not only the opposite but the enemy of poetry, in a war in which the victory, even the survival, of poetry is far from certain."[5]

Of course, there is ample evidence in Keats's poetry and letters to support such a claim. Both Bush and Abrams direct us to the oft-quoted toast of "confusion to mathematics" that Keats and Lamb drank at Haydon's "immortal dinner," where they asserted that Newton "had destroyed all the poetry of the rainbow by reducing it to the prismatic colours."[6] In addition, they, and many other critics, quote Keats's comment on science, or "philosophy," in *Lamia*:

> Do not all charms fly
> At the mere touch of cold philosophy?
> There was an awful rainbow once in heaven:
> We know her woof, her texture; she is given
> In the dull catalogue of common things.
> Philosophy will clip an Angel's wings,
> Conquer all mysteries by rule and line,
> Empty the haunted air, and gnomed mine—
> Unweave a rainbow, as it erewhile made
> The tender-person'd Lamia melt into a shade.
>
> (II, 229–38)[7]

It would be obtuse to deny that Keats utters such antiscientific, anti-intellectual, antirational sentiments, or to claim that they do not form an extremely important part of his thinking on art and creativity. Yet to cease an investigation of his attitude toward science with such quotations is to give only a partial picture. There are passages in the poetry and letters, less frequently quoted than these, that show another side of the poet, a side interested in "philosophy" and "knowledge."

In "Lines on Seeing a Lock of Milton's Hair," Keats states that "Pangs are in vain—until I grow high-rife / With old philosophy" (29–30), and on 24 April 1818 he writes to Taylor:

I was purposing to travel over the north this Summer—there is but one thing to prevent me—I know nothing I have read nothing and I mean to follow Solomon's directions of 'get Wisdom—get understanding'—I find cavalier days are gone by. I find that I can have no enjoyment in the World but continual drinking of Knowledge— . . . I have been hovering for some time between an exquisite sense of the luxurious and a love for Philosophy—were I calculated for the former I should be glad—but as I am not I shall turn all my soul to the latter. (*Letters* 1:271)

Lest we think that by "Philosophy" and "Knowledge" Keats means only metaphysics, one other passage, in his letter to Reynolds of 3 May 1818, should be examined:

Every department of knowledge we see excellent and calculated towards a great whole. I am so convinced of this, that I am glad at not having given away my medical Books, which I shall again look over to keep alive the little I know thitherwards. . . . An extensive knowledge is needful to thinking people—it takes away the heat and fever; and helps, by widening speculation, to ease the Burden of the Mystery.

(*Letters* 1:277)

This is a far cry from his earlier desire for sensations without thoughts and from the thrush's message to "fret not after knowledge" (*Letters* 1:233). It also shows that, for Keats, "knowledge" or "philosophy" includes medical science, and that knowledge is a necessary part of his more mature vision of the poet.

Increasing attention has been paid, in the last two decades, to Keats's desire for "philosophy" and "knowledge" as critics have become more aware of the intellectual capabilities of Romantic poets generally. Previously, however, when critics examined Keats's interest in "philosophy," their object was usually to demonstrate that he was intellectually immature or that he was moving in the wrong direction. They attempted to prove that his best poetry is sensual and that intellectualism led to inferior verse.[8]

Since the publication of works by scholars like C. D. Thorpe, Bernard Blackstone, and Earl Wasserman, this approach has been modified; there has been a much sharper critical focus on Keats's thought and a general debunking of the old attitude that Keats is simply a superb coiner of beautiful poetic phrases and narratives. Old attitudes are not easily laid to rest, however, and the fact remains that of the major Romantic poets, Keats is still portrayed as the least academic or intellectual in a formal sense, while his knowledge of science has been largely ignored by literary scholars.[9]

Critics who either take the position that Keats is antiscientific and anti-intellectual, or ignore his scientific knowledge and his desire for philosophy, tend to forget that the only formal advanced training Keats ever had was in science, or what was commonly called "natural philosophy." For six years of his brief life, from the summer of 1810 to the summer of 1816, Keats studied medicine, first as an apprentice in Edmonton and then as a medical student at Guy's Hospital in London. This period is equal in duration to that of his poetic creativity, from 1814 to 1820, yet his biographers have generally skimmed over it and literary critics have usually ignored or even denied the influence of his medical training on this thought.[10] This has been a grave oversight, for medical knowledge provided Keats not only with specific images and concepts that found their way into his poetry and letters, but also with ideas and attitudes that influenced his broader outlook on life.

In approaching Keats's poetry and letters from the perspective of his medical background, I am exploring an additional way of interpreting his work. I do not claim, however, that this is the only, or even the most rewarding, approach. A mind as literary as Keats's obviously is largely influenced by literary sources, but it seems impossible to deny that a mind as eclectic as his would also be influenced by the medical knowledge which took six years of his life to acquire. Of course, it is often difficult to say that some idea or image in the poetry or letters is exclusively literary or exclusively medical, and every scholar who works in the field of sources and influences should heed Wordsworth's warning:

> But who shall parcel out
> His intellect by geometric rules,
> Split like a province into round and square?
> Who knows the individual hour in which
> His habits were first sown, even as a seed?
> Who that shall point as with a wand and say
> "This portion of the river of my mind
> Came from yon fountain?"   (*Prelude*, II, 203–10)

Bearing such limitations in mind, I will attempt to demonstrate that Keats's medical knowledge was indeed one of the fountains that flowed into the river of his poetic mind, bringing with it ideas and images that often mingle with those from other sources, but that also sometimes remain distinct and independent. Where mingling occurs, however, it is usually impossible, because of the range and focus of this study, to indicate or elaborate upon every other influence or source that has been cited in interpreting specific images or ideas, although some attempt is made to point out the widely accepted or conventional interpretations. Sometimes the new information gained from Keats's medical background complements those conventional interpretations; at other times it contradicts them; at others still it illuminates passages of Keats's poetry and letters that critics have ignored or explained away with the excuse that the vocabulary or images are examples of his idiosyncratic means of expression, when in fact they are often adapted from medical science.

The reason that the influence of medical science on Keats's poetry and letters has not been fully documented is quite simply that the literary critics, with a few notable exceptions, lack the necessary medical knowledge to appreciate such influence. This is coupled with the fact that the Shelleyan and Pre-Raphaelite myth of Keats as a delicate, romantic spirit, which is incongruous with the portrait of Keats as a doctor, has died very hard.

Although I do not apologize for this lack of knowledge on the part of critics, I should point out that early nineteenth-century medicine is very different from modern medicine, and textbooks of the period are often rare and difficult to consult. Much of the information pertinent to Keats's medical training—the lectures he attended at Guy's Hospital, for example—exists only in manuscript form, and some books are extant in only a few copies.

It is perhaps not surprising that critics have overlooked much of Keats's medical knowledge when his biographers have paid so little attention to it, at least until fairly recently. Of the three important nineteenth-century biographers, Brown covers the medical training, which accounts for six years of Keats's life, in two pages, although what he has to say about it is very valuable;[11] Monckton Milnes has one sentence on the apprenticeship and one paragraph on the year at Guy's, in which he stresses only Keats's dislike of medicine;[12] and Rossetti devotes all of two pages of his biography to Keats's medical training, much of which is incorrect, designed to support the Pre-Raphaelite view that Keats was far too romantic, spiritual, and delicate ever to dissect bodies or mix medicines.[13]

Keats's medical training did not fare much better among biographers in the first half of this century. Sidney Colvin's huge *Life* devotes only seventeen pages to Keats's years with Hammond and at Guy's, with much erroneous information.[14] Amy Lowell, in her imaginative style, expands on this somewhat so that we get a slightly fuller coverage of the year at Guy's;[15] and Dorothy Hewlett gives us less than Lowell, although her facts are virtually the same.[16]

In fairness to these literary biographers, however, it should be observed that the medical men who have written on Keats—and there have been many—have not provided much more, or more accurate, information. Doctors, especially from Guy's, have always taken a strong interest and great pride in Keats as one of their own, so that numerous articles have been written by members of the profession on this aspect of Keats's life, some dating from the nineteenth century. Disappointingly, most of these articles have been derivative, often adopting their information from the literary biographies, so that they have added little to our understanding;[17] surprisingly, some of their ideas and "facts" concerning training at Guy's when Keats was there have been incorrect.

Such interest in Keats by the medical profession has resulted in two book-length studies of his training and illness. The first, which is probably the best known, is entitled *Keats as Doctor and Patient* by Sir William Hale-White, himself a Guy's man.[18] Hale-White's study is important because it sparked general interest in Keats's medical background, although some of his information has since proved wrong. The other study, which at times is so speculative as to border on fiction, and which adds little information to Hale-White's, is Walter Wells's *A Doctor's Life of John Keats*.

The first and only full-length study of Keats's medical training by a literary critic is Charles Hagelman's doctoral dissertation, "John Keats and the Medical Profession." Hagelman's study, which carefully examines and weighs the relevant evidence, dispels many misconceptions about Keats's medical training and provides much new information, some of which has found its way into public understanding through Aileen Ward's *John Keats: The Making of a Poet*.[19] Together with Ward, Bate has given a fair treatment of Keats's apprenticeship and year at Guy's,[20] but the only literary biographer who remains committed to a comprehensive understanding of the poet's medical training is Robert Gittings. In various articles,[21] as well as in his biography

John Keats,[22] Gittings has reinterpreted old material and un-
covered new until he has given us the most accurate picture of
Keats the medical student. I must state my indebtedness to his
and to Hagelman's work, without which a study such as mine
would have been much more difficult.

If biographical studies of Keats's medical background have
usually been unsatisfactory, critical studies of how that back-
ground influenced his poems and letters have been scarce.
Apart from a few minor notes,[23] the only studies in this area are
Pettit's article, "Scientific Correlatives of Keats' *Ode to Psyche,*"
Hagelman's article, "Keats's Medical Training and the Last
Stanza of the 'Ode to Psyche,' "[24] and Stuart Sperry's excellent
article "Keats and the Chemistry of Poetic Creation."[25] Many
critics have written on Keats's use of Robert Burton's *Anatomy of
Melancholy,*[26] and both Bernard Blackstone[27] and Desmond
King-Hele[28] have discussed the influence on Keats's poetry of
Erasmus Darwin's quasi-scientific poetry, which deals mainly
with botany. These studies, however, tend to be literary rather
than medical in focus, and Blackstone admits that he knows
little of Keats's medical background.

Although the prevailing attitude among critics is no longer the
traditional one that Keats was anti-intellectual—a shift that has
resulted in great interest in his knowledge of philosophy,
religion, politics, and so on—his scientific knowledge has not
yet been fully understood or documented. Many readers and
critics still think of Keats as being antiscientific,[29] and he himself
tended to propagate this view with his comments on Newton
and his prism. But as we have seen, Keats came to realize, as he
matured, that "philosophy," which includes science, was as
important to the poet as "sensations," and he was ultimately
glad that he had not given away his medical books. We too must
try to understand what was in those medical books if we are
to comprehend and appreciate fully his poetry and thought.
Unless we attempt to do so, we will miss an important aspect
of Keats's intellectual milieu.

Finally, in tackling a subject that involves both poetry and
science, it is helpful to remember that, despite some of the
statements made by Romantic poets, many thinkers in the early
nineteenth century still viewed the two fields of endeavor as

related or similar. For example, William Harvey, the great physiologist, states:

> On the same terms . . . as art is attained to, is all knowledge and science acquired; for as art is a habit with reference to things to be done, so is science a habit in respect to things to be known; as that proceeds from the imitation of types or forms, so this proceeds from the knowledge of natural things. Each has its origins in sense and experience, and it is impossible that there can rightly be either art or science without visible instance or example.[30]

And Sir Humphry Davy, the renowned chemist and good friend of Coleridge, comments:

> In the truths of the natural sciences there is, perhaps, a nearer analogy to the productions of the refined arts. The contemplation of the laws of the universe is connected with an immediate tranquil exaltation of mind, and pure mental enjoyment. The perception of truth is almost as simple a feeling as the perception of beauty; and the genius of Newton, of Shakespeare, of Michael Angelo, and of Handel, are not very remote in character from each other. Imagination, as well as reason, is necessary to perfection in the philosophical mind. A rapidity of combination, a power of perceiving analogies, and of comparing them by facts, is the creative source of discovery. Discrimination and delicacy of sensation, so important in physical research, are other words for taste; and the love of nature is the same passion, as the love of the magnificent, the sublime, and the beautiful.[31]

Keats may not often agree with these sentiments in his overt statements, as his diatribes against "consequitive reasoning" illustrate; yet in his own artistic endeavors he made use of images, ideas, and sometimes even the approach, the method of conceiving of things, that he learned during his medical studies. Ultimately, in *The Fall of Hyperion*, he described the poet as a physician, thus illustrating that he did not view the two subjects to which he devoted his life, first medicine and then poetry, as totally divorced.

CHAPTER I

Biography

It is impossible to trace how Keats's medical training influences his poetry and thought without first gaining a comprehensive understanding of the nature of that training. Such an understanding involves not only details of Keats's personal career, but also a broader awareness of the state of medical education in the early nineteenth century.

Keats's medical training probably began, indirectly, at John Clarke's Enfield school, where he was sent by his parents at the age of seven.[1] His parents had had ambitious dreams of sending their sons to Harrow, where the traditional education focused almost exclusively on Latin and Greek. Luckily for Keats, Clarke's school was modern, progressive, and liberal, modeled after the Nonconformist schools of the period.[2] Like most liberals, Clarke believed in the importance of science, and he counted among his friends Joseph Priestley, the greatest English chemist of his time.[3] It is interesting to note that two of the prizes Keats won at Clarke's school were Bonnycastle's *Introduction to Astronomy* and Kauffman's *Dictionary of Merchandize*, which deals extensively with minerals and other commodities of chemical origin.

Lowell points out that, as well as Latin and French, Clarke taught the "rudiments of science—astronomy, geology, botany probably, possibly a little physics."[4] Botany seems more definite than probable, however, judging from Charles Cowden Clarke's description of his father's school: "From the playground stretched a garden, one hundred yards in length, where in one corner were some small plots set aside for certain boys fond of having a garden of their own that they might cultivate according to their individual will and pleasure."⁵ Whether Keats was one of these boys we will never know, although his knowledge of botany suggests such an interest. He would certainly have participated in the half-holiday excursions, or field trips, on nearby Enfield Chase and into Epping Forest, both rich in flora and fauna.⁶ Murchie speculates that "probably this was the spot where John developed his fondness for 'Goldfinches, Tomtits, Minnows, Mice, Ticklebacks, Dace, Cock salmons and all the whole tribe of the Bushes and the Brooks', as he remembered to tell his sister in March 1819."⁷ In the letter to which Murchie refers, Keats demonstrates that, unlike Wordsworth who as a boy was enamored of, and awed by, the grandeur of nature, he was developing from an early age the scientist's interest in collecting and classifying specimens and in learning their names and characteristics. No doubt this interest was encouraged in Clarke's school along with the cultivation of vegetable gardens. In any case, Keats's firsthand knowledge of the fauna, and especially of the flora, would stand him in good stead when he came to study for an apothecary, one of whose functions was the concocting of medicines from plants. In addition, this interest in botany probably helped to cultivate Keats's sense of natural beauty, for Charles Brown points out that "from his earliest boyhood Keats had an acute sense of beauty, whether in a flower, a tree, the sky, or the animal world."⁸

In all previous biographies, including those by Hewlett, Bate, Ward, and Hagelman, it was assumed that Keats left school at Midsummer in 1811.⁹ Gittings has shown, however, that Midsummer 1810 is a far more likely date, since the strict ruling of the new Apothecaries Act of 1815 required a student to complete a five-year apprenticeship before beginning studies at a recognized hospital.¹⁰ When Keats registered at Guy's Hospital in October 1815 he produced the required testimonial from Hammond, his master, stating that he had completed the compulsory five-year term.

Whether and why Keats voluntarily took up medicine as a career have always been contentious issues. Medical men writing on Keats have assumed that he was forced into an apprenticeship against his will by his guardian, Richard Abbey.[11] This idea is a result of the Pre-Raphaelite view of Keats as a delicate spirit destined from birth for a poetic career, and it is not based on any fact. Literary biographers have given a similar version of the story, although they usually state that Keats acquiesced in, or at least did not object to, Abbey's suggestion of surgery as a suitable career for a middle-class boy.[12] Until Gittings, Hewlett was the only biographer to suggest that "it seems . . . unlikely that a boy of Keats's spirit would submit tamely to enter a profession he hated." She concludes, therefore, that "it seems probable that Keats had a genuine wish to become a doctor, and that it was not until he knew himself to be a poet that he decided to abandon the profession."[13]

Keats himself makes no statements about the choice of medicine, or about his apprenticeship, apart from his famous remark concerning the quarrel with Hammond.[14] The only contemporary comments we have come from Cowden Clarke:

When he left Enfield, at fourteen years of age, he was apprenticed to Mr. Thomas Hammond, a medical man residing in Church Street, Edmonton. . . . This arrangement evidently gave him satisfaction, and I fear that it was the most placid period of his painful life. . . .

In one of our conversations, about this period, I alluded to his position at St. Thomas's Hospital . . . for the purpose of discovering what progress he was making in his profession; which I had taken for granted had been his own selection, and not one chosen for him.[15]

Although these statements are inconclusive, they do suggest that Keats's choice of a career was his own, and all the circumstantial evidence points to his desire to be a doctor.

There are a number of possible reasons why Keats chose medicine as a career. First, in his last eighteen months at Clarke's school, from January 1809 to Midsummer 1810, his attitude toward life and work had undergone a dramatic change. According to Clarke, "In the early part of his school-life John gave no extraordinary indications of intellectual character,"[16] preferring sports and fighting; however, "during the last 12 months of his residence at Enfield one feature of his character came forth in full strength; his resolution and constancy. He determined to carry off all the first prizes in literature; and I think he succeeded throughout."[17] Keats's dedication to hard work reveals a general desire to succeed in life and a seriousness of purpose that prepared him to make a decision about his career at fourteen, a usual age for a boy of that period to decide on his future.

Even more important in coming to a decision, however, was the fact that Keats had spent the Christmas holidays of 1809–10 nursing his beloved mother, who was gravely ill with consumption. Haydon relates how Keats, apparently convinced that the medicines prescribed by Hammond, the surgeon, could save his mother, reserved the right of administering them for himself only. He cooked her meals, sat up nursing her at night, and read novels to her.[18] His efforts were to no avail, however, and in March 1810 she died, the fourth close relative who had died in the last six years: his father in 1804, his grandfather in 1805, his Uncle Midgley in 1807, and now his mother in 1810.

We know from Holmes's account that the death of his mother was a devastating blow to Keats and that he gave way to "impassioned prolonged grief."[19] It has often been observed that this loss matured Keats emotionally; I am convinced that it also intensified his desire to heal the sick, which resulted a few months later, in the summer of 1810, in his decision to become an apothecary-surgeon. Never a defeatist, he was determined more than ever to conquer disease, and his generally highminded and generous nature, attested to by Cowden Clarke, Brown, and Dilke,[20] found in medicine a specific means of helping others. For Keats, medicine offered a practical application of his new sense of purpose and of his altruistic ideals.

Medicine was, at the time, a varied profession, ranging from the apothecary to the physician. Training for the latter was out of the question for Keats, since it involved long years of very expensive study at a university. One could become an apothecary-surgeon, however, through an apprenticeship, the premium of which was within the range of Keats's financial legacy. A good apothecary-surgeon could make a fine living and become a respected citizen; it was an excellent choice for a middle-class boy, and Abbey probably agreed readily, especially since Keats already had a grounding in science and

Latin. Moreover, an apprenticeship with an Edmonton surgeon would allow him to remain near the only home he now had, his grandmother's, where his little sister, Fanny, was living. It was also near to Cowden Clarke, his closest friend. This was a much more attractive choice than going to London to work in Abbey's counting-house, the route taken by his two brothers, especially since Keats may have already disliked Abbey and was never interested in trade and finance.[21]

Having made up his mind, Keats was apprenticed for five years to Thomas Hammond of Edmonton, the apothecary-surgeon who had attended his mother and the students at Clarke's school. His premium was £210, which covered his room and board—he lived with Hammond at Wilston on Church Street, near to his grandmother's—as well as his training. In return Keats promised to fulfill a number of negative injunctions, including not to marry, not to gamble, and not to visit taverns or playhouses during his apprenticeship.

Little has been written about Keats's years as Hammond's apprentice, and much of that has been concerned with his introduction to poetry on his weekly afternoon off, spent with Cowden Clarke at Enfield.[22] In addition, biographers inevitably relate the only two incidents concerning this period of Keats's life that we know about. The first is the story told by R. H. Horne that, while a student at Clarke's school, he was dared to throw a snowball at Keats, who was sitting in Hammond's gig outside the school, waiting while Hammond attended a student. The fact that Horne gives a second, much romanticized version of the same story that is ludicrously hindsighted throws doubt on its validity,[23] but it does show that the apothecary's apprentice performed the duties of a servant in looking after his master's horses. Keats and Hammond's other apprentice were probably also responsible for keeping the surgery clean, ensuring that the medicine jars were well stocked, and delivering medicines to patients.

The second incident from this period about which we know is Keats's statement that in September 1819 it was seven years since his hand had "clench'd itself against Hammond" (*Letters* 2:208). Although it is generally accepted that, as Cowden Clarke says, "Keats's tastes [were] totally opposed to his master's,"[24] there is no evidence to support the wild claims that Keats broke off his apprenticeship with Hammond after their quarrel. Although the quarrel itself should not be surprising, given Keats's pugnacious nature, it did not, if Keats's dates are correct, lead to a break with Hammond in 1812.[25] George Keats's detailed discussion of Keats's expenses indicates, however, that Keats ceased to lodge with Hammond sometime during the apprenticeship and that his brother Tom, who had left Abbey's counting-house, lived with Keats, presumably in Edmonton.[26] Whether Keats left over a quarrel or to be with Tom we do not know.

Other statements about these years of Keats's life include Reynolds's claim that Keats "never referred to them, except to express his regret that he had undergone 'a one of them,'"[27] which was probably Keats's retrospective reaction when he found that medicine interfered with poetry; Taylor's claim that Hammond "did not . . . conduct himself as Mr. A[bbey] conceived he ought to have done to his young Pupil,"[28] which may indicate that Keats had reason to argue with Hammond; and Colvin's claim that a fellow apprentice said Keats was "an idle loafing fellow, always writing poetry,"[29] which without a cited source might be considered doubtful, especially since Brown says that before his eighteenth birthday, Keats's "leisure hours, which were few, had not been occupied in reading works of imagination; neither had he attempted, nor thought of writing a single line."[30]

The point to be emphasized, however, is that none of these statements tells us anything about Keats's duties as an apprentice, and most biographers give us little more. But before we can understand Keats's duties, a more detailed understanding of the medical profession is necessary.

The medical profession was divided into three areas: physicians, surgeons, and apothecaries. The physicians were men with degrees from Edinburgh, Cambridge, or Oxford, which gave them the title of "doctor" and the right to join the professional associations called "Colleges of Physicians." They were usually from wealthy families, and their high fees put their services out of the reach of the vast majority of the population. Moreover, although the Edinburgh College of Physicians had become involved in practical medical education during the eighteenth century, the London College of Physicians showed no such interest:

> The College remained a close corporation concerned with bolstering its own privileges rather than advancing education. . . . Close links were, of course, maintained with Oxford and Cambridge . . . but as medicine was hardly taught as a subject at either Oxford or Cambridge, such degrees were little indication of medical ability. This exclusive commitment to a system of medical education which both in form and content was outmoded meant that the College of Physicians as a body showed no interest in the teaching of clinical medicine in the London hospitals.[31]

While the physicians were looking after themselves and the wealthy, the care of the lower and middle classes, and the teaching of clinical medicine, were left to the surgeons and apothecaries who were, to all intents and purposes, the general practitioners of the nation.

The surgeons, whose medieval function had been blood letting, were joined with the barbers in the Guild of Barbers and Surgeons until in 1745 they separated to form the Corporation of Surgeons; in 1800 the Royal College of Surgeons of England was formed and granted a charter. The College of Surgeons took over the licensing functions from the corporation and examined candidates before they were granted licenses to practice as surgeons.

Unlike the surgeons, apothecaries did not need a license to practice. Originally they had been members of the medieval Guild of Grocers, but during a long and controversial evolution they had ceased simply to compound drugs and had become full-fledged general practitioners with the empirical ability to examine patients, diagnose diseases, and compound and administer remedies, much to the chagrin of the physicians.[32] As the duties of the apothecaries became more general, their overseeing body, the Worshipful Society of Apothecaries, ceased simply to police the administering of drugs and, by the late eighteenth century, had come to regard the education of apprentices as its chief duty.[33] To this end, and in order to gain the recognition they deserved, the society began petitioning for a licensing examination for apothecaries by the beginning of the nineteenth century.

The training of both surgeons and apothecaries, unlike that of physicians, was totally practical and consisted of a lengthy apprenticeship, originally of seven years but reduced by Keats's time to five. Once the apprenticeship was completed, the student could set up shop as an apothecary or could sit the licensing examination held by the Royal College of Surgeons to become a surgeon, which gave him the right to perform operations. In the seventeenth and early eighteenth centuries, the Corporation of Surgeons in London held lectures and dissections at their hall for the benefit of candidates. When the practice of teaching at the London hospitals increased, however, the corporation encouraged candidates to attend lectures there.[34] By the end of the eighteenth century the practical teaching at the hospitals was very good, but there was still no compulsion for students to attend. Moreover, it was difficult to administer the licensing examinations outside the London area, so many surgeons were not certified.

Under these circumstances, it is easy to see that the training received by an apprentice depended to a large degree on the knowledge and industry of his master. Thomas Hammond was a well-respected, well-trained apothecary-surgeon, one of a family firm of surgeons whose "older generation, like himself, were Members of the Corporation of Surgeons, its younger, Members of the newly-established Royal College of Surgeons."[35] Although only an apprenticeship was required, Hammond himself had been trained at Guy's, one of the great London teaching hospitals, where he had distinguished himself enough to be appointed dresser to William Lucas, Sr., a very good surgeon. Moreover, Hammond kept abreast of developments through his membership in the corporation and through his connection with Guy's, which served Keats well later on.

Hammond, then, was no country quack, but a well-established doctor with a practice so large that he could take on two apprentices. Even though recent evidence has shown that the Hammond family suffered from "habitual intemperance,"[36] there is no evidence that this was the case with Thomas

Hammond, or, if it was, that it affected his professional abilities. On the contrary, the fact that John Clarke, a well-educated man interested in science, called upon Hammond to treat his students speaks well of the doctor, for Clarke would hardly have tolerated an incompetent or a drunkard. Contrary to some opinion,[37] Keats received his training from a fully qualified master and probably went to Guy's with as good a knowledge of medicine as any of the other students.

In the area of surgery, Keats would have learned, first through observation and then by assisting, how to pull teeth, set broken bones, apply various plasters and bandages, bleed, either by the application of leeches or by venesection, and probably how to deliver babies. On the more strictly medical side, he would have learned from practical experience how to identify the symptoms of various diseases and disorders, including numerous fevers, and how to compound and administer their remedies. Most of the drugs used were of botanical origin and included such things as aconite, columbo, digitalis, jalap, opium, and so on. A few were also of mineral origin, including antimony, magnesia, and mercury. Obviously, this understanding of materia medica involved some theoretical knowledge along with practical knowledge of botany, but how much other textual knowledge Keats had is difficult to say. He probably also knew the basics of anatomy and physiology, which he may have gained from William Cullen's *First Lines of the Practice of Physic*, a very popular textbook of the day, but practical learning was far more likely to be stressed.[38] With Keats's quick mind and his determination once he decided to undertake a task, he probably learned a good deal from Hammond.

It should also be observed that in those days without anesthetics and without our modern stress on cleanliness and antiseptics, Keats would have been a daily witness to the human suffering, disability, fear, and sometimes death that accompany diseases and accidents. If at first he felt the horror and disgust, as well as the pity, that are natural for a boy of fifteen to feel, he must have become accustomed to, and if necessary have steeled himself against, such emotions over the five-year period. He was a normal, healthy boy with strong animal spirits and a fighting will who had seen much disease and death in his own family; he was not the delicate spirit that Shelley portrays in *Adonais*. It is not surprising, however, that he looked forward to the relief of the weekly walk to Enfield school to read poetry with Cowden Clarke, and the contrast between the world of medicine and the beautiful world of poetry must have been apparent to him from this early stage.

Two incidents occurred toward the end of Keats's apprenticeship, when he was probably contemplating setting up his own practice in Edmonton, to change the direction of his life. In 1814 his grandmother, Mrs. Jennings, died and his sister was sent to live with their guardian, Mr. Abbey, in Walthamstow. Thus, apart from the temporary lodging shared by Keats and Tom, there was no longer any family home in Edmonton, or anywhere for that matter. With George in London, there was little to keep Keats in Edmonton.

The second incident is less personal, but it affected Keats just as much. In the early years of the nineteenth century there was growing debate, both in Parliament and within the medical profession, about the state of medical practice in England. The problem was that since most of the public were treated by apothecaries who were not licensed, there was much opportunity for quacks to set up practice. In order to remedy this situation, Parliament and the apothecary-surgeons sought "a legislative enactment that would, by its gradual operation, secure for the service of the public properly educated practitioners, and for their branch of the profession [the apothecaries] that respectability and consideration to which its usefulness to society is so justly entitled."[39] To achieve this, George Brown, "a London practitioner and a qualified apothecary, took up the cause of medical reform . . . and organized an Association of Surgeon-Apothecaries (i.e. General Practitioners) of England with more than 3000 members."[40] The association appointed a general committee in 1812 to investigate reforms in education and certification.

The main question upon which the general committee had to decide was whether the existing Worshipful Society of Apothecaries should be given the duty of examining pupils for certification or whether a new "fourth" medical body, to be called the College of General Practitioners, should be established for this purpose. After eighteen months of investigation, the general committee in May 1814 "determined *not* to apply for the formation of a fourth medical body, for the purpose of examinations."[41] Instead, with the support of the College of Physicians, the Association of Apothecaries brought in a bill giving the Society of Apothecaries the right to examine "all persons applying for certificates to practise . . . in the science and practice of medicine, pharmacy, chemistry, materia medica, and medical botany."[42] For this purpose, the society appointed a board of examiners. The bill became "An Act for better regulating the Practice of Apothecaries throughout England and Wales" when it passed on 12 July 1815, at the same time as Keats was completing his five-year apprenticeship with Hammond.

This new Apothecaries Act is an important landmark in the history of English medicine. For nearly a century after its passage the London Society of Apothecaries used the powers given to it by the act to achieve the transition between medicine practiced as a trade, with only empirical training by apprenticeship, and the modern university-trained profession. Most nineteenth-century practitioners were trained according to the new act, and Keats was one of the first. In order to be licensed to practice, after finishing his five-year apprenticeship he would have to complete "a suitable attendance on the practice of an hospital"—defined as at least six months—and produce "testimonials of a sufficient medical and classical education, and of good moral conduct" from his master.[43] It is unlikely that this came as a total surprise to Keats since Hammond, a Guy's man and a member of the Corporation of Surgeons, must have been following the developments of the reform movement. Hammond probably advised Keats to do his hospital term at the United Hospitals of Guy's and St. Thomas's, not only because he was an ex-pupil of Guy's, but also because he had family connections on the hospital staff.[44]

John Flint South, who was a student at the United Hospitals from 1813 to 1815, points out that when a new pupil appeared at the beginning of the semester to pay his fees, he "was generally brought up by his father or master, often an old and loving pupil of the old school, and made known by him to the teachers to whom he felt he owed his professional success from his own instructions in former years."[45] Whether Hammond accompanied Keats to Guy's and introduced him around—perhaps to Astley Cooper—we cannot say, but because he was himself a Guy's man with staff connections the possibility of his having done so is strong.

Whether he was introduced by Hammond or not, however, the fact remains that in July 1816 Keats received his "Certificate to Practise as an Apothecary," which states that he had completed his five-year apprenticeship with Hammond and had attended the requisite courses at the United Hospitals. A page in the Register of Apothecaries' Hall for 1816 reads as follows:

July 25th 1816.
189 Mr. *John Keats of full age*—CANDIDATE for
a CERTIFICATE to practise as an APOTHECARY in *the Country*.
An APPRENTICE to Mr. *Thomas Hammond of Edmonton*
APOTHECARY FOR 5 Years
TESTIMONIAL from *Mr. Thomas Hammond*—

LECTURES.
2 COURSES on ANATOMY and PHYSIOLOGY.
2—THEORY and PRACTICE OF MEDICINE.
2—CHEMISTRY.
1—MATERIA MEDICA.

HOSPITAL ATTENDANCE.
6 MONTHS at *Guy's and St. Thomas's*—
as
MONTHS at
168 Examined by Mr. Brande & approved.[46]

The certificate is a standard form on which the details of the individual candidate were filled in.

As Keats's certificate indicates, the United Hospitals of Guy's and St. Thomas's, which ran the Borough Medical School, offered a comprehensive course of medical training which was not, as has been claimed, "a most casual affair" with "no formal lectures in surgery."[47] On the contrary, the syllabus, as advertised in the *London Medical and Physical Journal,* was extensive, with some excellent teachers:

The Autumnal Course of Lectures at these adjoining Hospitals will commence the beginning of October, viz.

At St. Thomas's.—Anatomy and the Operations of Surgery, by Mr. Astley Cooper and Mr. Henry Cline. Principles and Practice of Surgery, by Mr. Astley Cooper. At Guy's.—Practice of Medicine, by Dr. Babington and Dr. Curry. Chemistry, by Dr. Babington, Dr. Marcet, and Mr. Allen. Experimental Philosophy, by Mr. Allen. Theory of Medicine, and Materia Medica, by Dr. Curry and Dr. Cholmeley. Midwifery, and Diseases of Women and Children, by Dr. Haighton. Physiology, or Laws of the Animal Oeconomy, by Dr. Haighton. Structure and Diseases of the Teeth, by Mr. Fox.[48]

The courses were "so arranged, that no two of them interfere[d] in the hours of attendance; and the whole [was] calculated to form a complete course of medical and chirurgical instruction."[49] Because St. Thomas's was the senior partner, with a famous past, it allotted to itself the teaching of anatomy and surgery, the only lectures for which there was great demand before the 1815 act. Guy's had to be content with teaching the strictly medical subjects, which were not popular until the act made them compulsory, at which time Guy's became the most well-rounded medical school in London.

It is debatable whether Keats, on entering Guy's, intended to become a member of the Royal College of Surgeons or a licentiate of the Society of Apothecaries, but the fact that on Sunday, 1 October 1815, he registered at the Guy's Counting House for a twelve-month period suggests that he was aiming for the more ambitious title of surgeon, since an apothecary's license required only six months of hospital work.

Keats entered Guy's at a time when medical studies, especially surgery and anatomy, were enjoying a reputation for excellence. On a visit to London in 1814, Philibert Joseph Roux, a French doctor who was comparing the hospitals of London with those of Paris, was struck by the high quality of the surgery. This he attributed correctly to the influence of John Hunter, the controversial and revolutionary anatomist who made British surgery the best in Europe. Roux concluded that the hospitals of London were better equipped for their job than those of France.[50]

Biography

Two of Hunter's pupils were Henry Cline and Astley Cooper, both of whom helped to make the United Hospitals an excellent teaching institution. As Doubleday points out:

> The nineteenth century opened with a great advance in the anatomical and surgical work of the hospital and this must be indirectly attributed to the teaching of John Hunter. Henry Cline, jun., had attended his courses and introduced his methods into the teaching at St. Thomas's. Astley Cooper and Joseph Fox, two students who attended Cline's rounds, were destined to exert great influence at Guy's. . . . Cooper was a man full of energy, who often arrived at the hospital and dissected before breakfast; he assisted students by injecting bodies for them to dissect, and in 1800 he became surgeon to Guy's Hospital.[51]

Cooper was probably the most flamboyant and popular medical lecturer of his day, not only in England, but in all of Europe. John Flint South describes Cooper's appearance and method of teaching:

> A few moments before two Astley Cooper came briskly through the crowd, his handsome face beaming with delight and animation. He was dressed in black, with short knee-breeches and silk stockings, which well displayed his handsome legs, of which he was not a little proud. Almost to a minute he was in the theatre, where loud and continued greetings most truly declared the affectionate regard his pupils had for him. His clear silvery voice and cheery conversational manner soon exhausted the conventional hour devoted to the lecture; and all who heard him hung with silent attention on his words, the only sounds which broke the quiet being the subdued pen-scratching of the note-takers. . . . as he only talked of what he really knew from his own experience, what he taught was to be implicitly trusted.[52]

Testaments to Cooper's brilliance as a teacher are numerous, both from his contemporaries and from medical historians. Of him, the *British and Foreign Medical Review* wrote:

> As a teacher Sir Astley Cooper has never been excelled by any English surgeon. His discoveries were not hidden treasures; no sooner had he made them than he hastened, with liberal enthusiasm, and a winning affability, to diffuse a knowledge of them among a large class of pupils. The whole present generation of English surgeons may, indeed, be said to have studied directly or indirectly in his school; and, assuredly no

master was ever more beloved and honoured or sent more enthusiastic and grateful followers abroad into the world to propagate his doctrines.[53]

Brock claims that Cooper "came to be known as the greatest surgical teacher in Europe. His students came from Great Britain, Germany, Italy, Switzerland, France, Denmark, Sweden and America."[54] He was very popular in his profession, respected and esteemed by his peers, and he established Guy's as a famous school of surgery. The fact that Cooper, a surgeon rather than a university-educated physician, was chosen to treat the king—for which he was made a baronet in 1821—shows him to have been "the outstanding British surgeon of his time."[55]

Cooper himself never published his lectures, but they were so popular and in such demand that they were pirated and published in the *Lancet,* a medical journal. Later, in the mid-1820s, Frederick Tyrrell, who had been Cooper's apprentice, published the lectures with Cooper's permission; they were also published in America and translated into German. "Cooper's *Surgery* thus became the standard textbook of the day and held this position for many years after his death."[56]

Keats could hardly fail to have been impressed by Cooper's lectures, attended by up to four hundred students, which is perhaps why he kept his anatomy notes from Cooper's and Cline's course. The notes themselves indicate an industrious student, although we have no proof that Keats ever wrote up these hasty classroom notes into the elaborate forms used by some students. Perhaps even more important than the notes, however, is the fact that Keats adopted certain axioms and ideas from Cooper which are not strictly medical, but which are important to Keats's understanding of life and of poetry.

Keats was lucky that he attended Guy's when he did, for not only was Cooper in his prime, "but in 1814 really adequate accommodation was provided at St. Thomas's in a large building on ground to the north of the Hospital Courts, accommodation which comprised a large and handsome lecture theatre in the centre, flanked by the new dissecting room on one side and the Anatomical Museum on the other. The apprentices, the dressers and pupils from both hospitals dissected in the new building."[57] South gives a detailed account of these new anatomical facilities and explains that they were built largely through the influence and generosity of Cooper and Cline. The museum was one of the best in England because Cooper donated to it his whole private collection of dissected specimens.[58] Keats entered, then, a teaching hospital that had new facilities and an excellent staff.

It is difficult to prove exactly which courses in anatomy and physiology Keats attended. The new "Regulations for the Examination of Apothecaries" required a candidate "to produce certificates of having attended not less than two courses of Lectures on Anatomy and Physiology,"[59] and his certificate attests to his having fulfilled this requirement; but whether these two courses were Cooper's and Cline's course taken for two terms, as Gittings claims,[60] or whether he also attended Dr. Haighton's "Physiology, or Laws of the Animal Oeconomy," it is difficult to say. The problem is compounded by the fact that "the first twelve lectures given by Astley Cooper we were accustomed to call the physiological lectures . . . in which a slight sketch was given of the several structures of the body and the functions they were destined to be engaged in."[61] In addition, as the evidence indicates that Keats originally intended to be a surgeon, it is almost certain that he also attended Cooper's other course, "The Principles and Practices of Surgery," in the evening.

In the "Anatomy and Operations of Surgery" course, Cooper's twelve "physiological lectures" "were followed by about ten on the bones . . . also given by Cooper, and the various fractures, their characters and local treatment,"[62] after which Cline took over and lectured on the muscles, beginning with those of the head and face. Unlike Cooper, Cline "was a tall, sickly, and very plain man, marked with small-pox, and very shy" who taught "in a quiet monotonous tone." As his lectures went on for much longer than Cooper's, they were not so popular.[63] The fact that Keats made no notes on Cline's lectures—or, if he did, they have not survived—may indicate that he found them tedious and boring, but it does not prove Cameron's contention that Keats "probably did not attend them."[64] It is fair to say, however, that judging by the anatomical information that appears in Keats's poetry and letters, it was Astley Cooper's part of the course that he found most interesting.

Cooper's other course, "The Principles and Practices of Surgery," dealt in much more detail with methods of operating and of identifying diseases and disorders. His approach was extremely practical, to the extent that he used patients from the two hospitals to demonstrate specific diseases or disorders in the lecture theater. He also made extensive use of his excellent collection of specimens and dissections to demonstrate morbid pathology. This practical approach was revolutionary, for previously surgery had been taught as theory, an approach that Cooper abhorred. He insisted that knowledge can be gained only by observation and experience, an idea that always remained in Keats's mind.

Though it may be doubtful whether Keats attended Dr. John Haighton's lectures on physiology, it should be pointed out that Haighton was a distinguished man of science in his day, a fellow of the Royal Society who conducted much valuable research in such varied fields as obstetric surgery, the nervous system, and mathematics and astronomy. He was an excellent lecturer, although personally he was irritable and argumentative.[65] He was the first lecturer in physiology at Guy's, having been appointed to the post when it was created at the end of the eighteenth century.

While Keats was attending lectures on anatomy and physiology, he was also required to put his classroom knowledge into practice in the dissecting room, for, as Cooper pointed out in his first lecture, a pupil's "anatomical knowledge cannot be perfect unless he has frequently seen and assisted in the dissection of the human body."[66]

The anatomy demonstrator at Guy's when Keats was there was Joseph Henry Green, who later became Coleridge's friend and literary executor.[67] Green delivered as part of his duty "a regular course of practical anatomy in the theatre, which the pupils used to run into in their dissecting dresses. Such spare time as he had left was spent in demonstrating at the several tables in the dissecting-room."[68] Green himself outlines the necessity for having such a course:

Biography

It must be recollected that lectures, however necessary, are only calculated to give general ideas; whereas it is required of the practitioner, that his knowledge should be particular and even minute. It is not sufficient that he is merely acquainted with the presence of certain parts, but he must know precisely their situation and extent. The surgeon's knife may give health or death within the space of one hair's breadth. This kind of knowledge is to be acquired by actual dissection alone.[69]

Green urged his students to increase their anatomical knowledge by making preparations of a set of bones, the veins and arteries in an arm and leg, a male and female pelvis, and the nerves in a small subject.

Because the use of bodies for teaching anatomy was forbidden by law, the bodies for dissection were bought, for three or four guineas apiece, from body-snatchers, or "resurrection-men," who robbed local graves.[70] This practice was carried on at night, the resurrection-men bringing the bodies to the hospital naked in sacks, since stealing a shroud was a criminal offense, whereas stealing a body was only a misdemeanor. The gang of resurrection-men who regularly supplied Guy's was led by hard-drinking Ben Crouch and included his brother Jack, Bill Butler, and Jack and Bill Harnett.[71] As this was the only means of securing specimens, the ghoulish practice was supported by the hospital staff, especially Astley Cooper, who paid the body-snatchers' fines when they were caught and supported their families when they were sent to prison. So influential was Cooper with these men that he boasted he could obtain the body of any dead man in England if he so desired.[72]

The dissecting room itself must have been a gruesome place, with its bodies laid out on tables and its specimens in macerating tubs and bottles. The students, however, seem to have been immune to these sights and smells, for according to tradition they drank, cooked, and indulged in horseplay in the room, which they treated like a common room.[73] A contemporary account of the dissecting room, given by the uncle of the famous surgeon William Osler, is horrifying by present standards:

On entering the room, the stink was most abominable. About 20 chaps were at work, carving limbs and bodies, in all stages of putrefaction, &

of all colours; black, green, yellow, blue, while the pupils carved them apparently, with as much pleasure, as they would carve their dinners. One, was pouring Ol. Terebinth on his subject, & amused himself with striking with his scalpel at the maggots, as they issued from their retreats.[74]

Keats must have faced such scenes almost daily.

As well as attending the lectures on surgery and on anatomy and physiology at St. Thomas's, Keats was also required by the new act to attend courses in chemistry, botany, materia medica, and the practice of medicine, which were taught at Guy's by the physicians to the hospital.

As we have seen, according to his certificate to practice as an apothecary, Keats attended two courses of lectures on chemistry while at Guy's in 1815–16. This means that he attended one course during the autumn term, from October 1815 to mid-January 1816, and a second course during the spring term, from 20 January to mid-May 1816, for the syllabus published by St. Thomas's and Guy's announces only one course each term.[75] In both terms the course was taught by Dr. Babington, Dr. Marcet, and Mr. Allen. Both Babington and Marcet were full physicians at Guy's.

Babington, "a good-tempered, kindly Irishman," was "a very excellent practical teacher, who was listened to with great pleasure and advantage, as his lectures were full of experience and practical good sense."[76] Babington's main interest in chemistry was in minerals, and in 1795 he had published "A Systematic Arrangement of Minerals, Founded on the Joint Considerations of their Chemical, Physical, and External Characters." He was a founding member of both the Geological and Hunterian Societies, and later became a fellow of the Royal Society.[77]

Marcet, a native of Switzerland, was an experimental chemist of very high repute, a founding member of the Medico-Chirurgical Society, and a widely published fellow of the Royal Society.[78] Marcet was, in fact, the discoverer of a hitherto unknown substance which he named Xanthine.[79] The third lecturer, Allen, a well-known philanthropist, was traveling on the Continent in 1816, so it is unlikely that he taught Keats.[80]

That Keats attended two courses of lectures on chemistry illustrates that he was a conscientious student, for the new

"Regulations for the Examination of Apothecaries," set by the Court of Examiners of the Society of Apothecaries, demanded only that the candidate attend "one course of Lectures on Chemistry."[81] As in almost all his endeavors, Keats was preparing himself well.

Along with chemistry, Dr. Babington taught a course in the practice of medicine with Dr. James Curry, also an Irishman and also well respected in the profession. South describes Curry thus:

A man of very extensive reading and of very observant habits; his lectures went into the very bottom of things; he told of all that had been said and written by everyone who had handled the subjects on which he treated, but he dearly loved theorizing and criticizing. . . . He was one of the most fluent and attractive lecturers I have ever known; his language was unexceptionable, and his words flowed in an unbroken torrent; he could talk about anything and make everything full of interest.[82]

Despite this praise, however, Curry was criticized for prescribing calomel for almost any ailment, for which he was nicknamed "Calomel Curry." Unlike the benevolent Babington, with whom he lived, Curry was "irascible, peevish, and overbearing, but yet possessing an honesty of purpose, a strictness and integrity of conduct which could not but create an esteem towards him."[83]

According to Gittings, Keats took two courses in the theory and practice of medicine with Babington and Curry and one in materia medica with Dr. Cholmeley.[84] The Guy's syllabus, however, advertises "Practice of Medicine," taught by Babington and Curry, as one course, and "Theory of Medicine, and Materia Medica," taught by Curry and Dr. James Cholmeley, as a second course; it is almost certainly these two that Keats attended, perhaps taking one of them for two terms, which would account for the fact that his certificate states he completed two courses in medicine and one in materia medica. Cholmeley was a respected physician, although he was a difficult man to deal with and was very jealous of Astley Cooper, which did not help his popularity.[85] Like Curry, he too had a favorite medicine, in his case "the white mixture" (carbonate and sulphate of magnesia), which he prescribed freely.

Knowledge of materia medica was very important, because a large part of the apothecary's job was the compounding of drugs from botanical and mineral sources. To get the correct method and measurements for mixing these drugs, the student consulted the *Pharmacopoeia Officinalis Brittanica,* which compiled the methods and measurements approved by the Apothecaries' Societies of London, Edinburgh, and Dublin. Where these three bodies differed in their methods, the lecturer would give his recommendations.

The teaching of medicine and materia medica was also closely connected with the study of botany,[86] which from 1815 was taught to the students of the United Hospitals by William Salisbury, a well-known botanist:

Mr. William Salisbury, of the Botanic Garden, Sloane-street, at the recommendation of Drs. Babington and Curry, Richard Ogle, Esq. and other gentlemen, has lately adopted a mode of teaching Botany by making excursions into the fields near London, as was used to be practised by his late partner, Mr. William Curtis. It having become indispensably necessary for students in medicine to obtain a knowledge of this science, or at least so much of it as relates to an acquaintance with all the plants described in the materia medica, he is desirous of forming a regular establishment in the garden, for the purpose of rendering botanical information.[87]

Because of the outdoor nature of Salisbury's course, it was taught during the spring and summer; Keats would have taken it in the spring of 1816, a spring which, according to Salisbury, was "uncommonly backward."[88] The first meeting was held on Tuesday, 23 April, at the Red House Tavern in Battersea Fields, and field trips followed on Friday, 3 May, to Battersea Fields, Wandsworth Common, and Tooting; on Tuesday, 14 May, to Hampstead Heath, Cain Wood, and Highgate Archway; on Friday, 17 May, to Charlton and Woolwich Sand-pits and the Meadows opposite Blackwall; and on Friday, 24 May, to Richmond Park, Combe Wood, and Wimbledon Common. Trips were also planned for each Friday in June, to be deferred to the following Tuesday in the case of bad weather.[89] It was probably during or just after these June trips that Keats composed the three sonnets, "To one who has been long in city pent," "Oh, how I love!

on a fair summer's eve," and "To a Friend Who Sent Me Some Roses," all of which deal with the beauty of the countryside.

During the field trips, specimens were gathered and named, and afterwards the students met with Salisbury at a nearby inn to discuss the medicinal uses of each specimen. These excursions were, no doubt, a real pleasure to Keats, a relief from the squalid conditions of the Borough, and a reminder of the life he had had at Enfield with Cowden Clarke, where he had been introduced to botany during the field trips on Enfield Close. In addition to the excursions, Salisbury also gave a lecture at the Botanical Garden each Monday at 3:00 P.M. and encouraged the students to use the library and garden there.[90]

Of the other courses taught at Guy's, there is no evidence that Keats attended Dr. Haighton's midwifery lectures, Mr. Allen's lectures on experimental philosophy, or Mr. Fox's on the teeth. These courses were not required for the apothecary's examination, they do not appear on his certificate, and Keats would have had plenty of practical experience in drawing teeth and in obstetrics during his apprenticeship with Hammond. Of the courses he did take, he was certain to meet the lecturers personally, since each student was required to pay the lecturer directly for the course. For his courses, Keats paid a total of £33. 13s.[91]

The exact times at which the various lectures were given in 1815–16 cannot be stated with certainty, although we do know the hours of attendance during the late eighteenth century[92] and we possess a Guy's timetable for 1826.[93] Since the differences between these two accounts are minor, it is safe to assume that Keats's hours of attendance were similar, if not the same.

The day began at 7:30 A.M. (8:00 A.M. in 1826) with lectures on midwifery for an hour. At 10:00 A.M. on Monday, Wednesday, and Friday the lectures on the practice of medicine were given, and at 10:00 A.M. on Tuesday, Thursday, and Saturday the lectures on chemistry were held. Hospital attendance began at 11:00 A.M., at Guy's on Monday, Wednesday, and Friday, and at St. Thomas's on the other three days, with all students attending at both hospitals. The entire hospital was visited on Monday and Friday at Guy's, and on Tuesday and Saturday at St. Thomas's; Wednesday and Thursday were admitting and discharging day at the respective hospitals. Making the rounds of the hospital took an hour and a half.

In the afternoon, the anatomy lectures were given, from 2:00 to 4:00 during Keats's time,[94] after which the students dissected. On two days of the week—Tuesday and Friday in 1826—the theory of medicine was taught at 7:00 P.M., followed by the principles and practice of surgery at 8:00 P.M. On two other days—Monday and Wednesday in 1826—physiology lectures commenced at 6:30 P.M. By any standards, attendance at lectures and at the hospital constituted a long and tiring day.

The little firsthand information we have of Keats as a medical student attending lectures consists of the testimony of two fellow students and Keats's *Anatomical and Physiological Note Book*.[95] Those critics who have taken the time to read the *Note Book* usually agree that it shows Keats to have been a conscientious student.[96] Hewlett compares Keats's notes with those of a contemporary student, Joshua Waddington, and concludes that Keats's are scanty.[97] She does not distinguish, however, between classroom notes, in Keats's case, and notes that have been written up at a later date, as is the case with Waddington's. Critics also claim that the drawings of flowers in the margins of a couple of the pages in Keats's *Note Book* are evidence of his boredom during lectures.[98] But far from showing lapses of concentration, these may be botanical sketches, just as the drawings of skulls in the *Note Book* are obviously anatomical.

Even though Keats's notes show him to have been an industrious student, at least in Cooper's class, the contemporary accounts of him as a student are not favorable. The fuller, and more often quoted, account is given by one of Keats's roommates while he was at Guy's, Henry Stephens,[99] from whom we have gained much information about where and with whom Keats lived, and about what he was like as a student. Stephens claims that Keats "attended Lectures and went through the usual routine, but he had no desire to excel in that pursuit, In fact Medical Knowledge was beneath his attention. . . . No—Poetry was to his mind the zenith of all his Aspirations—The only thing worthy the attention of superior minds."[100] This record has shaped almost all subsequent accounts of Keats as a medical student, one who found medicine a hindrance to his poetic ambitions.

But Stephens's view must be placed in context. First, he did not know Keats until they were in their second term at Guy's, starting in January 1816, when Keats began to share rooms with Stephens and another student, George Mackereth.[101] It was not until the end of this term, during the summer of 1816, that Keats began to think of poetry as an alternative career to medicine, and even then it was only anatomy he told Cowden Clarke that he disliked:

He entered himself of St. Thomas's, but he could not knit his faculties to the study of anatomy. He attended the lectures; and he did not retain a word he had heard: all ran from him like water from a duck's back. His thoughts were far away—in the land of Faery. He was with "the lovely Una in a leafy nook"; or with "old Archimago leaning o'er his book." He said to me that a ray of sun-light came across the lecture-room, and he peopled it with the "gay beings of the element," glancing to and fro like the angels in Jacob's dream.[102]

Keats's dislike of anatomy may have stemmed from the horrifying conditions of the dissecting room, especially during the warmer months. It was perhaps for this reason that he gave up his original hopes of becoming a surgeon and instead sat the Licentiate of the Society of Apothecaries examination, which did not involve anatomy and surgery. It is more likely, however, that Keats's remarks to Stephens on poetry and medicine were tinged with a young man's desire to shock rather staid companions and to strike a pose similar to his dressing "à la Byron."[103] It should also be observed that Keats's own poetry and letters disprove Clarke's claim that "he did not retain a word he had heard" on anatomy. Moreover, Keats's notes of Astley Cooper's anatomy lectures seem to contradict Clarke's recollection.

The second account of Keats at Guy's by a contemporary student is that of Walter Cooper Dendy: "Even in the lecture-room of Saint Thomas's, I have seen Keats in a deep poetic dream; his mind was on Parnassus with the muses. And here is a quaint fragment which he one evening scribbled in our presence, while the precepts of Sir Astley Cooper fell unheeded on his ear."[104] Dendy then quotes what is known as the Alexander

Fragment, believed to be by Keats. The authenticity of Dendy's account, however, has been brought into doubt by B. Ifor Evans, who points out that hospital records show Dendy and Keats were not contemporary students—Dendy attended in 1813—and that even if Dendy was still connected with the hospital while Keats was there, it is unlikely that he still attended lectures.[105] Evans believes that Dendy wrote the Alexander Fragment himself, and supports his argument with other, obviously fictitious, stories about Keats that appear in some of Dendy's other writings. Even if, as Finney claims,[106] the fragment is by Keats, the story of its composition seems fictitious.

Stephens's and Dendy's accounts have led to many claims that Keats was a mediocre student whose real interest was poetry rather than medicine.[107] Even when they admit that Keats was a successful student, some biographers speculate that this was a result of his quick mind, or natural ability, rather than of his interest and industry.[108] Although these opinions of Keats are probably valid by the summer and autumn of 1816, when he had met Hunt and Haydon, they cannot be used as blanket statements about his years as a medical student. The concrete evidence we do have concerning his first two terms at Guy's unequivocally supports Brown's claim that Keats "was indefatigable in his application to anatomy, medicine, and natural history"[109] and Gittings's statement that "the medical profession was not distasteful to him in any way. . . . He had found his hospital training interesting and useful."[110] Keats himself wrote to George Felton Mathew in November 1815 that " 'tis impossible" for him to escape into poetry:

> far different cares
> Beckon me sternly from soft "Lydian airs,"
> And hold my faculties so long in thrall,
> That I am oft in doubt whether at all
> I shall again see Phœbus in the morning.
>
> ("To George Felton Mathew," 17–21)

These verses reveal a hard-working student, intent on becoming a surgeon.

The concrete evidence to which I refer as proof of Keats's interest and success in his medical studies consists of two facts:

in late October 1815 Keats was appointed a dresser at Guy's,[111] the first member of his class to be so honoured; and on 25 July 1816 he passed the examination to become a licentiate of the Society of Apothecaries.

Keats's dressership must be understood within the context of the hospital's organization in order to be appreciated fully. When a student attended a teaching hospital, he did not simply go to lectures, take notes, and dissect specimens. He was also required to "walk the wards," observing the surgeons and physicians as they made their rounds and treated patients. For this the student paid twenty-four guineas and became a surgical pupil for one year; Keats registered as such on 2 October 1815.[112] For this sum he could observe the surgeons and ask relevant questions. Wealthier and more ambitious students could become surgeon's apprentices, for which they paid the exorbitant fee of about three hundred pounds; in return, they gained many privileges in the hospital as well as the right to have private lessons with the surgeon to whom they were apprenticed; but the fee put this position beyond the vast majority of students, including Keats.

Between the positions of surgical pupil and surgeon's apprentice was that of dresser. Each of the three surgeons at Guy's was allowed to have four dressers, each of whom paid fifty pounds for a year's service.[113] In return, the dresser received a few privileges and a great many responsibilities. Since there were only twelve dressers in the whole hospital, and the positions were filled by appointment, a dressership was considered a great honor.

Each of the four dressers lived in the hospital at his own expense for a week at a time, during which period he acted virtually as house doctor.[114] On Wednesday, which was "taking-in day" at Guy's, the dresser on duty took charge of all his surgeon's cases, as South describes:

He attended to all the accidents and cases of hernia which came in during his week of office, and he dressed hosts of out-patients, drew innumerable teeth, and performed countless venesections, till two or three o'clock, as might be, till the surgery was emptied. . . . When the surgeon arrived the dresser on duty would show him, among

37

the outpatients, any case about which he needed further help or which he thought advisable to be admitted, as likely to issue in an operation. . . .

Cases of strangulated hernia, retention of urine, and all fractures or other accidents, were admitted at the discretion of the dresser. . . . That the patients were kindly, carefully and efficiently treated by the dressers as a rule I most unhesitatingly assert.[115]

Once these cases were warded, the surgeon began his rounds through both the male and female wards, accompanied by the dresser and any students who wished to observe. If the surgeon was well known and respected, the number of pupils following along would be large and the group often disorganized. During these rounds the dresser was privileged to carry a plaster box—containing plasters, bandages, and linseed meal—which was considered a mark of distinction, for it denoted the bearer's office. The surgeon gave his dresser the necessary instructions on how to dress wounds and administer drugs for each patient, and the more industrious dressers made notes for each case, although none were required. It was also the responsibility of the dresser to send for his surgeon in case of any emergency in the wards; the seriousness of the ailment was left to his discretion, and could include hemorrhages and other such occurrences. The dresser on duty would also be required to attend such emergencies at night; his was a position of no small responsibility.[116]

In addition, the dresser assisted the surgeon at operations, which were performed at both hospitals on Fridays (at noon at St. Thomas's and at one o'clock at Guy's), with usually two or three operations at each institution. Both operating theaters at St. Thomas's—one for males, the other for females—and the one at Guy's were too small, especially since the pupils of either hospital had the right to attend operations at both. This led to a continual confusion, crushing, and fighting for seats before and during the operation, especially if a well-known surgeon, like Astley Cooper, was operating or an important surgical technique was being performed.[117]

The theaters were semicircular to give the best possible view to observers, and rows of stepped, semicircular standings radiated out from the center. At the center of the theater stood the wooden operating table, underneath which there was a box of sawdust to catch falling blood, and on the side a table for the surgeon's tools—including knives, saws, tweezers, and scissors—and a wash basin in which the surgeon washed his hands after the operation. On the floor of the theater stood the operating surgeon and his dressers, along with any other surgeons and surgeons' apprentices who wanted to watch. The first two tiers of standings were reserved for the other dressers from both hospitals, and pupils occupied the remaining levels. According to South, during major operations "there was a continual calling out of 'Heads, heads,' to those about the table, whose heads interfered with the sightseers, with various appellatives, in a small way resembling the calls at the Sheldonian Theatre."[118] The scene was undoubtedly much more horrifying than it was comic, especially as no anesthetic was used on the patient.

After the operation the dresser was expected to dress the wound, and as his confidence and ability increased, he played a larger part in the surgery itself. He was also required to change the dressings during the postoperative period, which in a time before the use of antiseptics, when wounds festered very quickly, would mean daily changes. If the dresser had not seen enough pain, suffering, and death during his days as an apprentice, he would now see it on a grand scale.

How Keats came to be appointed a dresser on 29 October 1815, after being at Guy's for only a month, is not exactly clear. What is clear is that this was a great honor, and the choice must have been based to some extent on his merit. We know from South that the great Astley Cooper himself took an interest in Keats soon after Keats arrived at Guy's and arranged for him to live with two senior students, George Cooper, Astley Cooper's dresser (not a relative), and Frederick Tyrrell, a surgeon's apprentice.[119] These two students must have been a great help and inspiration to Keats, and it is almost certainly with their influence, and that of Astley Cooper, that he secured the dressership.[120] It is also probable that he had a strong recommendation from Thomas Hammond, who was related to Joseph Henry Green and who had been dresser to William Lucas, Sr. Within the close-knit world of influence it seems almost natural that Hammond's apprentice should become dresser to William Lucas, Jr. The appointment is also, however, a testament to Keats's hard work during his first month at Guy's.

Although he did not take up his dressership until 3 March 1816, it was most unfortunate for Keats that he was assigned to Billy Lucas.[121] William Lucas, Sr., had been a very good surgeon at Guy's, and it was because of his reputation and influence that his son Billy succeeded him in this position. The son, however, was very different from the father, as South attests:

A tall, ungainly, awkward man, with stooping shoulders and a shuffling walk, as deaf as a post, not over-burdened with brains of any kind, but very good-natured and easy, and liked by everyone. His surgical acquirements were very small, his operations generally very badly performed, and accompanied with much bungling, if not worse. He was a poor anatomist and not a very good diagnoser, which now and then led him into ugly scrapes.[122]

Astley Cooper, a man noted for his generosity, was horrified at Lucas's butchery: "He was neat-handed, but rash in the extreme, cutting amongst most important parts as though they were only skin, and making us all shudder from the apprehension of his opening arteries or committing some other error." [123] The dangerous operating techniques, under which patients suffered greatly, must have had an effect on Keats and have influenced his decision to give up surgery.[124] Luckily for the patients and Keats, however, Lucas rarely operated without Astley Cooper as an observer, in case anything went wrong.[125]

It has always been a popular speculation that had Keats been assigned as dresser to Astley Cooper instead of to Lucas, he might have stayed in medicine and become a successful surgeon. It should be pointed out, however, that Keats would still have seen Cooper operate every Friday, from his reserved place in one of the two front rows, and Cooper's brilliance may have made Keats realize his own shortcomings. Cooper was the most successful surgeon of his day in England and, as South says, "for operating with alacrity, and well at the same time, I have not known his equal; his great practical anatomical knowledge enabled him to operate without the least fear of getting into scrapes, which less facile anatomists would more carefully avoid by taking more time."[126] Cooper performed many innovative and spectacular operations during his career, and Keats probably saw him perform the first successful ligature of the abdominal aorta in 1816.[127]

Cooper was also noted for his encouraging and kind manner with patients, and for his "gentle sympathy, which won for him their immediate confidence and warm attachment."[128] Keats no doubt saw this bedside manner when he followed Cooper on his rounds at Guy's every Monday, Wednesday, and Friday, before he took up his duties as dresser for Lucas. No one could have been a better example of what a surgeon should be, but even he could not hold Keats's undivided attention on medicine.

On 25 July 1816 Keats presented himself at Apothecaries Hall at Blackfriars to take the examination for the Licentiate of the Society of Apothecaries certificate. The new Apothecaries Act required the passing of this examination before any candidate could practice as an apothecary.[129] We do not know whether Keats had already decided to abandon surgery by this time—an idea that seems unlikely, since he returned to Guy's to complete his year as dresser and to attend more courses in surgery in the autumn of 1816—or whether he wanted the L.S.A. as insurance in case he failed the examination for membership in the Royal College of Surgeons the following year. There is also the possibility that Abbey was pressuring him to complete his studies and begin practicing, since a large sum of money had already been spent on his training. The fact remains, in any case, that he passed the examination and thus became a qualified apothecary.

Until Gittings's biography, Keats's success in this examination was never recognized as the achievement that it was.[130] This was due mainly to the fact that Henry Stephens, in his account of Keats, claims that the examination was "more a test of Classical, than Medical—Knowledge,"[131] and that Keats passed on the strength of his Latin. Most readers failed to recognize in this part of Stephens's narrative his apparent jealousy of Keats because Keats had passed the examination when he, Stephens, failed in his attempt two months later. Contrary to Stephens's contention, the Court of Examiners of the Society of Apothecaries took the examination very seriously, and "during the first six months, the number rejected by the Court was large in proportion to the number examined, being about one in six." The court was confident that the act had achieved its purpose and "had already been productive of an increase of industry and application among the students of Medicine."[132] Although the examination did involve "translating parts of the Pharmacopoeia Londinensis, and Physicians' Prescriptions," the candidate was also examined in "the Theory and Practice of Medicine," in "Pharmaceutical Chemistry," and in "the Materia Medica."[133] The certificate, then, was no mere slip of paper. Keats's name appears in "A List of Certified Apothecaries" published in the *London Medical Repository* 6 (1816), with his address as Wilston, Edmonton, which was Hammond's home.

After he had passed his examination, Keats went off to Margate with Tom for a holiday, and the struggle between poetry and medicine had begun. In addition to needing a holiday, he may have gone to Margate in August 1816 to consult his old headmaster, John Clarke, about his future in medicine.[134] Keats's decision to give up medicine can hardly have been an easy one, since he had spent six years and a considerable sum of money preparing for the profession, and he may well have sought the advice of an older man whom he respected.

John Clarke was well prepared to give Keats advice on his future since Clarke's son-in-law, John Towers, was an apothecary and chemist practicing in London. In fact, Keats himself was well acquainted with Towers and his wife, Isabella Clarke, as Charles Cowden Clarke stayed with his sister and brother-in-law in London during 1816 and was often visited by Keats.[135] Cowden Clarke later recalled that Keats was the "kind playfellow" to the infant Charles Towers, his nephew.[136]

John Towers was a member of a respected family firm of dispensing chemists, Towers, Huskisson, and Huskisson, who remained in business on his own when the firm dissolved in 1808. He was particularly interested in botany and in theories of plant growth and physiology, with specific reference to heat and electricity. In 1819 he retired from London to the country to farm, and in 1830 he published *The Domestic Gardener's Manual;*

Biography

Being an Introduction to Gardening, on Philosophical Principles, which deals with much chemical and botanical theory. As Sperry speculates, it is very likely that Keats consulted Towers on topics in chemistry and botany while he was at Guy's,[137] and perhaps even later since he mentions seeing Towers as late as 1819 (*Letters,* 2:59).

But to return to Keats at Margate in 1816: whether he came to any decision about his future at this time we do not know, although, judging from a reference in his epistle "To My Brother George," he still considered medicine a useful and socially responsible occupation. In discussing his ambition to escape into poetic joy, Keats writes:

> Could I, at once, my mad ambition smother,
> For tasting joys like these, sure I should be
> Happier, and dearer to society. (110–12)

By late September he was back in the Borough, preparing for a new term of surgical lectures that began in October, and determined to complete his dressership, which extended until March 1817. By the time of his twenty-first birthday in October, however, Keats had decided in favor of poetry over medicine as a career, and soon afterwards he revealed his decision to his guardian, Richard Abbey.

It is difficult to know why Keats left medicine. A long-held opinion, championed by men like Hale-White, was that Keats's delicate nature was turned away from medicine by physical repugnance at hospital conditions of the time.[138] There is absolutely no evidence to support this view; Keats was probably no more and no less affected by the conditions than any other student,[139] and it seems unlikely that it would take him six years to decide medical conditions were repugnant.

There is also the probability that poetry itself was extremely appealing as a career by October 1816. Keats had recently met Hunt, Haydon, Hazlitt, and their literary set, who were no doubt encouraging him in the direction of poetry. He had also been introduced to the Olliers, who were interested in publishing new poets. The fact that his two longest poems to date, *Sleep and Poetry* and "I stood tip-toe . . . ," were written in the autumn of 1816 shows that he was devoting more and more time to this interest.

Despite this, however, Brown insisted that Keats "assured me the muse had no influence over him in his determination, he being compelled, by conscientious motives alone, to quit the profession, upon discovering that he was unfit to perform a surgical operation." The rest of Brown's statement is interesting and to the point:

He ascribed his inability to an overwrought apprehension of every possible chance of doing evil in the wrong direction of the instrument. "My last operation," he told me, "was the opening of a man's temporal artery. I did it with the utmost nicety; but, reflecting on what passed through my mind at the time, my dexterity seemed a miracle, and I never took up the lancet again."[140]

Keats's fear of failure as a surgeon, of destroying instead of saving life, is perfectly understandable, especially when we remember that in Billy Lucas he had a standing example of the butcher a poor surgeon could be.

In addition, Astley Cooper continually warned his students that

surgery requires certain qualities, without which no man can arise to celebrity in the Profession,—these are a good Eye, a steady hand, and above all a Mind which is not easily ruffled by circumstances which may occur during the Operation.[141]

But the quality which is considered of the highest order in surgical operations, is self-possession; the head must always direct the hand, otherwise the operator is unfit to discover an effectual remedy for the unforeseen accidents which may occur in his practice.[142]

His fear of doing harm with the scalpel apparently robbed Keats of such self-possession, and Cooper's lectures were not designed to reassure the timid or doubtful. In his introductory lecture to the course on surgery, Cooper listed numerous examples of surgeons whose incompetence resulted in the patient's death, including cases of venesection—the operation Brown describes Keats performing—where an artery was punctured instead of a vein.[143] He concluded: "I bring forward these examples to impress upon your minds that an imperative necessity exists for making yourselves well acquainted with anatomical science; without which you cannot conscientiously discharge your duty to society."[144] To a lazy or uncaring student, such warnings probably went unheeded; but to a conscientious student like Keats, acutely aware of the social responsibility of the medical profession, they perhaps increased self-doubt and fear of failure. This is particularly probable when seen in conjunction with Cooper's final warning, that a student's success depended upon his unbounded "zeal and industry" and that for this reason he should "be not multifarious or vacillating in [his] pursuits."[145] Since he was already vacillating between poetry and medicine, Keats must have felt impelled to make a final choice. Given his fears about his ability to operate, the growing encouragement from his literary friends, and the obvious contrast between the sordid, depressing hospital duty in the Borough and the intellectual stimulation at Hunt's Vale of Health, it seems inevitable that poetry was his choice. By November he was convinced, as he told his shocked guardian, Abbey, "that I possess Abilities greater than most Men, and therefore I am determined to gain my Living by exercising them."[146]

Even though the decision to abandon medicine was taken during the autumn of 1816, Keats continued his duties as dresser at Guy's until March 1817. His time, however, was occupied more and more by the Hunt circle, which after 11 December included Shelley and Horace Smith.[147] Hunt and Haydon urged Keats to gather some of his poems together for publication as a small volume, although Shelley advised him in vain to wait until he had a better collection of verse. This project occupied him through the winter months of early 1817. Auspiciously—perhaps ironically—the 1817 volume was published on 3 March, the same day that Keats's year as dresser to Guy's hospital came to an official end. One career was aborted and a new one was born. Shortly afterwards, Keats began work on *Endymion*.

Although he abandoned medicine as a career, Keats could not easily forget what he had heard and seen and learned during his six years of training. In private life, he continued to diagnose the pathological symptoms of friends and relatives.[148] Cowden Clarke remembered:

He once talked with me, upon my complaining of stomachic derangement, with a remarkable decision of opinion, describing the functions and actions of the organ with the clearness and, as I presume, technical precision of an adult practitioner.[149]

When he contracted tuberculosis, he diagnosed his own symptoms more accurately than did his doctors, who insisted first that he had a nervous condition and later that his ailment was seated in the stomach. After spitting up arterial blood in February 1820, he declared to Brown: "that drop of blood is my death-warrant."[150] But "his surgeon and physician both unhesitatingly declared that his lungs were uninjured. This satisfied me, but not him: he could not reconcile the colour of that blood with their favourable opinion."[151] Keats was, of course, correct, and a year later he was dead. His doctor in Rome, James Clark, was shocked to find his lungs deteriorated when an autopsy was performed, but Keats had known the nature of his disease all along.

As well as diagnosing occasionally, Keats, at various times when he was in need of money, reluctantly contemplated returning to medicine as a career.[152] Becoming a ship's doctor on an Indiaman remained an unattractive alternative to a failed poetic career; yet, ironically, he became a ship's doctor of sorts when journeying to Italy in 1820. One of the other passengers was a tubercular young lady, Miss Cotterell, whom Keats treated during the long, uncomfortable voyage.[153] The patience and success with which Severn says Keats treated the young lady under very adverse conditions suggests that he would have been a good doctor had he decided to follow such a career.

While providing him with the knowledge to diagnose his own ailments, and those of his friends and relatives, Keats's medical training also introduced him to certain images, metaphors, ideas, and ideals, which, as part of his intellectual equipment, would inevitably find their way into his poetry and letters. It remains to be shown how his knowledge of chemistry, botany, anatomy, physiology, pathology, and materia medica influenced Keats in his new career.

46

Biography

I will begin with chemistry because it is a convenient subject with which to introduce some of the general ideas and attitudes concerning science in the early nineteenth century and, more important, because in dealing with chemistry we gain insights into Keats's thoughts about poetic creativity, the process involved in producing art, before dealing with the poems themselves.

CHAPTER II

Chemistry

During the seventeenth and early eighteenth centuries, chemistry, as yet not very distinct from the related fields of biology and botany, was in a state of stagnation, lacking the kind of impetus Newton had given to physics and mathematics. Naturalists were still searching for some mysterious biochemical substance, usually called a "subtle fluid," which would explain the existence of life completely and finally. This onerous burden was placed on such "subtle fluids" as phlogiston, an invisible substance believed to flow in the blood. According to other theorists, animal magnetism and electricity were the life forces behind everything that lived and moved and had a being. These theories were often based on vague and loose analogies between very different life forms. They were much more satisfying to the imagination than to the reason, with empirical proof often being ignored or arbitrarily interpreted to suit a preconceived theory.

By the 1770s, however, scientists like Joseph Priestley, who exploded the myth of phlogiston, were claiming that advances in chemistry could be made only through rigorous empirical research, and not through vague theories postulated on a grand scale. Ironically, the revolution taking place in chemical studies by the end of the eighteenth century was not due to the discovery of the total explanation of life that had been sought previously; on the contrary, it was instigated by the acknowledgment that phenomena have only limited explanations. This allowed empirical researchers to concentrate on smaller, more specialized areas of science, an approach that led to the great discoveries of scientists like Sir Humphry Davy and his student Michael Faraday in the first half of the nineteenth century.

By the beginning of the nineteenth century, imagination and analogy had retreated before the advance of reason and empirical proof in the field of science. As Dr. John Haighton, who taught physiology at Guy's Hospital when Keats was there, states in his introductory lecture "On Life":

We are now to consider matter as possessed of vitality or the principle of Life. . . . Attempts have been made to give an idea of Life by analogy: as to the Spring of a Clock which gives movement to its different parts, others have compared it to Electricity which likewise gives motion to light bodies; and others again have compared it to Magnetism as communicated to Iron. But none of these analogies give us any adequate idea of Life.[1]

Haighton later claims that "arguing from Analogy is at all times fallacious."[2]

In his introductory discourse to "A Course of Lectures on Chemistry," delivered at the Royal Institution in January 1802, Sir Humphry Davy expands on the new developments in chemistry:

Before this time, vague ideas, superstitious notions, and inaccurate practices, were the only effects of the mind to establish the foundations of chemistry. Men either were astonished and deluded by their first inventions so as to become visionaries, and to institute researches after imaginary things, or they employed them as instruments for astonishing and deluding others. . . . These views of things have passed away, and a new science has gradually arisen. The dim and uncertain twilight of discovery, which gave to objects false or indefinite appearances, has been succeeded by the steady light of truth.[3]

The new attitude that truth is based solely on empirical proof, and that only limited explanations of life forces are possible, did not appeal to Romantic poets like Blake, who was still proclaiming the existence of a whole world in a grain of sand. As Ritterbush points out:

The Poet-Physician

To a thoughtful observer in the decades around 1800 the results of experiments would have fallen far short of accounting for the apparent qualities of organisms—their vital energies and the processes of growth and reproduction. . . . The resulting limits upon explanation have given rise to discomfort even to scientists, while to many thinkers of the Romantic period such limits were intellectually affronting—a challenge to their imaginations to devise comprehensive systems of explanation sufficient to account for all the phenomena of life.[4]

Even Romantic poets who had strong interests in science, like Goethe, were little interested in experiments and preferred to develop ideas through contemplation and intuition. They aspired to knowledge through direct insight and to explanations through the use of broad analogies between various life forms.

Keats's attitudes toward experimental proof and toward the use of analogy, however, were ambiguous. As a poet, he inevitably made extensive use of analogy, speculated at length about life, and insisted on the primacy of the imagination in grasping truth. Ironically, he adapted analogies from his scientific knowledge to describe aspects of his world of art, whereas previously scientists had adapted analogies from the sphere of the imagination to describe their "scientific" theories of immanence. Keats may have been turned away from medical science by the insistence of new men, like Astley Cooper and John Hunter, that any understanding of life forces can only be partial and limited, and must be devoid of wild speculation. He perhaps sought in poetry an intuitive understanding of life that nineteenth-century science no longer offered.

Yet certain aspects of Keats's thought show him clinging tenaciously to new scientific principles, especially his belief that "nothing ever becomes real till it is experienced" (*Letters* 2:81). As he progressed in poetry, he increasingly grew to believe that knowledge and truth had to be gained by observation, experience, and proof, an idea that involves a return to the principles he had been taught in medicine.

Exactly how rapidly these new approaches to chemistry and their resultant discoveries filtered down from research laboratories and learned societies to the level of practical medicine is debatable. But since Keats was taught by an eminent research chemist in the person of Alexander Marcet, it is safe to assume that he received a well-informed, up-to-date education in this field. As Babington and Allen point out in the introduction to their *Syllabus*, printed for their Guy's students attending the chemistry course, "Upon taking a retrospect of the last five and twenty years it will appear, that the discoveries within that period are so numerous and important,—the change which the Nomenclature has lately undergone is so essential and entire, that the Chemistry of the present day, compared with that of former times, may not improperly be considered as a new science expressed in new language."[5]

Babington takes this discussion of the new state of experimental chemistry a step further in his introductory lecture, "On Chemistry," delivered at Guy's and attended by Keats. He debates the merits of labeling chemistry an art or a science:

In searching for a satisfactory definition of the subject we are about to investigate, there appears, amongst the most celebrated Authors, who have treated of it, this remarkable difference, that by some it is regarded as little more than an Art, whilst others consider it, as a most important branch of Science. . . .

The Artist merely realizes what he knows beforehand to be practicable. The Man of Science satisfied of the practicability of the thing is little if at all solicitous whether it be realizes [*sic*] or not. The Artist is selfish, for he is constantly labouring for his own interest; he works from imitation & without principle. . . .

The Phylosopher or man of Science is in search of truth in order to make a general application of it to the benefit of his fellow creatures & values his experiments no further than as the[y] tend to the discovery or establishment of some general Law.[6]

I quote the passage at length for two reasons. First, it illustrates that the medical schools of Keats's day were not simply concerned with rudimentary remedies; they were still considering broad philosophical questions about the state of their science (or art), questions that probably would never be introduced by a modern teacher of chemistry.

Second, Babington's passage introduces a topic—the role of the artist versus that of the philosopher—that was to become of primary importance to Keats as his short career progressed. He never wanted to be a man of science "in search of truth," and he perhaps inwardly protested against Babington's claim that "the Artist is selfish," although he himself later told Shelley that "*an artist* . . . must have 'self concentration' selfishness perhaps" (*Letters* 2:322–23). But it is this very accusation—that "the Artist is selfish"—to which he returns in *The Fall of Hyperion* when Moneta, dismissing him as "a dreaming thing" (I, 168), asks: "What benefit canst thou do, or all thy tribe, / To the great world?" (I, 167–68). Keats's concept of the poet must finally be broadened to include Babington's idea of the philosopher as one who works for "the benefit of his fellow creatures." It is, then, no accident that Keats's final definition is that "a poet is a sage; / A humanist, physician to all men" (I, 189–90) and that he has Moneta proclaim, again using a medical image:

> "The poet and the dreamer are distinct,
> Diverse, sheer opposite, antipodes.
> The one pours out a balm upon the world,
> The other vexes it." (I, 199–202)

Although Keats is not consciously replying to Babington, it is apparent that his teacher had formulated for him, at a relatively early age, some important questions he would have to face later.

But let us return to the more mundane aspects of chemistry proper. With the exception of Stuart Sperry's excellent chapter "The Chemistry of the Poetic Process," [7] to which I am greatly indebted, no critic has paid much attention to Keats's knowledge of this science, an oversight that is difficult to comprehend when one realizes that the poet's vocabulary is full of words and metaphors whose meanings become wholly clear only within their chemical context. In particular, as Sperry has observed, Keats adapted certain chemical terms and theories as metaphors to explain his ideas concerning the creative process of writing poetry. Since medical chemistry is largely concerned with describing processes of change, combination, decomposition, and refinement, it is easy to recognize how Keats saw these processes as analogous to what occurs when the imagination works on various ideas, sensations, and emotions to produce poetry.

Chemistry

It is, of course, virtually impossible to say with any certainty whether Keats developed these analogies deliberately, or whether his knowledge of chemical terminology and processes became such an integral part of his intellectual equipment that the analogies were developed unconsciously. The precision with which he uses the terminology, however, suggests that it may very well have been a conscious effort. Such a suggestion gains support from the fact that Keats uses the terms mainly in letters to Benjamin Bailey, an Oxford academic who may well have been familiar with chemistry, and to his two brothers, to whom he probably explained his terms. As a theology student, Bailey would almost certainly have been familiar with scientific concepts, since "much popular science in English in the eighteenth century, and the first half of the nineteenth, was written as natural theology."[8]

It is also significant that Keats employs the chemical terms almost exclusively during the eighteen-month period immediately following the termination of his dressership at Guy's, from May 1817 to November 1818, when his knowledge of chemistry was fresh in his mind. In addition, by far the greatest concentration of these terms occurs in letters written between October 1817 and October 1818, immediately following Keats's stay in Oxford with Bailey. This suggests that Keats developed his ideas on poetic creativity in terms of chemistry through discussion with Bailey, and so used this terminology with the confidence that his friend would grasp his meaning. Once the correspondence with Bailey was dropped at the end of 1818, Keats's use of the chemical terms ceases almost completely.

Because the chemical analogies are concentrated in this relatively brief eighteen-month period of correspondence, it is not imperative to examine their development in a strictly chronological fashion. In fact, one more easily comprehends Keats's meaning if a single term or metaphor is traced through a number of letters, and occasionally in poems, while recognizing that other chemical terms and metaphors are being used at the same time in a cumulative effect.

The objection can, of course, be raised that many words in a professional terminology have similar meanings to, or source affinities with, those same words as used in common speech. Thus readers without any specialized knowledge of chemistry have grasped a general understanding of what I designate as Keats's chemical terms and phrases. Such understanding has often been vague, however, which leaves me convinced that knowledge of the specific chemical definitions of certain terms enhances and renders more precise our comprehension of some of Keats's more difficult images and phrases.

As I have indicated, Keats used his knowledge of chemistry mainly to describe the workings of the creative, poetic process. He was not, of course, the only writer to do so. Wordsworth had employed the analogy previously: "The imagination is . . . that chemical faculty by which elements of the most different nature and distant origin are blended together into one harmonious and homogeneous whole."[9] Later in the century, J. S. Mill would claim:

> The laws of the phenomena of the mind are sometimes analogous to mechanical, but sometimes also to chemical laws. When many impressions or ideas are operating in the mind together, there sometimes takes place a process of a similar kind to chemical combination. . . . These therefore are cases of mental chemistry: in which it is proper to say that the simple ideas generate, rather than that they compose, the complex ones.[10]

The analogies as expressed by Wordsworth and Mill, though acceptable, are obvious, almost forced, the deliberate attempts of literary minds to discover neat comparisons. They are based on a loose grasp of ideas concerning chemical composition. Keats's use of chemical analogies, however, is not so simple-minded, nor is it obvious, which may explain why it went unnoticed for so long. On the contrary, it is complex, subtle, and amazingly accurate, demonstrating a mind so familiar with its subject that slipping into chemical terminology and ideas is natural.

Closer to Keats's use of chemical terms and concepts is T. S. Eliot's view of the artist, which I strongly suspect to be influenced by his reading of Keats's letters. Eliot writes:

> The progress of an artist is a continual self-sacrifice, a continual extinction of personality. . . . It is in this depersonalization that art may be

said to approach the condition of science. I therefore invite you to consider, as a suggestive analogy, the action which takes place when a bit of finely filiated platinum is introduced into a chamber containing oxygen and sulphur dioxide. . . . The analogy was that of the catalyst. When the two gases previously mentioned are mixed in the presence of a filament of platinum, they form sulphurous acid. This combination takes place only if the platinum is present; nevertheless the newly formed acid contains no trace of platinum, and the platinum itself is apparently unaffected: has remained inert, neutral, and unchanged. The mind of the poet is the shred of platinum. It may partly or exclusively operate upon the experience of the man himself; but, the more perfect the artist, the more completely separate in him will be the man who suffers and the mind which creates; the more perfect will the mind digest and transmute the passions which are its material.[11]

Keats, as I will demonstrate, comes to the same conclusion about the artist's mind being a catalyst that transmutes materials into the more refined state of poetry. But whereas Eliot's analogy is very consciously developed, and thus essentially artificial, Keats's analogies are natural, organic outgrowths of a mind trained to think in such a vocabulary. Thus Keats does not feel the necessity to explain his metaphors as Eliot does.

Perhaps the most obvious use Keats makes of chemical concepts to illustrate imaginative creativity appears in a letter to Haydon on 8 April 1818, in which he describes the difficulties an artist must go through in order to create a work of beauty: "The innumerable compositions and decompositions which take place between the intellect and its thousand materials before it arrives at that trembling delicate and snail-horn perception of Beauty—I know not you many havens of intenseness—nor ever can know them" (*Letters* 1:264–65). As Sperry has indicated,[12] Keats here draws on the very definition of chemistry that Babington and Allen outline on the opening page of their *Syllabus* for the chemistry course at Guy's:

From the consideration of the peculiar properties of *Matter* arises its distribution into different *Kinds;* and from the action of *these* upon each other the various *Combinations* and *Decompositions,* the study of which constitutes the province of CHEMISTRY.

The Poet-Physician

CHEMISTRY therefore defined, *The Science of the Composition and Decomposition of the heterogeneous particles of Matter:* or "that which teaches the intimate and reciprocal action of bodies upon each other."[13]

For Keats, the creative process, like the chemical one, involves the artist's imagination bringing various materials— natural objects and the sensations they evoke—into "combinations and decompositions," or what Babington and Allen later call analysis and synthesis,[14] in order to form new, often purer, finer materials. Combination and decomposition are facilitated by the process of chemical attraction, which "is a principal agent in all chemical operations and phenomena."[15] Chemical attraction occurs exclusively between the particles of dissimilar, or heterogeneous, bodies, drawing them together into unity; "at the End of the process we find the result to be a compound totally differing from either of the Bodies employed."[16] This phenomenon is a perfect metaphor for the workings of the imagination, which draws together various thoughts and feelings into a new creative whole.

The process, as Keats describes it, involves various "havens of intenseness," or "intensity," a term that also derives from his understanding of chemistry. The *O.E.D.* defines the scientific meaning of "intensity" as "the degree or amount of some quality, condition, etc.; force, strength, energy; degree of some characteristic quality, as brightness, etc.; *esp.* in *Physics,* as a measurable quantity." In chemistry, "intensity" often refers to the degree, or level, of heat necessary to bring about a chemical or physical change in substances. Joseph Priestley explains that "heat assists the solvent power of almost all menstrua; so that many substances will unite in a certain degree of heat, which will form no union at all without it."[17] Heat also assists the decomposition of many substances. Not all combination and decomposition require external changes in heat intensity, however; often the temperature change is internally generated by the bodies themselves.[18]

That Keats uses the word "intensity" with this scientific meaning becomes clear at the end of the famous "Pleasure Thermometer" passage in Book I of *Endymion*:

Chemistry

> But there are
> Richer entanglements, enthralments far
> More self-destroying, leading, by degrees,
> To the chief intensity: the crown of these
> Is made of love and friendship.　　(I, 797–801)

In a letter of 30 January 1818 to John Taylor (*Letters* 1:218), Keats himself draws attention to the image of the thermometer, an instrument that measures the degrees of intensity of heat. The image is used in *Endymion* as a metaphor to describe the various levels of human feeling. It is interesting to note that as the degree of intensity is increased, the amount of "self" that is destroyed also increases—"love and friendship" being self-less—an idea that also fits the chemical analogy since the intensity of heat applied determines the evaporation of impurities from the substance being heated. As Babington points out, "All Bodies are capable of being evaporated by heat tho' the degree of heat, requisite to be applied, varies in different Bodies as well as in the same matter under different Circumstances."[19] The greater the "intensity" of heat, then, the greater will be the number of "disagreeables," or selfish propensities, evaporated off.

Keats employs this metaphor again at the end if 1817 when writing to George and Tom about Benjamin West's painting *Death on the Pale Horse:* "But there is nothing to be intense upon; no women one feels mad to kiss; no face swelling into reality. the excellence of every Art is its intensity, capable of making all disagreeables evaporate, from their being in close relationship with Beauty & Truth" (*Letters* 1:192). The intensity of art, like that of heat, is capable of burning off or evaporating all impure or disagreeable elements in a substance or a work, thus leaving it purified.

Yet the chemical analogy here has gone unnoticed by many prominent critics. Bate, for example, argues that Keats's "intensity" is synonymous with Hazlitt's "gusto," the "power or passion defining any object."[20] Hazlitt had in fact written an essay on West's *Death on the Pale Horse,* which appeared in the *Edinburgh Review,* to which Bate directs us. In this essay, however, Hazlitt mentions the term "gusto" only once, and never

57

discusses "beauty," "truth," or "intensity." If Keats is influenced by Hazlitt, it is much more likely that he has in mind the critic's essay on another of West's paintings, *Christ Rejected:*

Perhaps in the entire body of Mr. West's production, however meritorious the design and composition often are, there is not to be found, a single instance of exquisite sentiment, or colour, or drawing; not one face or figure, hand or eye, which can be dwelt upon as an essence in its kind; as carrying truth, or beauty, or grandeur, to that height of excellence to which they have been sometimes carried, and beyond which the mind has no wish or conception that they should go. In fact, Mr. West's pictures are made up of a great quantity of indifferent materials, formally put together. . . . If there was anything in the world which could have touched Mr. West's pencil, it must have been the intense feeling, and "power of love sublime," conveyed in the passage which he has the temerity to quote. —"Woman, behold thy Son, and turning to the beloved disciple—Behold, thy Mother." . . . but no such thing.[21]

Although one should recognize the influence of Hazlitt's general ideas about West on Keats's criticism of *Death on the Pale Horse,* one still misses the point of Keats's proclamation about art if one fails to see it within its chemical context. It may well be that Hazlitt's reference to "intense feeling" triggers Keats's comment on the "intensity" of art. But, with his chemical knowledge, Keats develops the concept further, viewing the intensity of art as thermal energy which evaporates—there is no such chemical process mentioned by Hazlitt—"disagreeables," or impurities, until only the purified work is left. Beauty and truth act as catalysts in the purification, until only the very essence of the subject being painted remains.

But the process of evaporation is not the only one that Keats draws on in his attempts to formulate his understanding of imaginative creativity. He continually uses the words "distill," "sublime," "abstract," and "digest," which, as Sperry has pointed out,[22] are chemical terms to describe processes that are similar to evaporation. Babington and Allen state in their *Syllabus* that "to the head of *Evaporation* may also be referred the processes of *Distillation,* and *Sublimation.*"[23] And in his "Lectures," Babington explains that "*Distillation* is only a process of Evaporation in a proper Apparatus that the Vapor may again be condensed,"[24] and "*Sublimation* Is where the Saline substance is of a Volatile Nature we proceed to apply Heat to it in a particular Vessel, where what is Volatile may be saved."[25] In other words, sublimation is a dry form of distillation. To "abstract" in the chemical sense is "to separate an essence or chemical principle by distillation," whereas to "digest" is "to prepare by boiling or application of heat; to dissolve by the aid of heat and moisture" (*O.E.D.*). Richard Stocker, the apothecary at Guy's, states in his translation of the *Pharmacopoeia* that "in DIGESTION the Dublin College mean, unless it is otherwise directed, a gentle heat to be employed."[26]

All these processes utilize heat (Keats's "intensity" of art) to resolve substances, usually chemical compounds, into their component parts, with the principal object of refining or purifying them, and then collecting the purified product, which is often a "spirit" or an "essence," two terms to which I will return. This process provides Keats a perfect metaphor with which to describe his ideas concerning the creative processes of art.

Before examining these terms in Keats's work, however, I should illustrate their frequent use by Babington and Allen with a few simple quotations from the *Syllabus* and the "Lectures on Chemistry":

Of Alcohol

Repeated distillation and digestion on dried *Muriate of Lime* or on *Potash*, necessary to bring *Alcohol* to its utmost degree of purity.[27]

Urea,—procured from fresh *Urine* in the form of crystalline plates, by evaporating it to the consistence of syrup, digesting this when cold in *Alcohol*, distilling the solution so as to separate and collect the spirit, and allowing the residuum to crystallise by cooling.[28]

Acid of Vinegar

Vinegar may be purified in many ways but the most common & best is by simple distillation.[29]

Acid of Phosphorus

It may be decomposed by mixing it with Charcoal & distilling when there will come over Phosphorus in it's own particular form.[30]

Stocker also makes frequent mention of these terms in the *Pharmacopoeia*, which describes the methods for mixing medicines. His recipe for purified opium, for example, is:

The Poet-Physician

> Take of Opium cut into small pieces a pound,
> Proof Spirit twelve pints.

> Digest in a gentle heat, frequently shaking, until the Opium is dissolved; then filter the liquor, and let it be distilled in a retort to separate the Spirit; pour out the residual liquor, and let it be evaporated until the extract has acquired the proper consistence.[31]

Keats first employs these chemical terms in a letter to Bailey in October 1817. Complaining of his attraction to indolence, he states: "This leads me to suppose that there are no Men thouroughly wicked—so as never to be self *spiritualized* into a kind of *sublime* Misery—but alas! 't is but for an Hour" (*Letters* 1:173).[32] Keats speculates that even wicked men must have some part of their baser selves "spiritualized," sublimated, or distilled into the purer form of "sublime" Misery, or Spirit of Misery, if only for a brief time. Here, however, the terms do not refer specifically to the creative, or artistic, process.

In his letter of 27 June 1818, written to Tom from the Lake District, Keats does introduce these terms in discussing poetry. He writes:

> What astonishes me more than any thing is the tone, the coloring, the slate, the stone, the moss, the rock-weed; or, if I may so say, the *intellect*, the countenance of such places. The space, the magnitude of mountains and waterfalls are well imagined before one sees them; but this countenance or *intellectual tone* must surpass every imagination and defy any remembrance. I shall learn poetry here and shall henceforth write more than ever, for the *abstract* endeavor of being able to add a mite to that mass of beauty which is harvested from these grand *materials*, by the *finest spirits,* and put into *etherial* existence for the relish of one's fellows. (*Letters* 1:301)

The "abstract endeavor" Keats discusses here is not some vague, aesthetic goal, but a specific desire to "abstract," in the chemical sense of "distill," the "grand materials," which are the physical aspects of nature he sees around him, into "etherial existence," which is a more purified, refined, perfected state, the state of poetry. In chemistry this state is brought about only by the "finest spirits," which correspond to the purest, most *refined* imaginations. Thus Keats implies that the imagination itself must be distilled, purified, before it can abstract material objects into great art which exists on a higher, more *spiritual* plane. This higher plane is what he elsewhere calls a "finer tone" (*Letters* 1:185), which is derived from the concept of distilling as a process of refining.

What Keats says about this landscape in the Lake District, before he discusses his "abstract endeavor," is also of interest. Previously he had written to Haydon about the artist's "innumerable compositions and decompositions which take place between the intellect and its thousand materials before it arrives at that trembling delicate and snail-horn perception of beauty"; but here the "materials"—"the coloring, the slate, the stone, the moss. . . . The space, the magnitude of mountains and waterfalls"—have their own "intellect," or "intellectual tone," which "must surpass every imagination and defy any remembrance." Ironically, Keats is saying that the very material landscape of the Lake District which inspires him to artistic endeavor needs no human intellect or imagination to refine, distill, or abstract it into a state of art; it already exists in a "finer tone," in a state of self-created pure beauty that defies improvement by the human imagination. It is poetry incarnate, reality more ethereal than imagination could make it. It is no wonder, then, that he exclaims, "I shall learn poetry here."

That Keats talks about "materials" or "worldly" things being distilled or "sublimated" by the imagination into a "spiritual" or "ethereal" (themselves chemical terms) state of beauty illustrates that he does not use the eighteenth-century distinction, still prevalent in Wordsworth's poetry, between the sublime and the beautiful. For him sublimation leads to beauty which is above greatness, as he points out in a somewhat insulting comment on Americans to George and Georgiana in October 1818:

Those American's are great but they are not *sublime* Man—the humanity of the United States can never reach the *sublime*—Birkbeck's mind is too much in the American Stryle [*sic*]—you must endeavour to infuse a little *Spirit* of another sort into the Settlement, always with great caution, for thereby you may do your descendents more good than you may imagine. If I had a prayer to make for any great good, next to Tom's recovery, it should be that one of your Children should be the first American Poet.　　　　　　　　　(*Letters* 1:397–98)

Again it is the poetic imagination that can sublimate the ordinary material of the settlement into "ethereal existence" through the infusion of refined "spirit." This must be George and Georgiana's "abstract endeavor."

It should be pointed out, however, that critics have usually viewed Keats's concept of the "sublime" in a very traditional literary fashion. Thomas Weiskel, for example, has placed Keats in the tradition of "the Romantic sublime" that develops from Longinus, through the Renaissance poets, especially Milton, and the literary, philosophical, and religious writers of the eighteenth and nineteenth centuries in England and Germany, to psychological Freudian concepts of "sublimation."[33] Stuart Ende has taken the same literary and psychological approach, but has focused exclusively on Keats within this tradition.[34] Although the approach of these critics is valid and valuable, it does not involve any close examination of Keats's use of the word "sublime" in his letters, which supports my contention that, without an understanding of the chemical process of sublimation as a form of distillation, Keats's meaning cannot be wholly ascertained.

The familiar chemical terms associated with the process of distillation appear again a few days later in the same letter to George and Georgiana, this time in Keats's discussion of his prospects for marriage:

Notwithstand your Happiness and your recommendation I hope I shall never marry. Though the most beautiful Creature were waiting for me at the end of a Journey or a Walk; though the carpet were of Silk, the Curtains of the morning Clouds; the chairs and Sofa stuffed with Cygnet's down; the food Manna, the Wine beyond Claret, the Window opening on Winander mere, I should not feel—or rather my Happiness would not be so *fine*, as my Solitude is *sublime*. Then instead of what I have described, there is a *Sublimity* to welcome me home. (*Letters* 1:403)

It is interesting to note that Keats was probably going to write "I should not feel so happy as . . . ," but he deliberately changed his expression to include his now commonly used chemical terminology. He boldly claims that even the most refined material possessions associated with conjugal bliss cannot compensate for the refinement, the sublimity, of his distilled moods of solitude, in which poetic creation occurs and in which he possesses not merely a few beauties, but all the distilled or abstracted beauty of the world: "The roaring of the wind is my wife and the Stars through the window pane are my Children. The mighty *abstract* Idea I have of Beauty in all things stifles the more divided and minute domestic happiness" (*Letters* 1:403).

Keats's discussion of domestic happiness at this point is influenced by two earlier passages in his letters. The first is his description, given to George and Georgiana a few days earlier, on 14 October 1818, of the Reynolds's cousin, Jane Cox, who is perhaps the subconscious cause of his discussion about matrimony:

She has a rich eastern look; she has *fine* eyes and *fine* manners. When she comes into a room she makes an impression the same as the Beauty of a Leopardess. She is too *fine* and too concious of her Self to repulse any Man who may address her— . . . I always find myself more at ease with such a woman; the picture before me always gives me a life and animation which I cannot possibly feel with any thing inferiour.   (*Letters* 1:395)

The admiration Keats feels for the refined beauty and living energy displayed by this Charmian is very similar, I think, to the strangely attached and yet detached interest of a scientific observer who is not at all interested in applying any moral qualities to such energy.

Keats illustrates these same ideas with sharper focus in a later letter to George and Georgiana, written on 19 March 1819:

Though a quarrel in the streets is a thing to be hated, the *energies* displayed in it are *fine*; the commonest Man shows a grace in his quarrel—By a superior being our reasoning[s] may take the same tone—though erroneous they may be *fine*—This is the very thing in which consists poetry; and if so it is not so *fine* a thing as philosophy—For the same reason that an eagle is not so *fine* a thing as a truth.   (*Letters* 2:80–81)

This letter has caused much confusion among critics, sometimes resulting in the erroneous claim that Keats was turning away from poetry in favor of philosophy as a superior pursuit in life.[35] Such a view is based on a moral understanding of the word "fine" as a synonym for "good." Keats's comparison of the relationship between poetry and philosophy to that between an eagle and a truth, however, demonstrates conclusively that he does not use "fine" with any moral connotations. Philosophy is in no sense better or more virtuous than poetry, just as a truth cannot claim moral superiority over an eagle.

Keats's meaning becomes clear only when "fine" is understood within its scientific context of refining metals and liquids. The *O.E.D.* defines "fine" in a scientific sense as:

Free from foreign or extraneous matter, having no dross or other impurity; clear, pure, refined.
a. Of metals: Free from dross or alloy.
b. Of gold or silver: Containing a given proportion of pure metal, specified respectively in 'carats' or 'ounces'.
c. Of liquids: Free from turbidity or impurity, clear. Also occas. of air: Pure.[36]

What Keats means in his pronouncement is that philosophy is more refined, distilled, or purified than poetry, in that it is totally intellectual, just as a truth is totally abstract (or abstracted); neither has any material basis, any dross. Poetry, on the other hand, like the eagle, is, for Keats, rooted in the materials from which it is formed, energies like those displayed in "a quarrel in the streets" or a woman like Jane Cox, whom he calls "a fine thing speaking in a worldly way." These "energies" or "things" can themselves be refined, but they never cease to be fundamentally earthy or material.

This introduces an important question in our consideration of Keats's understanding of poetic creativity as a process of distillation, refinement, or purification. Does such a process lead ultimately to the imagination soaring beyond material experience into transcendent, or even transcendental, divine states of experience that are divorced from the real world? Although Keats is constantly aware of such a danger, and succumbs to it himself in his early escapist romances, the final answer to the question is a resounding *no*. For Keats, poetic creativity is ultimately rooted in material existence, in sensations perceived from concrete objects, even though those sensations and the imaginative speculations they evoke are distilled into art. He is always concerned with the "eagle," rarely with the abstract "truth." In this respect, it is interesting to note that even Keats's conception of heaven involves "having what we call happiness on Earth repeated in a *finer* tone and so repeated—And yet such a fate can only befall those who delight in sensation rather than hunger as you [Bailey] do after Truth" (*Letters* 1:185).

The other letter recalled by Keats's discussion of marriage and his claim that "the roaring of the wind is my wife and the Stars through the window pane are my Children" is an early one to Haydon on 11 May 1817, in which he writes about "looking upon the Sun the Moon the Stars, the Earth and its contents as *materials* to form greater things—that is to say *ethereal* things—but here I am talking like a Madman greater things that our Creator himself made!!" (*Letters* 1:143). It is clear that Keats is here speculating about the way art is formed, and Sperry claims that "'etherealization,' or the way in which material forms are 'put into etherial existence,' is close to the heart of his [Keats's] notion of poetic creativity."[37] It is important, therefore, that we comprehend exactly what Keats means by the words "ethereal" and "material," for they are vital to his understanding of poetry. Despite this importance—or perhaps because of it—there is no general consensus as to their meanings. This is in part due to the fact that Keats himself uses the term "ethereal" with a variety of meanings.

Sometimes he uses "ethereal" in its conventional sense of "pertaining to ether," which, according to ancient and mythical cosmological speculation, is "the clear sky; the upper regions of space beyond the clouds; the medium filling the upper region of space, as the air fills the lower regions" (*O.E.D.*). This is precisely the meaning he would have found in Bonnycastle's *Introduction to Astronomy*, which he won as a prize at Clarke's school: "ETHER, a fine subtile fluid, which is supposed to fill the whole celestial space between the heavenly bodies and our atmosphere."[38] Thus we get Keats's lines: "Lovely the moon in ether, all alone" (*Calidore*, 157); "E'en like the passage of an angel's tear / That falls through the clear ether silently" ("To one who has been long in city pent," 13–14); and "From the clear space of ether, to the small / Breath of new buds unfolding" (*Sleep and Poetry*, 168–69).

From this definition of "ether" comes the related, but less specific, meaning of "ethereal" as "light, airy, attenuated; heavenly, celestial" (*O.E.D.*). This is Keats's meaning when he requests that "Sweet Hope, ethereal balm upon me shed" ("To Hope," 5), and in *Endymion* when he asks the heavenly muse to "let a portion of ethereal dew / Fall on my head, and presently unmew / My soul" (I, 131–33). In fact, it is with this common meaning of "heavenly, celestial"—and sometimes "spirit-like" (*O.E.D.*)—that Keats uses the adjective "ethereal" most often in his poetry.[39]

With this definition of ether as "the medium filling the upper regions of space, as the air fills the lower regions," George Bornstein has conducted an extensive study of "Keats's Concept of the Ethereal," focusing primarily on *Endymion*, in which his main argument is:

The supra-natural (but actually existent) sphere of ether above the earth furnished Keats with a metaphor to describe his poetry, just as terrestrial nature furnished him with the metaphors for the poetry itself. Ethereal poetry would have the same relation to ordinary reality that ether had to air: it would be purer, higher, and free from mutability.[40]

Employing this same idea, but literally rather than metaphorically, and claiming that Keats obtained his understanding of ether from a study of alchemy and magic in writers like Agrippa, Blackstone writes that "ethereal"

is indeed a key word for Keats. Its antonym is "material"; the distinction is very like that drawn between the "subtle" and the "gross" bodies in Hindu metaphysics. The alchemical process, in the Great Work, distils the ethereal from the material substance. . . . The process of nature, participated in by man the magus as an under-agent of what in *Endymion* Keats will call the "throned seats unscalable," is continuously transmuting gross into subtle bodies.[41]

Though his argument contains his usual flashes of brilliance and incomprehensibility, Blackstone here seems to be fishing for sources in very distant waters.

It was Davies who first suggested that Keats might be using the word with a chemical meaning: "Keats uses ethereal in a variety of senses. When applied to physical things and actions it can mean having the insubstantiality and rarity of *ether*, delicate, refined, volatile. It seems to be derived from Keats's medical studies in which he would have found ether contrasted with heavy spirits."[42] That Keats was aware of the chemical difference between ethereal and heavy spirits is evidenced in his comments to George and Georgiana about claret:

For really 't is so *fine*—it fills the mouth one's mouth with a gushing freshness—then goes down cool and feverless—then you do not feel it quarelling with your liver—no it is rather a Peace maker and lies as quiet as it did in the grape—then it is as fragrant as the Queen Bee; and the more *ethereal* Part of it mounts into the brain, not assaulting the cerebral apartments like a bully in a bad house looking for his trul and hurrying from door to door bouncing against the waistcoat; but rather walks like Aladin about his own enchanted palace so gently that you do not feel his step—Other wines of a *heavy and spiritous* nature transform a Man to a Silenus; this makes him a Hermes.

(*Letters* 2:64)

This passage is a strange and wonderful mixture concocted from Keats's eclectic knowledge of chemistry, physiology, mythology, oenology, and prostitution.

Sperry greatly expands upon the eighteenth-century scientific understanding of ether as a "subtle" or "imponderable" fluid, "a substance of great elasticity and subtilty, believed to permeate the whole of planetary and stellar space, not only filling the interplanetary spaces, but also the interstices between the particles of air and other matter on the earth" (*O.E.D.*). The theory of this fluid was developed by Descartes and Newton to account for the movement of forces without physical contact and was explained in the early nineteenth century by Sir Humphry Davy.[43] Sperry goes on to show that "the notion of an ethereal matter forever at work in the world's atmosphere and bringing about continual changes in its elements offered Keats a useful and suggestive parallel to the operation of the spirit of poetry."[44]

Although Sperry's argument is well taken, it should be pointed out that the definition of ether he uses is, strictly speaking, from astronomy and physics rather than from chemistry. While at Guy's Keats did not take any course in physics, and in his "Lectures" Babington never refers to ether as a subtle fluid. Instead, he discusses it within the context of its chemical definition: "the colourless, light, volatile liquid, resulting from the action of sulphuric and other acids upon alcohol, whence it was also known as *Sulphuric, Phosphoric,* etc. *ether*" (*O.E.D.*). As Priestley explains, "If spirit of wine be distilled with almost any of the acids, the produce is a liquor which has obtained the name of *Aether,* from its extreme lightness and volatility, being much lighter, and more volatile, than any other fluid that we are acquainted with."[45] And Babington states that "Sp of wine unites with the different acids; hence our different *Aethers.*"[46]

The production of these ethers from the distillation of rectified spirits is outlined at great length in both Babington's "Lectures" and Stocker's *Pharmacopoeia.*[47] It is this process that Keats seems to have in mind when he talks of "looking upon the Sun the Moon the Stars, the Earth and its contents as materials to form greater things—that is to say ethereal things," and of "that mass of beauty which is harvested from these grand materials, by the finest spirits, and put into etherial existence." Within the context of the chemical metaphor, Keats's "materials" are equivalent to the acids that are mixed with rectified spirits (Keats's "the finest spirits") to form ether (Keats's "ethereal things") by distillation. The "materials" are physical things of beauty and the sensations they produce, which are refined by the imagination ("the finest spirits") to produce poetry ("ethereal things"). The poetic process, like the chemical, is one of distillation or purification; but as always, Keats's poetry is rooted in the phenomenal world.

Stocker outlines in further detail the distillation process in which Keats discovered an apt metaphor to explain the workings of the imagination:

Chemistry

Put the Nitrate of Potash into a tabulated retort placed in a cold water bath, and pour on it gradually, and at different times, the Sulphuric Acid and Spirit, previously mixed together and allowed to cool. Without any external heat . . . The Ethereal Spirit will begin to distil over, the assistance of fire not being required. . . . Pour the ethereal liquor, which thus spontaneously distils, into a glass stopped vial.[48]

This description of the production of nitric ether fits perfectly Keats's concept of how poetry is created, not only because it involves a process of distillation,[49] but for two other reasons. First, that the reaction occurs spontaneously coincides with Keats's idea that "if Poetry comes not as naturally as the Leaves to a tree it had better not come at all" (*Letters* 1:238–39). Second, that the process generates its own energy in the form of heat—no external heat being necessary—complies with Keats's claim that "the excellence of every Art is its intensity, capable of making all disagreeables evaporate" (*Letters* 1:192) and that "the Genius of Poetry must work out its own salvation in a man. . . . That which is creative must create itself" (*Letters* 1:374). The process also involves "the innumerable compositions and decompositions which take place between the intellect and its thousand materials" before the beauty of art is formed (*Letters* 1: 264–65).[50]

Thus far I have discussed Keats's concept of the "ethereal" in a number of letters where the term occurs in conjunction with other chemical terms. By far the most obvious reference to the "ethereal" in the context of chemical reactions, however, appears in an early letter, written on 22 November 1817 to Bailey. This letter, written not long after Keats returned from visiting Bailey at Oxford, is studded with clusters of chemical metaphors and analogies, some of which I have already examined in discussing Keats's claim that heaven will be earthly happiness experienced in a "finer tone." A little earlier in the letter he postulates the idea that "Men of Genius are great as certain ethereal Chemicals operating on the Mass of neutral intellect—by [for but] they have not any individuality, any determined Character" (*Letters* 1:184). Just as acids can combine with rectified spirits to form ethers, so too ethers can react with other chemicals to form active substances.

But whereas it is obvious that Keats is again comparing how a poet or "Man of Genius" creates to the workings of a chemical reaction, it is not perfectly clear what he means by "the Mass of neutral intellect." The phrase has often been interpreted as meaning the minds of the readers upon whom the poetry works, although Bornstein suggests that it refers to the poet's mind, which must be in a neutral state of "negative capability" before creativity can proceed.[51] Blackstone, however, with whom I concur, believes that the phrase refers to the "grand materials" of the phenomenal world, which are distilled by "ethereal Chemicals" in order to form poetry. The "ethereal Chemicals" are, then, the poets' imaginations, which are already in a state of refinement. This reading of the phrase "Mass of neutral intellect" gains support from the fact that Keats later calls the "grand materials" of the Lake District aspects of its "intellect" which are "harvested . . . by the finest spirits" to create poetry.[52]

That Keats's "Men of Genius" have no "individuality," no "determined Character," suggests that they act like catalysts in the creative process of transmuting material "things" into art: they instigate the process but do not themselves enter into combinations with the other substances to form the finished product. As Humphry Davy states in his discussion of "ethereal matters" (Keats's "ethereal Chemicals," the imagination): "their principal effects seem rather to depend upon their communicating motion to the particles of common matter, or modifying their attractions, than to their actually entering into combination with them."[53] This catalytic role is precisely parallel to Keats's view of the genuine poet: he must, with his imagination, distill materials and sensations into art, but at the same time he must not allow his own moral, religious, or philosophical views to inform the poetry. Poetry must never be didactic: "We hate poetry that has a palpable design upon us" (*Letters* 1:224). Like the "ethereal Chemicals," the genuine "Man of Genius" will never allow his ego to enter into his art; instead, he acts as a catalyst or a stimulant that is ultimately invisible in the work itself.

Having made these statements about the poetic process, and

declared his faith in the imagination as opposed to "consequitive reasoning," Keats goes on to tell Bailey in this letter of 22 November that a "philosophic Mind" must balance both intuitive imagination and rational knowledge: "and therefore it is necessary to your eternal Happiness that you do not only drink this old Wine of Heaven which I shall call the redigestion of our most ethereal Musings on Earth; but also increase in knowledge and know all things" (*Letters* 1:186).

In calling poetry the "old Wine of Heaven" or "the redigestion of our most ethereal Musings on Earth," Keats again makes use of a chemical metaphor. In chemistry, to "digest" means to bring to maturity using heat, usually by "keeping bodies for a considerable time immersed in a fluid at a higher temperature than that of the atmosphere, in order that combinations may take place that could not else have been effected."[54] Babington, in his lecture on the spirit of wine (Keats's "old Wine of Heaven"), writes: "It may be purified by repeated distillation & converted to a state of Alkohol by *digesting* it over mild & caustic vegetable Alkali in certain proportions & submitting it to further distillation which must be conducted *slowly & gradually*."[55] Similarly for Keats, his "ethereal [distilled, purified] Musings" must be digested and redigested, maturing passively over long periods of time in order to form the new combinations that are poetry. As he says elsewhere, "Nothing is finer for the purposes of great productions, than a very *gradual* ripening of the intellectual powers" (*Letters* 1:214).

The importance of states of passivity to the creative process of "etherialization" is emphasized by Keats about a month later—on 19 February 1818—in a letter to Reynolds. He speculates:

I have an idea that a Man might pass a very pleasant life in this manner—let him on any certain day read a certain Page of full Poesy or *distilled* Prose and let him wander with it, and muse upon it, and reflect from it, and bring home to it, and prophesy upon it, and dream upon it—untill it becomes stale—but when will it do so? Never— When Man has arrived at a certain ripeness in intellect any one grand and *spiritual* passage serves him as a starting post towards all "the two- and thirty Pallaces" How happy is such a "voyage of conception,' what delicious diligent Indolence! A doze upon a Sofa does not hinder it, and a nap upon Clover engenders *ethereal* finger-pointings.

(*Letters* 1:231)

It has long been recognized that Keats's idea of "diligent Indolence" is influenced by Wordsworth's concept of "wise passiveness," in which the artist remains in a state of passive receptivity while experiencing sensations that trigger trains of association in his mind.[56] It is important to understand, however, Keats's belief that imaginative speculations need not be initiated by physical sensations: "spiritual passages" of "full Poetry or distilled Prose" can themselves trigger speculations that launch the reader on his own "voyage of conception." As the distilled product of intense imaginative experience, the spirit of literature—in a chemical rather than an esoteric sense, the purest passages—acts as a catalyst to help generate the creative process of "etherealization" in the reader's own mind. In this context, the speculations and musings that the poetry initiates in the reader's mind are "ethereal finger-pointings," gentle directions to aid in the reader's creative process of distillation. Poetry, as Keats proclaims elsewhere, must be "great & unobtrusive" (*Letters* 1:224); instead of didactically teaching, it must act as a catalyst that assists the reader in his own generative act which, like the poet's, occurs in a state of passivity.

Having discussed the process of creating ethers, I should perhaps attempt to explain what Keats means by "ethereal things." He outlines his thoughts on this subject at length in a letter to Bailey on 13 March, about three weeks after his discussion of "diligent Indolence":

As Tradesmen say every thing is worth what it will fetch, so probably every mental pursuit takes its reality and worth from the ardour of the pursuer—being in itself a nothing—Ethereal thing may at least be thus real, divided under three heads—Things real—things semireal—and no things—Things real—such as existences of Sun Moon & Stars and passages of Shakspeare—Things semireal such as Love, the Clouds &c which requires a greeting of the Spirit to make them wholly exist—and Nothings which are made Great and dignified by an ardent pursuit—Which by the by stamps the burgundy mark on the bottles of our Minds, insomuch as they are able to "*consec[r]ate whate'er they look upon.*" (*Letters* 1:242–43; Keats's italics)

This passage, in which Keats is more analytical than usual, has never, to my mind, been fully explained, although Sperry does an admirable job of fitting it into the general context of Keats's thought.[57] In describing the three stages of ethereal reality—which seems almost a contradiction if we take "ethereal" to mean "heavenly"—Keats is explaining the degree of imaginative input necessary, on the part of the artist, to distill or refine "grand materials" into the "etherial existence" which is artistic beauty. Again, the concept of distilling chemical ethers lies beneath his explanation.

At the first or highest level of reality, that of the ethereal-real, are things that are already really ethereal; that is, they are already in their purest, most refined or abstracted form and thus, like the landscape Keats saw in the Lake District, do not require any input from the poet's imagination to distill them. It is easy to see why Keats includes "passages of Shakspeare" in this category since, for him, Shakespeare's was poetry already refined to its highest intensity. More difficult to understand is his reason for including "existences of Sun Moon & Stars" when he had earlier talked of "the Sun the Moon the Stars, the Earth and its contents as materials to form greater things—that is to say ethereal things." But we must realize that the operative word here is "existences"—"of Sun Moon & Stars"—which indicates that they already "wholly exist" or are in "etherial existence," presumably put there by previous artists, and so are no longer merely "grand materials." Of course, the sun, moon, and stars also exist in the classical mytho-cosmological "ether," the region above the clouds, which fits nicely with Keats's argument.

The second category, that of the ethereal-semireal, includes things which are at present only half-ethereal and so they require some input from the imagination "to make them wholly exist" or ethereally exist. That Keats calls the imagination "the Spirit" points up the chemical metaphor, for it is spirit of wine, or rectified spirit, that is mixed with acid to distill ether. The choice of the verb "greet" is also exact, for it implies a mutual interplay between the semireal (material-ethereal) thing and the "Spirit"; the onus is not totally on the imagination to make the thing real. "Clouds" are included in this category because they are formed by a process of evaporation—a form of distillation without heat—and condensation; they are between the "material" state of water and the "ethereal" state of pure vapor. And within the classical concept of ether, clouds exist at the transition point between the atmosphere and the ether, and so are semiethereal. Love also involves a mixture of material, or sensual, passion and refined emotion, and so needs a "greeting of the Spirit" to distill it into totally ethereal existence, where it becomes "disinterestedness."[58]

The third category, that of ethereal nothings, is made up of material things that as yet have no ethereal existence and so are totally dependent on the "ardent pursuit" of the poet's imagination to sublimate them into artistic beauty, greatness, and dignity. This is obviously the most difficult process of distillation, and as Babington points out, when an acid is reluctant to give off ether, "it may be made to afford more ether, by the addition of one third of very strong *ardent spirit*."[59] It is probably this process that Keats has in mind when he talks of the "ardent pursuit" of the "Spirit"-imagination to etherealize material things; without this stronger chemical, no distillation would take place, no ether would be formed.

It is this "ardent pursuit" of the imagination that "stamps the burgundy mark on the bottles of our Minds," by which I understand Keats to mean "produces the best poetry or artistic beauty." We have already seen him refer to poetry as the "old Wine of Heaven," and he had recently written to Reynolds a verse letter entitled "Hence burgundy, claret, and port" in which he claims that "there's a beverage brighter and clearer," given by Apollo, which again refers to the best, spiritual poetry.[60] The choice of wine as a symbol for poetry is itself appropriate since wine is formed by a process of distillation and fermentation over a long period, which accords with Keats's idea of a "gradual ripening of the intellect."[61] Babington explains the process of fermentation:

Before we speak of Spi of Wine . . . I think it necessary to mention Fermentation from which it is produced. The word Fermentation, in an e[n]larged sense, is used to denote that change of the principles of organic bodies, which begins to take place spontaneously as soon as their vital functions have ceased.[62]

That fermentation occurs spontaneously and is conditional on a certain amount of heat is similar to Keats's comments about the "intensity" of art and his claim that poetry must be created spontaneously, like leaves growing on a tree.

Keats uses the same image of literature being distilled from "materials," put into "etherial existence," and then fermented in a humorous passage written on 24 March 1818 about Milton's attack on Salmasius. On learning that Milton rolled in a certain meadow before writing the attack, and that no nettles grew there afterwards, Keats states: "This accou[n]t made me very naturally suppose that the nettles and thorns *etherialized* by the Scholars rotary motion and garner'd in his head, thence flew after a new *fermentation* against the luckless Salmasius and accasioned his well known and unhappy end" (*Letters* 1:254). Again the harvesting image is linked to the chemical concepts, and the idea that the "etherealizing" of the thorns is produced by Milton's "rotary motion" probably derives from the fact that in the production of some ethers it is necessary to shake the mixture to begin spontaneous distillation.[63] Keats calls the change in these thorns "a new fermentation" since the rectified spirit used to form the ether must itself have originally been fermented. In the fashion of fermentation, the nettles were spontaneously transformed, in Milton's mind, into the words that produced what Keats would call "distilled Prose," but the distillate of nettles is a stinging spirit, as Salmasius discovered.

The comment on Milton, however, is not Keats's first reference to fermentation. In January 1818 he wrote to Bailey: "The best of Men have but a portion of good in them—a kind of *spiritual yeast* in their frames which creates the *ferment* of existence—by which a Man is propell'd to act and strive and buffet with Circumstance" (*Letters* 1:210). As Babington points out, it is sometimes necessary to add yeast to facilitate fermentation and the resultant "remarkable change" it brings about in the process of maturing spirits.[64] In Keats's metaphor, the good in a man acts as the yeast to help him mature through facing the problems of life. He makes use of the same concept again to describe the maturing of the imagination in his preface to *Endymion:* "The imagination of a boy is healthy, and the mature imagination of a man is healthy; but there is a space of life between, in which the soul is in a ferment, the character undecided."

The image of yeast is particularly appropriate for describing the troubled and turbulent changes from youth to maturity, since with the addition of yeast to a fluid "the fluid becomes turbid and frothy."[65] But with maturity, "yeasting youth / Will clear itself, and crystal turn again" (*Otho the Great* III, ii, 178–79), just as spirits become clear after fermentation. The confusion of adolescence will have passed and been replaced by mature clarity of thought.

In discussing imaginative creativity as a process of distillation, the words "essence" and "essential" have occurred, often in conjunction with chemical terms. But because they are such problematical terms in Keats criticism, I have refrained thus far from attempting to define them. They do, however, have chemical definitions of their own, and Babington's lectures on "Vegitable Inflamables"—which include spirit of wine and ethers—contain a section on "Essential Oils and Resins." The essential oils "differ only from the Resins in being thinner & containing the finer & more volatile, whilst the latter are the more coarse parts"[66] of fluids from fragrant vegetables. The essential oils are separated from the resins "by distillation with water" in which "the finer & more volatile" oils rise, leaving the resin behind.

It is this process of distilling essences from vegetables that often seems to be at the back of Keats's mind when he uses the words "essential" and "essence." The first example occurs when he writes to Bailey on 22 November 1817—in a letter filled with chemical analogies—that "I have the same Idea of all our Passions as of Love they are all in their *sublime,* creative of *essential* Beauty—In a Word, you may know my favorite Speculation by my first Book and the little song I sent in my last" (*Letters* 1:184–85). The latter reference is to the "Song of Sorrow" in Book IV of *Endymion,* where Keats introduces the idea, later developed to its fullest in the "Ode on Melancholy," that sorrow and joy, like all passions, are, when "sublime"—sublimation being a form of distillation—an essence of beauty or "essential Beauty." In this distilled, refined form all passions are unified just as essential oils, "by repeated distillation . . . are brought nearly to resemble each other."[67] And again Keats points out that this purifying and synthesizing are carried out by the imagination, which sublimates passions into their essential state of beauty or art.

This idea is repeated in a marginal note in his copy of *Paradise Lost*, where Keats says that Milton "is 'sagacious of his Quarry,' he sees Beauty on the wing, pounces upon it and gorges it to the producing his *essential* verse."[68] Here he coins a mixed metaphor drawing on his knowledge of chemical and physiological "digestion" as a means of expressing how the poetic mind creates fine beauty. Two other marginal notes in *Paradise Lost*, which Keats was studying with Dilke during the winter of 1817–18, a period when chemical metaphors abound in his letters, also reveal his use of chemical terms to describe how Milton rarefies material beauty into the "essential Beauty" of poetry. He states that Milton "*refines* on his descriptions of beauty, till the sense aches at them," and that his description of a vale "is a sort of Delphic *Abstraction*—a beautiful thing made more beautiful."[69]

As well as mentioning the "Song of Sorrow" to Bailey, Keats also mentions his "first Book" of *Endymion* as a place where his speculations about "essential Beauty" are outlined. Presumably he is referring to the well-known "Pleasure Thermometer" passage, which deals with the whole question of "essence" and which is, after the "Beauty-Truth" statement in the "Ode on a Grecian Urn," the most problematical and controversial passage in Keats's poetry. The passage, which he discusses in a letter to Taylor on 30 January 1818, runs:

> Wherein lies happiness? In that which becks
> Our ready minds to fellowship divine,
> A fellowship with essence; till we shine,
> Full alchemiz'd, and free of space. Behold
> The clear religion of heaven!   (I, 777–81; *Letters* 1:218)

Finney, following Colvin, de Selincourt, Bridges, and Murry, has given the passage the "traditional" neo-Platonic interpretation in which "essence" means the Platonic Ideal, and the Pleasure Thermometer is a type of ladder up which the poet must progress in his quest for Ideal Beauty.[70] More recently, Newell Ford, following Pettet, has rejected this Platonic reading of "'essence' in its transcendental sense," claiming instead that "Keats was almost unquestionably using the word 'essence' as a synonym for 'a thing of beauty' or 'shape of beauty'" in a very material sense.[71]

In arguing over the meaning of "essence," these critics have missed the point, brought out by Sperry, that "the chief key to [the passage's] significance, as indicated by the word 'alchymized,' is its relation to chemical theory."[72] This becomes even more apparent in Keats's comment that "it [the passage] set before me at once the gradations of Happiness even like a kind of Pleasure Thermometer," the thermometer being the instrument used to measure the different intensities of heat needed to produce different chemical reactions. Similarly, the Pleasure Thermometer demarcates the different levels of intensity of various pleasures, and just as the purest distillate is produced by the greatest intensity of heat, so too the most intense pleasure is the purest, presumably produced by the purest imagination, since what he is describing is essentially a creative process.

As always for Keats, this creative process originates in sensations gained from physical objects. Thus, at the lower degrees of happiness or pleasure are the feel of a rose leaf and the sound of music:

> Feel we these things?—that moment have we stept
> Into a sort of oneness, and our state
> Is like a floating spirit's. (I, 795–97)

The sensations are already being distilled into the form of a rarefied "spirit," be it chemical or mythical. But they can be purified even further:

> But there are
> Richer entanglements, enthralments far
> More self-destroying, leading, by degrees,
> To the chief intensity: the crown of these

Chemistry

Is made of love and friendship, and sits high
Upon the forehead of humanity.   (I, 797–802)

His use of the terms "degrees" and "intensity," together
with his description of the passage as outlining the gradations of a "Pleasure Thermometer," indicates immediately that
Keats is describing a process analogous to chemical distillation,
in which the purest distillate is "love and friendship." Here he
describes, in relation to pleasure, what he has already
described, a month earlier, within the context of art: that "the
excellence of every Art is its intensity, capable of making all
disagreeables evaporate, from their being in close relationship
with Beauty & Truth" (*Letters* 1:192).[73] Within the moral context, the "disagreeables" are "self," and so they must be evaporated off before pure "love and friendship" remain.

But even this crown of "love and friendship" can be separated further:

All its more ponderous and bulky worth
Is friendship, whence there ever issues forth
A steady splendour; but at the tip-top,
There hangs by unseen film, an orbed drop
Of light, and that is love.   (I, 803–07)

This level of love is the ultimate "fellowship with essence" that
Keats describes earlier, and the separation of friendship and
love is analogous to the separation of resins from essentials
oils. The resins are "the most coarse parts" just as friendship is
the "more ponderous and bulky worth"; and the essential oils,
"the finer & more volatile" parts corresponding to love, are
separated from them by further distillation. In this metaphorical context, the image of love as "an orbed drop" that "hangs
by unseen film" is an exact description of a drop of pure distillate as it condenses on the lip of a retort to drip into a beaker.
Keats makes the substance even more refined by calling it "an
orbed drop / Of light," but the image—like much of the
language here—is derived from his observation of chemical
processes.

Why Keats places love, by which he obviously means passionate, sexual love, above friendship is debatable, although

we should not forget that he is discussing gradations of "pleasure." It should be observed, however, that on 13 January 1818—the same month in which he writes Taylor about the Pleasure Thermometer—he writes to Tom and George that "disinterestedness" is the highest quality in a man: "Not thus speaking with any poor vanity that works of genius were the first things in the world. No! for that sort of probity & disinterestedness which such men as Bailey possess, does hold & grasp the *tip top* of any spiritual *honours*, that can be paid to any thing in this world" (*Letters* 1:205). Again the image of levels of refinement is used, but this time to describe gradations of "honours" rather than of "pleasures."

Keats makes similar use of chemical terminology in other passages of *Endymion*, the only major poem he wrote while his medical training was still fresh in his mind. After Endymion has met Cynthia and been deserted by her, he describes his change of feelings from ecstasy to melancholy in terms of essences, which are volatile, light, and refined, and heavy spirits, which are turbid:

> Now I have tasted her sweet soul to the core
> All other depths are shallow: essences,
> Once spiritual, are like muddy lees,
> Meant but to fertilize my earthly root,
> And make my branches lift a golden fruit
> Into the bloom of heaven.   (II, 904–09)

The chemical metaphor changes subtly into a botanical one, but the concept of refinement remains, with the "muddy lees" which fertilize the "earthly root" being transmuted, through the process of upward growth, into golden, heavenly fruit of love.

Even when the word "essence" loses its chemical meaning and denotes simply "immaterial being," it is usually linked with the idea of purifying heat, as in the description of sunrise near the beginning of *Endymion:*

> For 'twas the morn: Apollo's upward fire
> Made every eastern cloud a silvery pyre
> Of brightness so unsullied, that therein
> A melancholy spirit well might win

Chemistry

Oblivion, and melt out his essence fine
Into the winds.   (I, 95–100)

In *Isabella*, his next major poem after *Endymion*, Keats also makes occasional use of chemical images and terms, the most obvious being the liquors with which Isabella anoints Lorenzo's severed head:

Then in a silken scarf,—sweet with the dews
    Of precious flowers pluck'd in Araby,
And divine liquids come with odorous ooze
    Through the cold serpent-pipe refreshfully,—
She wrapp'd it up.   (409–13)

Hagelman comments: "This description of a distilling aparatus is engagingly expressed. The 'serpent-pipe' is the condensing coil, and in order for it to function effectively, it must be kept cool. . . . Keats undoubtedly saw and probably operated one in his chemistry courses at Guy's Hospital."[74] Hagelman has not noticed, however, that Babington's description of this piece of apparatus, used for distillation, is remarkably like Keats's. Babington writes: "Alembic or Common Still corresponds in principle with the Retort, but has a Refrigerator, in which *cold* water may be kept, in this there is also a *Serpentine tube* called a Worm, thro' which the Steam passes from the Still."[75]

Again in *Isabella*, Lorenzo's ghost describes his feelings on seeing Isabella in a passage that brings together a number of chemical terms:

"Thy beauty grows upon me, and I feel
A greater love through all my essence steal."

The Spirit mourn'd "Adieu!"–dissolv'd, and left
The atom darkness in a slow turmoil.   (319–22)

The first two lines Keats quotes in a letter to Fanny Brawne in February 1820, and the concept of the lover dissolving when separated from his loved one takes on very personal connotations for him. While at Winchester in the late summer and early autumn of 1819, he writes to Fanny: "I cannot think of you without some sort of *energy*—though mal a propos—Even as I leave off—it seems to me that a few more moments thought of you would *uncrystallize* and *dissolve* me—I must not give way to it—but turn to my writing again" (*Letters* 2:142). And in October, he writes again: "You have *absorb'd* me. I have a sensation at the present moment as though I was *dissolving*—I should be exquisitely miserable without the hope of soon seeing you" (*Letters* 2:223). Thoughts of Fanny engender in Keats a "sort of energy," corresponding to heat within the context of the chemical analogy he is using,[76] which uncrystallizes and dissolves him. As Babington explains, "Crystallizability is a property which all Bodies have of assuming a particular configuration in returning from the fluid to the solid state."[77] To uncrystallize or dissolve is, then, to return to the fluid state, or to melt, with the added implication of being broken down into one's formative parts or component elements, since most crystals are compounds. To avoid this, Keats says, he must "turn to my writing," which implies that in his writing, which is opposed to Fanny's influence, he finds crystallization and unity. The idea of a poem as a crystallization of thought is particularly apt for Keats since, in Babington's words, "every kind of Matter has its own distinct & separate crystallization by which it may be distinguished from every other Body."[78] Similarly, each poem is a unique combination of elements—sensations and their resultant associations and speculations—which unite to form a work of art analogous to a crystal.

In discussing his understanding of chemistry in relation to his thoughts on poetry, I am not claiming that Keats developed a unified and coherent system of poetics based on his knowledge of chemistry, although it is interesting to speculate that his understanding of chemistry, which he gained before delving deeply into poetics, may have helped him to formulate his speculations on the workings of the imagination. His ideas on poetry, however, were always fluid and developing; he abhorred dogmatic system. What I am claiming is that, in his knowledge of chemistry, Keats found a ready-made vocabulary that helped him to understand and to explain many of his more difficult ideas concerning the poetic process, a vocabulary so familiar to him from his medical training that he used it naturally.

Chemistry

Ultimately, for Keats the creation of poetry involves the combination—akin to chemical combination—of various sense impressions, associations, and speculations, which come together in a receptive mind where they mature, or ferment, over a period of time, and where they are distilled by the spontaneous workings, the intensity, of the imagination into a more spiritual, sublime, ethereal form called art—the concrete, crystallized product of which is a unique poem.

CHAPTER III

Botany

The study of botany in the early nineteenth century was closely connected with the study of chemistry, as Sir Humphry Davy outlines:

Natural history and chemistry are attached to each other by very intimate ties. For while the first of these sciences treats of the general external properties of bodies, the last unfolds their internal constitution and ascertains their intimate nature. . . . botany and zoology as branches of natural history, though independent of chemistry as to their primary classification, yet are related to it so far as they treat of the constitution and functions of vegetables and animals. How dependent in fact upon chemical processes are the nourishment and growth of organized beings.[1]

In medical education, the connection between botany and chemistry was particularly close, since both subjects were studied in relation to materia medica. Most medicines were either botanical or mineral in origin, and it was necessary to know their chemical properties and reactions in order to compound them. In addition, much chemical theory concerning life forces and subtle fluids like electricity and magnetism was applied to plant life. Elaborate analogies were built by seventeenth- and eighteenth-century naturalists between human, animal, and plant forms and processes of growth,[2] and although the whole system of argument from analogy was attacked and rejected in the early nineteenth century, chemistry and botany remain closely related fields of study.

Botany

Botany, of course, has always been an important part of medical science, dating back to ancient cultures; the earliest known remedies for illnesses are herbal. Often, however, the specific study of plants and vegetables has been subsumed by the larger, more generalized subject of "natural philosophy," whose focus has often tended to be philosophical and religious, concerned with hierarchies of being and other such esoteric topics, rather than with strict scientific investigation.

During the middle and late eighteenth century, however, interest in botany as a science grew rapidly, owing largely to the work of Carl Linnaeus (1707–78), the renowned Swedish botanist. Linnaeus took on the herculean task of describing and categorizing all plants according to their class, order, genus, and species. His encyclopedic works of taxonomy, such as the *Genera Plantarum*, went through many editions between 1740 and 1770, and were credited with bringing order to the chaotic field of botany.

In Britain, the study of botany became fashionable, especially after Captain Cook returned from his voyage in the *Endeavour* in 1771, bringing with him many exotic plants. The Royal Botanic Garden at Kew was founded, and in 1776 William Withering published a Linnaean account of British botany, *A Botanical Arrangement of All the Vegetables Naturally Growing in Great Britain*.

The scientist and poet Erasmus Darwin also became very interested in botany, translating Linnaeus's *Systema Vegetabilium* as *A System of Vegetables* (1783) and then popularizing the Linnaean system in his huge poem *The Botanic Garden* (1791). As a physician, Darwin was interested in medical botany, as he points out in *Principia Botanica,* a short introduction to Linnaean botany that he wrote under his son Robert's name. Discussing botany, he states, "Neither is any part of natural history more useful for the most important purposes of life, as *food, drink, raiment, &c.* but what is still more valuable, *health;* for it supplies us with a very essential part of *Materia medica.*"[3]

Thus the study of botany was an extremely important aspect of medical training when Keats attended Guy's in 1815, much more important, in fact, than it is today when pharmaceutical manufacturing has become completely divorced from the medical practitioner. As an apothecary, Keats would be expected to compound medicines for his patients, mainly from botanic ingredients. As William Salisbury, the lecturer on botany at Guy's, pointed out to his pupils: "It is therefore high time that those persons who are engaged in the business of pharmacy should be obliged to become so far acquainted with plants, as to be able to distinguish at sight all such as are useful in diet or medicine."[4] In his introduction to materia medica James Curry states that the student must know:

1st. the names adopted by the Colleges of London, Edinburgh, and Dublin; —the most common Synonyma, and the Etymon of each when ascertainable. —2dly, the Linnean Class, —Order, —Genus, —and Species; —and also, if the article by [sic] a vegetable, its *Natural Order*, with a view to shew how far there is a connection between the *botanical character*, and *medical virtue* of plants. —3dly, the Natural History of the Article; —the country, soil, and situation producing it; the modes by which it is obtained; —and the processes it undergoes before it is brought hither.[5]

Although it is obvious from this statement that Keats was expected to know a great deal about the botanic origins of medicines, it is more difficult to ascertain exactly what he learned from William Salisbury. This is due to the nature of Salisbury's course, which was taught in a series of field trips, so that no formal lectures remain, although Salisbury did publish detailed lists of specimens observed on each field trip.[6] In addition, in 1816, the year Keats attended his course, he published a text on botany entitled *The Botanist's Companion*, which undoubtedly contains much of the information he taught his students. Students probably also consulted the many works of the famous botanist Robert Thornton, who had taught at the United Hospitals before Salisbury.

It is probably safe to assume that Keats obtained his knowledge of botany from these sources, all of which were Linnaean in approach. He may also have gained additional information from friends like Cowden Clarke and Clarke's brother-in-law, John Towers, although Towers's published works on botany did not appear until the 1830s and 1840s.[7] Leigh Hunt's sister-in-law, Elizabeth Kent, whom Keats met at the Vale of Health, was also a keen botanist[8] and published a book on the subject, *Flora*

Domestica, in 1823. A number of people in Keats's circle were interested in the subject, then, and it is likely that they discussed botanical questions from time to time.

Keats's interest in botany and gardening continued, in fact, through his brief life, and he encouraged a similar interest in his sister, Fanny. On 31 March 1819, he writes to her: "I shall be going to town tomorrow and will call at the Nursery on the road for those roots and seeds you want, which I will send by the Walthamstow stage" (*Letters* 2:49). And two weeks later, on 12 April, he writes to Fanny again: "I ordered some bulbous roots for you at the Gardeners, and they sent me some, but they were all in bud—and could not be sent, so I put them in our Garden There are some beautiful heaths now in bloom in Pots—either heaths or some seasonable plants I will send you" (*Letters* 2:51).

That Keats conceived of the botanist in the Linnaean sense of a taxonomist is evidenced in a comment he makes, in a letter to Sarah Jeffrey on 9 June 1819, about working as a doctor on board an Indiaman: "To be thrown among people who care not for you, with whom you have no sympathies forces the Mind upon its own resourses, and leaves it free to make its speculations of the differences of human character and to class them with the calmness of a Botanist" (*Letters* 2:115). At various points in his career, Keats longed for the scientist's calm detachment in observing life's energies, and he regretted that his own emotions often destroyed the ability for such detachment, leaving him in a state of melancholic depression.

Yet flowers and plants remained a continual source of pleasure for the poet, as he explains to James Rice on 14 February 1820, when he knew he was dying:

How astonishingly does the chance of leaving the world impress a sense of its natural beauties on us. Like poor Falstaff, though I do not babble, I think of green fields. I muse with the greatest affection on every flower I have known from my infancy—their shapes and colours as are new to me as if I had just created them with a superhuman fancy.
(*Letters* 2:260)

And on his deathbed in Rome, Keats told Severn: "I could get away from suffering. —in watching the growth of a little flower; . . . perhaps the only happiness I have had in the world—has been the silent growth of Flowers."[9] If nothing else, the botanical studies at Clarke's school and at Guy's under Salisbury encouraged in Keats an interest that remained for him a constant pleasure.

Establishing Keats's interest in the subject and his sources of botanical knowledge is easier, however, than circumscribing the boundaries of the subject itself. Where does a specific interest in botany as a science stop and a much more general interest in nature, which has always been recognized in Keats's poetry, begin? It is virtually impossible to discuss the works of any Romantic poet without dealing with his concept of nature and his use of botanical images; it is equally impossible, within the scope of this study, to comment on every use Keats makes of flowers, trees, and plants in his poetry, or even to attempt to adumbrate his whole approach to nature. My focus must be limited to fairly detailed images and ideas that can be traced to Keats's medical knowledge, although occasionally I will point out other possible sources, especially in the poetical works of Erasmus Darwin, which are themselves quasi-scientific. Further, because of this focus on specific images, metaphors, and concepts, I cannot pretend to offer thorough interpretations of all the poems with which I will be dealing. A knowledge of botany and morphology in the late eighteenth and early nineteenth centuries can, however, help us to appreciate more in certain of Keats's natural images than merely their rich sensuousness.

The only critic who, to my knowledge, has attempted to trace the sources of Keats's botanical images and ideas in any detail is Bernard Blackstone.[10] In *The Consecrated Urn,* he develops some excellent insights into Keats's understanding of nature, but at times his arguments are very tenuous, and he ends by admitting:

One would like to know a good deal more than one does know about Keats's schoolboy and later education: how much he would be expected to read in natural and physical science, for instance; what elements of physics, natural history, meteorology were included in his syllabus; where he got his knowledge of morphology, his interest in the connectedness of plant form with human form.[11]

Botany

I believe that it is possible to answer some of Blackstone's queries and thus gain new insight into Keats's poetry.

The influence of Keats's interest in botany is evident in even a cursory reading of his early poems like *Sleep and Poetry* and "I stood tip-toe . . . ," both of which abound in detailed natural images. His study of botany during the summer of 1816 probably increased Keats's already keen powers of observation, and the fruits of his observations are evident in the density of detail in these early poems. It is also probable that the study of botany was the only part of his medical training that Keats found compatible with the sensuously rich poetry he was reading and imitating at the time, the poetry of Wordsworth, Spenser, and the Elizabethans. Much of the natural beauty he found described here he would have discovered in reality on the field trips for his botany course, although the technical accuracy of his own descriptions ultimately surpasses that of his models.

From the opening lines of "I stood tip-toe . . ." Keats's acute observation of things botanical and his delight at being out in the country become apparent through his detailed and accurate images of flowers:

> I stood tip-toe upon a little hill,
> The air was cooling, and so very still,
> That the sweet buds which with a modest pride
> Pull droopingly, in slanting curve aside,
> Their scantly leaved, and finely tapering stems,
> Had not yet lost those starry diadems
> Caught from the early sobbing of the morn.   (1–7)

Here the poeticism of the dew described as "starry diadems" of tears shed by a personified morn is combined with the keen observation of the "scantly leaved, and finely tapering stems" in what is a strange and and unique mixture. Later, a marigold is described as a "round of starry folds" (47), an exact description of the specific star shape of the marigold which also captures its overall circular form.

From marigolds, Keats passes on to sweet peas:

> Here are sweet peas, on tip-toe for a flight:
> With wings of gentle flush o'er delicate white,

And taper fingers catching at all things,
To bind them all about with tiny rings.   (57–60)

Apart from the very accurate image of the "tiny rings"of the
sweet peas' tendrils, there is also the image of the flowers "on
tip-toe for a flight," which Miriam Allott correctly suggests
"are like butterflies."[12] This is no casual comparison, however, but a botanically accurate description, since the pea
blossom belongs to the class of flowers called "papilionaceous." As Erasmus Darwin states, "The flowers of this class
[Genista] are called papilionaceous, from their resemblance to
a butterfly, as the pea-blossom."[13] Robert Thornton defines
"PAPILLIONACEOUS *(Papilionacea),* having four petals, of
different shapes and sizes, placed so as to resemble a butterfly
on the wing."[14]

But in "I stood tip-toe . . . ," Keats is not interested just in the
visible form of plants and flowers; his intense imagination traces
them back to the very initiation of their growth, in roots and
bulbs:

And let a lush laburnum oversweep them,
And let long grass grow round the roots to keep them
Moist, cool and green; and shade the violets,
That they may bind the moss in leafy nets.

A filbert hedge with wild briar overtwined,
And clumps of woodbine taking the soft wind
Upon their summer thrones; there too should be
The frequent chequer of a youngling tree,
That with a score of light green brethren shoots
From the quaint mossiness of aged roots:
Round which is heard a spring-head of clear waters.   (31–41)

Already Keats is interested in the cyclic potential for growth out
of death—the green shoots springing from aged roots—that
would be of major importance to his later understanding of life.
He is also correct in surrounding the dormant bulb and root
with the moisture and cool temperatures necessary for plant
development.

These thoughts concerning new plant growth would later
crystallize in a minor poem "Shed no tear":

Botany

> Shed no tear—O shed no tear!
> The flower will bloom another year.
> Weep no more—O weep no more!
> Young buds sleep in the root's white core.   (1–4)

The image of the bud lying dormant in the root is based on a common misconception among botanists, which is explained in detail by Darwin:

A BULB, (bulbus) is a large sort of bud produced under ground, placed upon the *caudex* part of the root of certain herbaceous plants; hence called *bulbus* plants; all of which are perennial, that is, perpetuated by their *bulbs* or ground *buds*, as well as by seeds; they are therefore improperly called roots, being only the *hybernacle* [winter lodgment] of the future shoot.[15]

Thus the speaker of Keats's poem tells the listener not to cry, for what he describes is a perennial flower, whose "Young buds sleep in the root's white core," waiting to be awakened in the spring. Robert Thornton, in his *Temple of Flora,* has a magnificent, full folio page drawing of just such a root with the bud enclosed, which Keats may well have seen. Of course, Darwin's dry explanation cannot compare with Keats's line, nor am I claiming that Keats is writing a botanical treatise, but Darwin's explanation and Thornton's drawing do explain the knowledge behind Keats's image.

Keats's use of the word "core" in this line is also a careful choice based on his botanical knowledge. As Darwin explains, "The CORCULUM (from cor, a heart) is the essence of the seed, and principle of the future plant."[16] And under "Terms applicable to the Seed," Thornton lists the "HEART *(Corculum),* the rudiment of the young plant within the seed."[17] Thus the young bud in Keats's image is at the "core" of the root.

This botanical meaning of the word "core" becomes, in fact, quite commonly employed by Keats. When, in *Isabella,* he describes the heroine as she "Hung over her sweet basil evermore, / And moisten'd it with tears unto the core" (423–24), he does not mean that the moisture sank to some vague center in the pot; rather, it goes to the very heart of the basil's seed, which Keats equates with Lorenzo's head. Again, in "To Autumn," when the sun and autumn conspire to "fill all fruit with ripeness to the core" (6), it means to the very heart of the fruits' seeds, where ripeness and growth commence.

There are other words in Keats's vocabulary whose meanings have been misunderstood because they have not been explained in a botanical context. The best example of this is his use of the word "luxury" or "luxuries." This brings us back to "I stood tiptoe . . . ," where the speaker states:

> I was light-hearted,
> And many pleasures to my vision started;
> So I straightway began to pluck a posey
> Of luxuries bright, milky, soft and rosy.   (25–28)

De Selincourt glosses Keats's use of "luxuries" as being "concrete and abstract," which is of little help in understanding the poet's meaning; Allott defines it in this instance as "pleasures," which is undoubtedly part of its meaning, the "luxuries" being metaphorically equivalent to the pleasures Keats sees before him. To grasp the concreteness of the image, however, it is imperative that the word be understood as a botanical term rather than as a vague equivalent to "pleasures." Again Darwin explains:

Under this head of *Inflorescence* may be explained LUXURIANT FLOWERS, (commonly called double flowers). . . . A *luxuriant* flower is supposed generally to be owing to superabundant nourishment. . . . a greater exertion of luxuriancy may produce . . . several heads of flowers, each growing out of that immediately below it.[18]

Keats's "posey / Of luxuries bright, milky, soft and rosy" is a cluster of such flowers of excessive growth, the emphasis on their milkiness stressing their superabundant nourishment.

This is not the first time Keats employed the term in a definitely botanical sense, however. In his earliest extant poem, "Imitation of Spenser," he writes:

> And all around it dipp'd luxuriously
> Slopings of verdure through the glassy tide,
> Which, as it were in gentle amity,
> Rippled delighted up the flowery side;
> As if to glean the ruddy tears, it tried,
> Which fell profusely from the rose-tree stem!

Botany

> Haply it was the workings of its pride,
> In strife to throw upon the shore a gem
> Outvieing all the buds in Flora's diadem.   (28–36)

Keats's emphasis on the profusion of plant growth and the desire to produce a bud that outshines Flora's diadem should have indicated to his readers the botanical meaning of "luxuriously."[19]

Finally, Keats uses "luxury" as a pun, meaning both pleasure and an abundant flower, in *Isabella*. After Lorenzo has been murdered, Isabella indulges in her grief:

> She weeps alone for pleasures not to be;
> Sorely she wept until the night came on,
> And then, instead of love, O misery!
> She brooded o'er the luxury alone.   (233–36)

Here "luxury" obviously means the pleasures of grief, but the image is also a brilliantly concrete foreshadowing of Isabella's later brooding and weeping over the basil plant, which grows into the most luxuriant basil ever seen.

Another word in Keats's vocabulary which has a previously unrecognized botanical meaning is "simple" when it describes flowers. The use of "simples," meaning medicinal herbs, is obvious in the doggerel verses "Two or three posies / With two or three simples," but what exactly does Keats mean by "simple flowers" in "Imitation of Spenser":

> Which, pure from mossy beds, did down distill,
> And after parting beds of simple flowers,
> By many streams a little lake did fill,   (5–7)

or in *Sleep and Poetry*: "Find a fresh sward beneath it, overgrown / With simple flowers" (258–59)? The word makes sense only as a botanical term. As Darwin explains: "*Complete flowers* are either *simple* or *aggregate*; *simple* when no part of the *fructification* is common to many flowers or florets, but is confined to one only; *aggregate*, when the flower consists of many florets collected into a head by means of some part of the *fructification* common to them all."[20] Under "Botanical Terms Applicable to the Corolla," Thornton makes the same distinction between

93

simple and compound flowers: "SIMPLE *(Simplex)*, not a compound flower . . . COMPOUND *(Composita)*, made up of distinct florets on a common receptacle."[21]

That Keats was not only familiar with botanical science during this period, but comfortable and confident enough to use his specialized knowledge to create nice jokes for his friends is demonstrated in a letter he wrote to Reynolds on 18 April 1817, while he was staying at Carisbrooke: "Will you have the goodness to do this? Borrow a Botanical Dictionary—turn to the words Laurel and Prunus show the explanations to your sisters and Mrs. Dilk and without more ado let them send me the Cups Basket and Books they trifled and put off and off while I was in Town" *(Letters* 1:133). Keats's mock argumentative joke is based on dictionary descriptions of the flowers of these trees as having no cups,[22] which puts them in the same situation as himself.

Sleep and Poetry, like "I stood tip-toe . . . ," is one of those early poems in which Keats revels in natural description for its own sake. But, although the structure of these poems is loose, allowing the poet to roam freely from one topic to another, the images remain remarkably concrete and intricate and, as in "I stood tip-toe . . . ," some of them are fully comprehensible only within the context of Keats's specialized knowledge of botany. Two such images concern the belief that plants breathe, a controversial concept that was denied by Linnaeus. Darwin outlines the two sides of the argument: "The LEAVES, which are said by Linnaeus, to be *muscles* or organs of motion of a plant; by others, the organs by which perspiration and inspiration are performed."[23] That Keats is aware of this concept of plants breathing becomes clear in a brief rhetorical question concerning the power of imagination:

> Has she not shewn us all?
> From the clear space of ether, to the small
> Breath of new buds unfolding? (167–69)

Earlier in *Sleep and Poetry,* the speaker describes poetic inspiration as derived from the breath of bay trees; the bays literally breathe into, or inspire, the poet:

> O Poesy! for thee I grasp my pen
> That am not yet a glorious denizen

Of thy wide heaven; yet, to my ardent prayer,
Yield from thy sanctuary some clear air,
Smoothed for intoxication by the breath
Of flowering bays, that I may die a death
Of luxury, and my young spirit follow
The morning sun-beams to the great Apollo
Like a fresh sacrifice; or, if I can bear
The o'erwhelming sweets, 'twill bring to me the fair
Visions of all places.   (53–63)

Here Keats has incorporated a number of ideas, both mythical and scientific, concerning the bay or laurel. According to ancient myth, the bay or laurel is associated with Apollo, and the infusion of the leaves was believed to induce poetic frenzy similar to that described by Keats.[24] He was no doubt familiar with such myths, but he would also have known from his botanical training that the bay actually breathes or exhales a sweet-smelling essential oil ("The o'erwhelming sweets") which acts as a stimulant or intoxicant to the mind. As Salisbury explains:

LAURUS *nobilis*, BAY-TREE. *Leaves and Berries. L.*—In distillation with water, the leaves of bay yield a small quantity of very fragrant essential oil; with rectified spirit, they afford a moderately warm pungent extract.[25]

Thornton gives a similar description but emphasizes the stimulating nature of the oil:

COMMON SWEET BAY. This tree is a native of the south of Europe, but bears the winter of this climate perfectly well. Both leaves and berries contain a considerable quantity of essential oil, which renders them aromatic stimulating substances.[26]

In describing the intoxicant as powerful enough to produce "a death / Of luxury," however, Keats probably has in mind the effects of the laurel, which is often called a bay. Salisbury explains:

PRUNUS *Lauro-cerasus*. THE COMMON LAUREL.—The leaves of the laurel have a bitter taste, with a flavour resembling that of the kernels of the peach or apricot; they communicate an agreeable flavour to aqueous and spiritous fluids, either by infusion or distillation. The distilled water applied to the organs of smelling strongly impresses the mind with the same ideas as arise from the taste of peach blossoms or apricot kernels: it is so extremely deleterious in its nature, and sometimes so sudden in its operation, as to occasion instantaneous death.[27]

Keats's appeal for death and his desire for visions produced by "the breath / Of flowering bays" are couched in the public language of classical myth with which his readers would have been familiar. For Keats, however, they are not simply vague imaginings; rather, they are realistic requests made concrete by the foundation of scientific knowledge that supports the mythic structure.

In early poems like the "Imitation of Spenser," "I stood tiptoe . . . ," and *Sleep and Poetry*, Keats is interested in describing nature for its own sake; there is not much symbolic or metaphorical meaning in his natural images, although the connections among natural richness, calm passiveness, and poetic creativity, to which I will return, are already beginning to germinate. This interest in natural phenomena, especially botanical phenomena, probably reflects the keen powers of observation that Keats developed on the excursions with Salisbury into the fields around London. It results, in these early poems, in extended and detailed descriptions of plants, flowers, and other things natural, which in their length and focus are unlike anything we find in the later poems.

These lengthy descriptions have often been misunderstood, however, and have sometimes been criticized as an inherent weakness in the poetry. For example, the following passage from *Calidore* has been attacked by Amy Lowell as weak and inaccurate:

> Green tufted islands casting their soft shades
> Across the lake; sequester'd leafy glades,
> That through the dimness of their twilight show
> Large dock leaves, spiral foxgloves, or the glow
> Of the wild cat's eyes, or the silvery stems
> Of delicate birch trees, or long grass which hems
> A little brook.   (46–52)

Lowell writes:

Lacking any clear vision of the scene, he makes it up out of words only. There could hardly be a greater number of factual errors, all contained in a few lines, than there are in this passage. . . . Because an island is tufted, is no reason for it to cast a "soft shade." Fox-gloves are not spiral. Wild cat's eyes can scarcely have been "pleasant things" to observe staring at one.[28]

The errors Lowell describes are her own. First, "wild cat's eyes" are a type of wild flower and not a feline's organs of vision. Second, the pistil of the foxglove, or digitalis, is spiral and is described by Darwin as "a serpent-wreathed wand."[29] Keats's images are, then, far more accurate than critics such as Lowell have recognized.

Another common accusation leveled against Keats's early poetry is that it is too heavily influenced by the language and imagery of Leigh Hunt. In fact, words like "luxury" are often touted as being Huntian and weak; yet, as I have shown, Keats sometimes uses the word with a very specific botanical meaning. A quotation from one of Hunt's poems on flowers and plants, "Lines Written on a Sudden Arrival of Fine Weather in May," will show how much more detailed and accurate Keats's botanical images are than those of the elder poet:

> For lo! no sooner have the chills withdrawn,
> Than the bright elm is tufted on the lawn;
> The merry sap has run up in the bowers,
> And burst the windows of the buds in flowers;
> With song the bosoms of the birds run o'er;
> The cuckoo calls; the swallow's at the door;
> And apple-trees at noon, with bees alive,
> Burn with the golden chorus of the hive.
> Now all these sweets, these sounds, this vernal blaze,
> Is but one joy, expressed a thousand ways:
> And honey from the flowers, and song from birds,
> Are from the poet's pen his overflowing words.   (12–23)[30]

The passage is typical of Hunt's natural descriptions in its catalogue form and its generalized description of plants and insects. There are few of the fine, intricate details of observation that we find in Keats's poetry.

The other "nature" poet who strongly influenced Keats at this time was Wordsworth. Although no one would deny that Wordsworth's descriptions of nature are acute and accurate, it is safe to say that in his poetry he does not show the keen interest in the minute details of the organs of botanical growth—the bulbs, roots, petals, and buds—that Keats does. In his poetry, Wordsworth generally evokes the grand, sublime scene, and the awe-inspiring aspects of nature, in a way that Keats does not until after a visit to the Lake District and Scotland in 1818.

When Wordsworth does focus on a specific plant, flower, or tree, it is often for a metaphorical purpose in which the natural object serves to illustrate some moral quality, like patience or fortitude, that men should emulate. Examples of such poems are numerous; they include "The Oak and the Broom," "To the Daisy," "To the Same Flower," "To the Small Celandine," "The Primrose of the Rock," and "To a Snowdrop." Even in the famous "I wandered lonely as a cloud," Wordsworth is more interested in demonstrating the workings of emotions recollected in tranquillity than he is in the daffodils themselves. As Douglas Bush observes, "so preoccupied was Wordsworth in philosophizing what he saw, one may doubt if he was able to surrender himself so completely and ecstatically to the beauty of nature for its own sake, if he could become, as Keats could, a stalk of waving grain."[31] Blackstone makes a similar comparison between the two poets: "What flowers meant for Keats has already become apparent in the course of this study. They do not give him thoughts too deep for tears: indeed, they do not give him thoughts at all. He watches, and he feels. He feels the life of the flower, is the flower."[32]

Wordsworth's close analogies between the human and botanical realms do have their roots in eighteenth-century botanical theory, but his focus still remains very different from that of Keats. No matter how metaphorical Keats's descriptions of nature may become, he never uses them for the almost purely didactic purposes that Wordsworth often does, nor is he primarily concerned with the human relationship to nature.

To make these comparisons is not, however, to deny or lessen the influence of Hunt and Wordsworth on Keats. My principal aim is to demonstrate that Keats had a fund of botanical knowledge, gained from his study of medicine, which they either did not have or, if they did, did not use to the same extent.

Of course, understanding the exact meanings of individual words or images in Keats's early poems does not necessarily enhance our larger understanding of his poetry, but it does show Keats to be a more muscular poet than has often been thought. He uses words for specific meanings, not simply for their sound or their effect of richness, although the rich texture of the early verse does echo his thoughts and feelings about nature in all its multiplicity and vitality.

Thus far I have dealt with Keats's understanding of botany from the scientific viewpoint of his medical training. But this was not his only approach to the subject; he also approached the natural world from the standpoint of myth and, as Blackstone has shown, of magic or the occult, in which trees and plants have numerous associations and symbolic meanings that may or may not be connected with scientific truths. I have already referred to D'Avanzo's discussion of Keats's use of laurel leaves as a symbol of poetic inspiration, which is based on the fact that laurels are an intoxicant. D'Avanzo also discusses Keats's use of the oak as a similar symbol,[33] his interpretation in both instances being founded upon Keats's understanding of Greek and Roman lore, as is Evert's interpretation of Keats's use of certain flowers.[34] Blackstone has suggested, however, that Keats was also influenced by Celtic symbolism as explained in Edward Davies's *Celtic Researches* (1804), although he has not traced many specific instances of influence.[35]

Apart from using symbolic meanings of specific botanical species in his poetry, Keats also uses plants and trees as more general symbols and metaphors. One of his most important botanical metaphors is of the flower as a vital, but passive, being that exists in a state akin to negative capability. The metaphor appears in an important letter to Reynolds dated 19 February 1818:

It has been an old Comparison for our urging on—the Bee hive—however it seems to me that we should rather be the flower than the Bee—for it is a false notion that more is gained by receiving than

The Poet-Physician

giving—no the receiver and the giver are equal in their benefits—The f[l]ower I doubt not receives a fair guerdon from the Bee—its leaves blush deeper in the next spring—and who shall say between Man and Woman which is the most delighted? Now it is more noble to sit like Jove [than] to fly like Mercury—let us not therefore go hurrying about and collecting honey-bee like, buzzing here and there impatiently from a knowledge of what is to be arrived at: but let us open our leaves like a flower and be passive and receptive—budding patiently under the eye of Apollo and taking hints from every noble insect that favors us with a visit—sap will be given us for Meat and dew for drink—I was led into these thoughts, my dear Reynolds, by the beauty of the morning operating on a sense of Idleness.

(*Letters* 1:232)

The main thrust of this passage, heavily influenced by Wordworth's concept of "wise passiveness," is that calm, passive receptivity, in which the mind is open to sensations that will trigger trains of associations and speculations, is an integral part of the creative process. The poet, like the flower, must remain alive and alert to sensations, rather than run around after knowledge like the bee, an idea that echoes Keats's concept of "*Negative Capability*, that is when man is capable of being in uncertainties, Mysteries, doubts, without any irritable reaching after fact & reason" (*Letters* 1:193).

The image of the flower as a symbol of both vitality and passivity may have been influenced by Wordsworth's numerous poems—for example, "To the Daisy," "To the Celandine"—that praise flowers for their passive receptivity to all aspects of life, and by Plato's discussion of "Plants" in the *Timaeus*:

For whatever participates of life we may justly and with the greatest rectitude denominate an animal. But this [plants] which we are now speaking of participates the third species of soul, which we place between the praecordia and the navel: and in which there is neither any thing of opinion, reason, or intellect; but to which a pleasant and painful sense, together with desires, belongs. For it continually suffers all things. But when it is converted in itself, about itself, and, rejecting external, employs its own proper motion, it is not allotted by its generation a nature capable of considering its own concerns by any thing like a reasoning energy. On this account it lives, and is not different from an animal; but, becoming stably rooted, abides in a fixed position, through its being deprived of a motion originating from itself.[36]

Since Keats had been reading Plato with Benjamin Bailey at Oxford in September 1817, the passage was probably still fresh in his mind when he wrote his letter to Reynolds in February 1818.

Plato's claim that the plant not only is alive but also has "a pleasant and painful sense, together with desires" was probably itself of great interest to Keats, who makes a similar claim when he compares the pleasure received by the bee and flower, respectively, to the pleasure received by a man and a woman during sexual union: "The flower I doubt not receives a fair guerdon from the Bee—its leaves blush deeper in the next spring—and who shall say between Man and Woman which is the most delighted? "[37] The whole idea that plants have not only life, but also sensibilities, passions, and sexual appetites was common in late eighteenth-century botany, and was one of the strongest analogies between plants and human beings. The concept forms the basis for Linnaeus's sexual botany, which classifies plants according to their gender, marriage habits, promiscuity, and so forth. In the nineteenth century, these analogies were attacked by scientists like Sir Humphry Davy, but they remained particularly appealing to the Romantic poets, who were strongly attracted by the similarities between human beings and plants. This can be seen in poems like Shelley's *The Sensitive Plant,* and in Wordsworth's "faith that every flower / Enjoys the air it breathes" ("Lines Written in Early Spring," 11–12).[38]

Keats himself makes use of analogies based on the belief that plants experience sensations. In one of his letters from Scotland, written to Tom on 26 July 1818, he talks of the inhabitants handling Brown's "Spectacles as we do a sensitive leaf" (*Letters* 1:347). A later comparison between men and plants is much more tentative, however, couched in the language of supposition as if Keats has doubts about the validity of these analogies. He discusses men's inability to escape suffering and be happy:

The Poet-Physician

The point at which Man may arrive is as far as the paralel state in inanimate nature and no further—For instance suppose a rose to have sensation, it blooms on a beautiful morning it enjoys itself—but there comes a cold wind, a hot sun—it cannot escape it, it cannot destroy its annoyances—they are as native to the world as itself: no more can man be happy in spite, the world[l]y elements will prey upon his nature.   (*Letters* 2:101)

The analogy here is conscious and deliberate, but Keats may have phrased it as a supposition for readers not familiar with the Linnaean idea that plants experience sensation.

For Linnaeus, however, flowers were not simply alive and sensitive; they were also sexual beings:

The organs of generation, which in the animal kingdom are by nature generally removed from sight, in the vegetable kingdom are exposed to the eyes of all. . . .
The calyx is the bedchamber, the corolla the curtains, the filaments the spermatic vessels, the anthers the testes, the pollen the sperm, the stigma the vulva, the style the vagina, the germen the ovary, the pericarp the fecundating ovary, and the seed the ovum.[39]

Darwin's *Loves of the Plants* was a popularization in verse of Linnaeus's theory.

Although Keats disliked Darwin's poetry, and probably felt that Darwin had taken the sexual analogies to a ridiculous conclusion, he himself uses flowers as sexual metaphors and similes, although not in the elaborate style of the older poet. An early example of the metaphorical connection between erotic passion and flowers, especially roses, occurs in the sonnet "Had I a man's fair form" in which Keats complains that he is "no knight," "no happy shepherd" to proclaim his love:

> Yet must I dote upon thee,—call thee sweet,
> Sweeter by far than Hybla's honied roses
> When steep'd in dew rich to intoxication.
> Ah! I will taste that dew, for me 'tis meet,
> And when the moon her pallid face discloses,
> I'll gather some by spells, and incantation.   (9–14)

102

The sweet rose with its rich dew, which the speaker wants to taste, becomes a substitute for the woman of his desires; in his mind, the two are intertwined.

Similarly, in *Endymion*, Book II, the rose becomes a symbol of the woman with whom Endymion is in love, and whom he follows unceasingly. Early in Book II, the hero, "Brain-sick" with love and the sorrow it brings,

> is sitting by a shady spring,
> And elbow-deep with feverous fingering
> Stems the upbursting cold: a wild rose tree
> Pavilions him in bloom, and he doth see
> A bud which snares his fancy: lo! but now
> He plucks it, dips its stalk in the water: how!
> It swells, it buds, it flowers beneath his sight.   (53–59)

The sensuous budding of the rose not only rekindles Endymion's love and desire, but also releases a butterfly, itself a symbol of the loved one's soul or psyche, which leads him on his journey to ultimate consummation. The passage is interesting because it anticipates the "Ode to Psyche" in which the three aspects of Psyche, flowers, and erotic passion coalesce:

> 'Mid hush'd, cool-rooted flowers, fragrant-eyed,
>   Blue, silver-white, and budded Tyrian,
> They lay calm-breathing on the bedded grass;
>   Their arms embraced, and their pinions too;
>   Their lips touch'd not, but had not bade adieu,
>   As if disjoined by soft-handed slumber,
>   And ready still past kisses to outnumber
> At tender eye-dawn of aurorean love.   (13–20)

The lush, rich growth of the plants, flowers, and trees echoes the creative passion of Cupid and Psyche, a passion that is itself ultimately a metaphor for the creativity of the poet's imagination, as D'Avanzo has asserted.[40]

Again, in *The Eve of St. Agnes*, the consummation of love between Madeline and Porphyro is described thus: "Into her dream he melted, as the rose / Blendeth its odour with the violet,— / Solution sweet" (320–22). And in *Lamia* Keats returns to the comparison of the relationship of a man and a

woman to that of a bee and a flower when he describes the
love between Hermes and the Nymph:

> But the God fostering her chilled hand,
> She felt the warmth, her eyelids open'd bland,
> And, like new flowers at morning song of bees,
> Bloom'd, and gave up her honey to the lees.　(I, 140–43)

Of course, the metaphorical link between flowers and sexuality is common in literature, stretching from the medieval
Romance of the Rose to Blake's "The Sick Rose," and Keats does
use the conventional analogies like that between flowerbeds
and lovers' beds. But Keats sees much more than symbolic
connections between plant growth and human passion:
because he is so acutely aware, in a biological sense, of the
procreative power of sexual love, he actually claims there is a
cause-and-effect relationship between human love and nature's
fecundity as a whole. In *Endymion*, he states:

> Just so may love, although 'tis understood
> The mere commingling of passionate breath,
> Produce more than our searching witnesseth:
> What I know not: but who, of men, can tell
> That flowers would bloom, or that green fruit would swell
> To melting pulp, that fish would have bright mail,
> The earth its dower of river, wood, and vale,
> The meadows runnels, runnels pebble-stones,
> The seed its harvest, or the lute its tones,
> Tones ravishment, or ravishment its sweet,
> If human souls did never kiss and greet?　(I, 832–42)

Human passion actually generates growth, fruition, ripeness in
nature. Byron was completely off the mark when he said that
the passage was "sentimental,"[41] although Keats's language
may be weaker than his meaning. Bailey, who knew Keats
very well at the time, understood what the passage meant
even though his Christian sensibilities could not accept the
idea. He complained about *Endymion*'s "inclination . . . to that
abominable principle of *Shelley's*—that *Sensual Love* is the principle of *things*. Of this I believe him to be unconscious, & can
see how by a process of imagination he might arrive at so false,

delusive, & dangerous conclusion."[42] Although his claim that Keats did not understand what he was saying is obviously a poor excuse, Bailey is perhaps correct in seeing Shelley's atheistic influence at work here in the idea that sensual love generates all life forms into growth and fruition.

But for Keats the relationship between love and creativity in nature does not end here: it continues into the realm of poetic creativity. After all, the poet is himself a god who generates in poetry the same growth and ripeness that love creates in nature. As Keats tells Haydon when discussing the creative process, "but here I am talking like a Madman greater things that our Creator himself made!!" (*Letters* 1:143). The poet is himself godlike, an idea that finds support in the fact that the supreme poet is Apollo.

Apollo is, however, more than just an artistically creative poet: as the sun, he is also the generative force in the processes of natural growth, as we saw when Keats talked of flowers "budding patiently under the eye of Apollo" (*Letters* 1:232). Both Evert and Blackstone have traced the creative power of Apollo in so much detail that further consideration is unnecessary here;[43] suffice it to say that, as Apollo's representative on earth, the poet has tremendous creative power that extends to the realm of nature, as Keats explains in "I stood tip-toe . . .":

> In the calm grandeur of a sober line,
> We see the waving of the mountain pine;
> And when a tale is beautifully staid,
> We feel the safety of a hawthorn glade:
> When it is moving on luxurious wings,
> The soul is lost in pleasant smotherings:
> Fair dewy roses brush against our faces,
> And flowering laurels spring from diamond vases;
> O'er head we see the jasmine and sweet briar,
> And bloomy grapes laughing from green attire;
> While at our feet, the voice of crystal bubbles
> Charms us at once away from all our troubles:
> So that we feel uplifted from the world,
> Walking upon the white clouds wreath'd and curl'd.
> So felt he, who first told, how Psyche went

> On the smooth wind to realms of wonderment;
> What Psyche felt, and Love, when their full lips
> First touch'd. (127–44)

Here, as elsewhere, Keats unites his three dominant metaphors of sensual love, natural fruition, and poetic creativity. He virtually equates the creative power of the three realms, portraying them as interchangeable. We have already seen the three forces united when Endymion, who is both poet and lover, forces the rose into bloom by holding it in the cold stream of water. This is an image that Keats had employed before in "I stood tiptoe . . ." to describe the imaginative power of the poet, the workings of the creative process. After again discussing the sexual attraction of a woman, the poet asks:

> What next? A tuft of evening primroses,
> O'er which the mind may hover till it dozes;
> O'er which it well might take a pleasant sleep,
> But that 'tis ever startled by the leap
> Of buds into ripe flowers. (107–11)

Once more Keats describes the creative process of the imagination in terms of organic growth. The poet's mind "hover[s]" over the primroses until it falls into a trancelike state of calm passivity, which Keats describes elsewhere as a state of "diligent indolence" akin to negative capability. It is in this state of calm receptivity that the poet's senses are suddenly "startled," alerted, "by the leap / Of buds into ripe flowers," a metaphor for poetic creation. The image is one of an electric impulse or discharge as the flower is created—an accurate description, since it was believed by some theorists that electric fluid was the life force in plants as well as in human beings.

I cannot agree with Blackstone when he says of this passage: "The flower is 'forced,' as it were, into growth under the poet's eye,"[44] although it was generally accepted that the application of external electricity could stimulate plant growth.[45] Surely the point of the passage is that the growth is natural rather than "forced"; the process is organic, not artificial. As Keats himself explains in the third axiom about poetry, "If Poetry comes not as naturally as the Leaves to a tree it had better not come at all" (*Letters* 1:238–39).

Of course, the idea of poetry as organic growth is not original to Keats; it was a common concept among both the German and English Romantics.[46] The difference between Keats and many of the other poets, however, is that, because of his intimate knowledge of the processes of organic growth, gained from his study of biology and botany, the relationship between organic growth and poetic creativity ceases to be simply a neat, if vague, analogy and becomes instead a strong metaphorical identification. For example, in a letter of 27 April 1818 to Reynolds, he writes: "I lay awake last night—listening to the Rain with a sense of being drown'd and rotted like a grain of wheat—There is a continual courtesy between the Heavens and the Earth. —the heavens rain down their unwelcomeness, and the Earth sends it up again to be returned tomorrow" (*Letters* 1:273–74). The cycles of weather—and of life—go on continually, yet at this time Keats was in a state of depression as Tom was ill at Teignmouth and he feared that his poetic ability was failing as he went into a torpid state of unhealthy indolence. He knew inherently from his study of botany, however, that a state of dormancy—often lasting through the whole winter—is necessary before growth, renewed creativity, can occur. Decay of the seed is necessary before the plant begins to grow. The concept is a crude foreshadowing of his later philosophical idea of "dying into life," which becomes so important in the two *Hyperions*. The seed dies into the land and will flourish as a new plant, an idea that Keats develops at length in *Isabella*, the poem on which he was working when he wrote this letter to Reynolds.

From an artistic perspective, this dormant state of passivity, or indolence, is a precondition of imaginative creativity; it is necessary before poetic growth can begin, before ripeness occurs. Sometimes Keats fears, however, that he may not live long enough for poetic ripeness, the perfection of growth and health, and he had expressed those fears to Reynolds a few months earlier, on 31 January 1818, in the sonnet "When I have fears . . .":

The Poet-Physician

> When I have fears that I may cease to be
> Before my pen has glean'd my teeming brain,
> Before high piled books, in charactry,
> Hold like rich garners the full ripen'd grain.
>
> (1–4; *Letters* 1:222)

Keats knows his imagination is as fecund as nature, but he worries whether that potential will ever come to fruition.

In another sonnet, written before 13 March 1818, shortly after "When I have fears . . ." and at around the same time as the "Axioms" on poetry, Keats focuses on man's mind in relation to nature, especially the seasons:

> Four seasons fill the measure of the year;
> Four seasons are there in the mind of man.
> He hath his lusty spring, when fancy clear
> Takes in all beauty with an easy span:
> He hath his summer, when luxuriously
> He chews the honied cud of fair spring thoughts,
> Till, in his soul dissolv'd, they come to be
> Part of himself. He hath his autumn ports
> And havens of repose, when his tired wings
> Are folded up, and he content to look
> On mists in idleness: to let fair things
> Pass by unheeded as a threshold brook.
> He hath his winter too of pale misfeature,
> Or else he would forget his mortal nature. (*Letters* 1:243)

In many ways the sonnet anticipates "To Autumn," which looks back to summer and forward to winter while evoking "the songs of spring." And like "To Autumn," it stresses the poet's state of receptivity, passivity, calm reflection, and speculation while the creative process of growth runs its natural course. But the sonnet differs from "To Autumn" in that Keats is as yet not reconciled to the idea of the mind's winter, and the couplet remains its weakest aspect.

Again, the comparison between the seasons and the stages of man's life is a literary commonplace that stretches all the way back to Ovid.[47] But Keats's version of this analogy is different from others, as Evert has observed, because of "his focus on the growth of the mind, rather than on the mere facts of physical vigor and decay."[48] Evert suggests that this emphasis on the mind—specifically the imagination—in the relation to natural growth is a result of the dual role of Apollo as maturer of the imagination (in his role as god of poetry) and of nature (in his role as sun god).[49] Although this is a valid observation, I believe that the focus on "the mind of man" demonstrates Keats's interest in organic form as well as process, and is probably peculiar to him because of his knowledge of anatomy and morphology—the study of organic, as opposed to mechanical, form.

Blackstone has argued that Keats was interested in the form of the seed as an earthly correlative of the divine form of the urn,[50] an idea that originates in hermetic magic. It is more evident, however, that he was attracted to the seed as a correlative of the form of the mind, brain, or skull, as both are spherical, organic shapes. As Philip Ritterbush explains: "The sphere was the most nearly ideal of the forms of transcendental morphology and, according to that system of beliefs, its shape served to distinguish living nature from crystal growth. Whatever manifested the spherical form was alive."[51] This belief that organic shapes are spherical or globular, as opposed to mechanical or crystalline forms, which were believed to be angular and linear, is more directly connected to the fields of anatomy and physiology and so is dealt with in more detail in the following chapter. Suffice it to say here that Keats's emphasis on the spherical forms of seeds, eggs, and skull has its roots in eighteenth- and early nineteenth-century physiological theory, which helps explain why he viewed the seed, egg, and skull as organic, and hence creative, forms. The correspondence between these three creative forms becomes abundantly clear in *Isabella,* a poem I will deal with shortly.

One of the best examples of Keats's use of the mind-skull as an organic, creative sphere, however, occurs in the "Ode to Psyche," where poetic creativity is expressed in the metaphor of the garden in the mind of man:

> Yes, I will be thy priest, and build a fane
> In some untrodden region of my mind,
> Where branched thoughts, new grown with pleasant pain,
> Instead of pines shall murmur in the wind:
> . . . .

The Poet-Physician

And in the midst of this wide quietness
A rosy sanctuary will I dress
With the wreath'd trellis of a working brain,
    With buds, and bells, and stars without a name,
With all the gardener Fancy e'er could feign,
    Who breeding flowers, will never breed the same.

(50–53, 58–63)

Keats again expresses the fecundity and infinite variety of the poetic imagination in terms of natural growth and creativity. The spring and summer flowers of the mind will bloom forever; the imagination and nature are metaphorical echoes of each other. The passage is also interesting for its conception of the paradoxical state of "diligent indolence," the "working brain" actively creating "in the midst of this wide quietness." Such calm passivity, as far as Keats is concerned, is a necessary element for creative ripeness, fruition, and flowering to occur.

Despite his fascination with the fecundity of the mind in relation to nature, however, Keats could not for long avoid contemplation of the destructive aspect of nature with which he must have been so familiar in his study of medicine. Early in his poetic career he felt that the destruction he saw in nature was not within the "proper bound" of poetry, which should deal exclusively with beauty. As he states in *Sleep and Poetry*, the object of poetry is not to "feed upon the burrs, / And thorns of life," but to "be a friend / To sooth the cares, and lift the thoughts of man" (244–47).

The desire that poetry should soothe, should transcend destruction, is perhaps natural in a medical student whose primary aim was to prolong life and relieve suffering. Yet as a naturalist Keats could not banish the destruction he saw everywhere in nature, and this problem came to a head in "To J. H. Reynolds, Esq.":

Oh never will the prize,
High reason, and the lore of good and ill,
Be my award. Things cannot to the will
Be settled, but they tease us out of thought.
Or is it that imagination brought
Beyond its proper bound, yet still confined, —
Lost in a sort of purgatory blind,

110

Cannot refer to any standard law
Of either earth or heaven? —It is a flaw
In happiness to see beyond our bourn—
It forces us in summer skies to mourn:
It spoils the singing of the nightingale.   (74–85)

Moreover, not only is there incomprehensible decay in nature; there is also absolute cruelty:

                    I was at home,
And should have been most happy—but I saw
Too far into the sea; where every maw
The greater on the less feeds evermore: —
But I saw too distinct into the core
Of an eternal fierce destruction,
And so from happiness I far was gone.
Still am I sick of it: and though to-day
I've gathered young spring-leaves, and flowers gay
Of periwinkle and wild strawberry,
Still do I that most fierce destruction see,
The shark at savage prey—the hawk at pounce,
The gentle robin, like a pard or ounce,
Ravening a worm.   (92–105)

Reason cannot adequately explain these natural cycles of life, growth followed by decay, creation by destruction, and Keats seems to have momentarily lost his faith in negative capability, his willingness to accept "uncertainties, Mysteries, doubts" (*Letters* 1:193). He wants desperately to understand in order "to ease the Burden of the Mystery" of life, as he writes to Reynolds two months later on 3 May 1818 (*Letters* 1:277).

Keats's fear of, and disgust at, the cruel destructiveness in nature may have been influenced by his reading of Erasmus Darwin's *Economy of Vegetation*, where Darwin discusses this very topic in a passage that would undoubtedly have interested Keats as a botanist and naturalist:

If we may compare the parts of nature with each other, there are some circumstances of her economy which seem to contribute more to the general scale of happiness than others. Thus the nourishment of animal bodies is derived from three sources: 1. the milk given from the mother. . . . 2. Another source of the food of animals includes seeds or eggs. . . . 3. But the last method of supporting animal bodies by the destruction of other living animals, as lions preying upon lambs, these upon living vegetables, and mankind upon them all, would appear to be a less perfect part of the economy of nature than those before mentioned, as contributing less to the sum of general happiness.[52]

Later, in Canto III, Darwin discusses "the warrior Shark" (79) — Keats's "shark at savage prey" — and the sturgeon, who:

> Ambush'd in weeds, or sepulcher'd in sands,
> In dread repose He waits the scaly bands,
> Waves in red spires the living lures, and draws
> The unwary plunderers to his circling jaws.   (III, 73–76)

As Keats knew, "Every maw / The greater on the less feeds."

At the end of "To J. H. Reynolds, Esq.," Keats claims that he will "from detested moods in new romance / Take refuge" (111–12), and the romance he refers to is *Isabella*, the next poem he wrote after the epistle. But if he thought that he was going to escape in *Isabella*, Keats must have been sadly disappointed, for the romance is itself an intricate discussion of life cycles of creation and destruction. It is a biological—one is almost tempted to say a botanical—romance that goes straight to "the core / Of an eternal fierce destruction." Keats transfers to the human realm what he saw in nature, so that the images of animals feeding on animals in the epistle become images of men feeding on men.

It would be wrong to claim that Keats's intention was to write a biological romance. After finishing *Endymion*, which celebrates the love of a mythical shepherd for a goddess, he undoubtedly intended to come to terms with "the agonies, the strife / Of human hearts" (*Sleep and Poetry*, 124–25) in *Isabella*. The love of Isabella and Lorenzo seems, however, to be an inevitable biological attraction rather than a meeting of passionate spirits, an idea heightened by the botanical images Keats employs to describe its natural, organic growth:

> "Love! thou art leading me from wintry cold,
> Lady! thou leadest me to summer clime,
> And I must taste the blossoms that unfold

In its ripe warmth this gracious morning time."
So said, his erewhile timid lips grew bold,
    And poesied with hers in dewy rhyme:
Great bliss was with them, and great happiness
Grew, like a lusty flower in June's caress.

Parting they seem'd to tread upon the air,
    Twin roses by the zephyr blown apart
Only to meet again more close, and share
    The inward fragrance of each other's heart.   (65–76)

Their love buds in the spring, will grow to fruition and ripeness in the summer, and, inevitably and ironically, will run its
seasonal course to death in the winter.

Moreover, the cruelty of nature we saw in "To J. H. Reynolds, Esq." is at work here in the animalistic brothers who are
"the shark" and "the hawk" of the human realm. They thrive
on the destruction of beings who are weaker—if only finan-
cially and socially—than themselves:

For them the Ceylon diver held his breath,
    And went all naked to the hungry shark;
For them his ears gush'd blood; for them in death
    The seal on the cold ice with piteous bark
Lay full of darts; for them alone did seethe
    A thousand men in troubles wide and dark.   (113–18)

Afraid that Isabella's love of Lorenzo will thwart their plans to
use her in marriage for their own gain, "these men of cruel
clay / Cut Mercy with a sharp knife to the bone" (173–74)—the
image smacks of anatomical dissection—and kill Lorenzo,
returning his body to the forest, which seems ironically fitting
for this "lusty flower" of a lover. In death he is surrounded by
"Red whortle-berries" (298), "beeches and high chestnuts"
(300); he is now absorbed in the natural world, "Upon the
skirts of human-nature dwelling" (306).

In grief over Lorenzo's absence, Isabella falls into a kind of
late-autumn decay as she follows through her cycle of life:

In the mid days of autumn, on their eves
    The breath of Winter comes from far away,
And the sick west continually bereaves

> Of some gold tinge, and plays a roundelay
> Of death among the bushes and the leaves,
>   To make all bare before he dares to stray
> From his north cavern. So sweet Isabel
> By gradual decay from beauty fell.   (249–56)

The dance of vegetational death has begun in Isabella and is completed when she discovers Lorenzo's body. Grasping his glove,

> She kiss'd it with a lip more chill than stone,
>   And put it in her bosom, where it dries
> And freezes utterly unto the bone
>   Those dainties made to still an infant's cries.   (371–74)

Her maternal milk, the sap of life, has been frozen; the winter of their love is complete with the thwarting of the procreative function.

But because this love is botanical, a vegetational resurrection is possible for Lorenzo. Isabella digs to "the kernel of the grave" (383), and Keats's choice of the word "kernel" is important for it is the center of the seed from which new growth will come, "the embryon [which] is in a torpid or insensible state,"[53] and it lies dormant in the ground-grave during winter. "The kernel of the grave" is quite literally Lorenzo's head, which Isabella cuts off and carries home. In this image the organic, spherical forms of the seed and the head, both so prominent in Keats's poetry, are perfectly united. They are literally, rather than metaphorically, identical.

Isabella plants Lorenzo's head in a pot, just like a seed, "cover'd it with mould" (415), sets a basil plant over it, "And moisten'd it with tears unto the core" (424). As we have seen, Keats's choice of the word "core" is precise, derived from the botanical word "corculum," which is the very center, or essence, of the seed from which future growth develops. And the now unfrozen water of life is necessary to plant growth. At this point Keats employs a certain degree of poetic license, for on a literal level the basil has sprouted from another seed before Isabella plants it over Lorenzo's buried head. But, because the basil, far from being simply a means of hiding the head, symbolizes the vegetational resurrection of Lorenzo, Keats virtually portrays it as sprouting anew from the head-seed, the "kernel of the grave":

> And so she ever fed it with thin tears,
>   Whence thick, and green, and beautiful it grew,
> So that it smelt more balmy than its peers
>   Of basil-tufts in Florence; for it drew
> Nurture besides, and life, from human fears,
>   From the fast mouldering head there shut from view:
> So that the jewel, safely casketed,
> Came forth, and in perfumed leafits spread.   (425–32)

Creation springs from destruction, growth from decay; life triumphs over "Winter chill" (450).

Correspondingly, Isabella's procreative maternal instincts are revived in her care of the basil:

> And when she left, she hurried back, as swift
>   As bird on wing to breast its eggs again;
> And, patient as a hen-bird, sat her there
>   Beside her basil, weeping through her hair.   (469–72)

The image of the eggs is important, not only for portraying Isabella's maternal love, but also because in anatomy the skull is often compared to an egg. As Andrew Fyfe points out, "The *General Figure* of the *upper* part of the Cranium is compared to that of an Egg."[54] In the image of Lorenzo's head, over which Isabella broods like a mother hen, the motifs of skull, seed, and egg, so commonly associated in botany and anatomy, coalesce to enhance Keats's theme of new growth out of death that is symbolized by the luxurious basil. Life triumphs, if only biologically and momentarily, for it is quickly snuffed out again by the brothers, who prey on anything weaker than themselves. When they succeed in stealing the basil, Isabella pines to death.

Isabella may not be a brilliant poem—Keats himself disliked it—but it does exorcise the horror he felt at the destruction and decay in nature. It helps Keats to reaffirm his faith in the cyclical flux of nature and so paves the way for his calm acceptance in early 1819 of all aspects of life. And its forcefulness is built largely on Keats's accurate use of botanical images.

The Poet-Physician

On 19 March 1819, Keats writes to George and Georgiana what is in fact a detailed answer to the fears he expressed in the epistle "To J. H. Reynolds, Esq.," an answer based on the calm acceptance of destruction as an integral part of the forces of life:

I have this moment received a note from Haslam in which he expects the death of his Father. . . . This is the world—thus we cannot expect to give way many hours to pleasure—Circumstances are like Clouds continually gathering and bursting—While we are laughing the seed of some trouble is put into the wide arable land of events—while we are laughing it sprouts is [for it] grows and suddenly bears a poison fruit which we must pluck—Even so we have leisure to reason on the misfortunes of our friends.

Again, Keats conceptualizes the destructive forces of life in terms of natural, botanical metaphors. He still feels sorrow at Haslam's news, yet he is striving toward a feeling of "disinterestedness," the ability to sympathize with all men equally, that will allow him to see beyond personal pain, to appreciate the whole of life. He continues:

Yet this feeling [disinterestedness] ought to be carried to its highest pitch, as there is no fear of its ever injuring society—which it would do I fear pushed to an extremity—For in wild nature the Hawk would loose his Breakfast of Robins and the Robin his of Worms The Lion must starve as well as the swallow—The greater part of Men make their way with the same instinctiveness, the same unwandering eye from their purposes, the same animal eagerness as the Hawk— . . . I go among the Feilds and catch a glimpse of a stoat or a fieldmouse peeping out of the withered grass—the creature hath a purpose and its eyes are bright with it—I go amongst the buildings of a city and I see a Man hurrying along—to what? The Creature has a purpose and his eyes are bright with it.   (*Letters* 2:79–80)

Far from being disgusted by the similarities between men and animals, Keats now admires the instinctive alertness and sense of purpose in both. He contemplates this raw energy with the cool detachment of a scientific observer, and now seems unperturbed by the prospect of death itself, for in this same letter he copies out the sonnet "Why did I laugh tonight?," concluding boldly that "death is life's high meed."[55] This is a very different view of death from that expressed in "To J. H. Reynolds, Esq." and in *Isabella*.

Keats followed "Why did I laugh tonight?" with a short, often ignored song, probably written in early April 1819, in which a bird, foreshadowing the nightingale, tries to console two brothers who have lost a third:

> Shed no tear—O shed no tear!
> The flower will bloom another year.
> Weep no more—O weep no more!
> Young buds sleep in the root's white core.   (1–4)

I have already examined the botanical accuracy of these images, the concept of the buds of perennial flowers surviving the winter by being housed in the hybernacle, or bulb, of the plant. The bird's consolation is based on this fact of the seasonal return of life in the spring, symbolized by the new flower, so that the death of winter is no longer horrifying.

Keats's acceptance of death and winter is most strongly expressed in the ode "To Autumn," the culmination of his creativity in which his poetry, like the season, is at its richest and ripest. Through concentration on details of the fruit, the flowers, and the bees, Keats creates an exquisitely vivid, lush, and colorful picture. It is a depiction of perfection, of fulfillment, of ripeness, of growth reaching its climax:

> Season of mists and mellow fruitfulness,
>   Close bosom-friend of the maturing sun;
> Conspiring with him how to load and bless
>   With fruit the vines that round the thatch-eves run;
> To bend with apples the moss'd cottage-trees,
>   And fill all fruit with ripeness to the core;
>   To swell the gourd, and plump the hazel shells
> With a sweet kernel; to set budding more,
> And still more, later flowers for the bees,
> Until they think warm days will never cease,
>   For summer has o'er-brimm'd their clammy cells. (1–11)

In the last stanza of "To Autumn," the images of "the stubble-plains," the "full-grown lambs," and the "gathering swallows" all suggest that the richness of growth and harvest is over and that winter is on its way. Even the gentle image of "the soft-dying day" indicates approaching death, here symbolized by a diurnal, rather than a seasonal, image.[56]

Keats realizes that natural beauty is transient, perfection momentary, and death inevitable. But his awareness of these things in no way detracts from the rich, sensuous beauty of the scene; instead it heightens that beauty, as Keats has managed to capture autumn in its most intense and poignant moment. He has come a long way from the dark questions and desperate cries of the epistle "To J. H. Reynolds, Esq.," which were evident in his poetry as recently as the "Ode to a Nightingale." Now the prospect of death, the destruction of the year, is met with calm, passive acceptance, symbolized in the second stanza by the "diligent indolence" of the personified figure of autumn. In her relaxed postures, "sitting careless on a granary floor" (14), or "Drows'd with the fume of poppies" (17), she both fully appreciates the beauty of the season and calmly accepts its passing away. She is truly exercising negative capability, and so is similar to the poet himself. It is Keats's final vision of life.

In tracing the influence of Keats's botanical knowledge on his poetry and correspondence, I have moved from the examination of very specific images of flowers, plants, and trees in his early poetry to a much broader consideration of his understanding of life forces in the later poems and letters. In this broadening of approach I do not mean to imply that Keats ceased to use precise botanical images in his later work; a glance at the vividly accurate images of the poisonous plants "Wolf's-bane, tight-rooted" and "nightshade, ruby grape of Proserpine"[57] in the first stanza of the "Ode on Melancholy" will dispel any such notions. He still draws on his botanical knowledge for excellent images, and his powers of observation are still acute.

But as Keats matured, both artistically and philosophically, he moved beyond the bounds of simply observing nature for its sensuous beauty and began to consider difficult questions concerning the forces of life and death in the natural world, questions that often led him into severe depression until he learned to accept pain, suffering, and death as an integral part of the cycle of life. In examining this development, I have been forced myself to move beyond the bourne of botany proper, but throughout I have tried to demonstrate that Keats's knowledge of botany and morphology taught him to observe nature closely and assisted him in his attempts to understand its forces of growth and decay, the forces that make up the very flux of life. Botany formed part of the "extensive knowledge [that] is needful to thinking people—it takes away the heat and fever; and helps, by widening speculation, to ease the Burden of the Mystery" of life (*Letters* 1:277). As Joseph Priestley says, "The object of experimental philosophy is the knowledge of nature in general";[58] without such knowledge, Keats's understanding of life could not have developed so far so fast.

CHAPTER IV

Anatomy and Physiology

In a certain sense, anatomy and physiology are the easiest of Keats's medical subjects to study since his *Anatomical and Physiological Note Book* is still extant.[1] The fact that this notebook from Astley Cooper's course is the only one that has survived from Keats's days as a medical student may suggest that this subject held a particular interest for him. On the other hand, there is less evidence of anatomical and physiological knowledge in the poetry and letters than there is of chemical or, in a more general way, pathological knowledge. This is perfectly understandable, however, when we realize that chemistry and pathology provided Keats with concepts and metaphors that were much more readily adaptable to poetic needs and meanings than those of anatomy. This is not to say, however, that evidence of anatomical and physiological knowledge is absent from the poetry and letters; rather, certain areas of the subject seem to have dominated Keats's interest in this field, and ideas and images from these crop up quite frequently.

I have already described in some detail Keats's anatomy, physiology, and surgery teachers—Sir Astley Cooper, Henry Cline, Jr., Joseph Henry Green, and possibly Dr. John Haighton; some discussion of the textbooks Keats used in these subjects is now necessary. In Green's course of dissections the standard textbook was *The London Dissector* by an anonymous author, which South says "kept its place as the text used by most of the students till Green published a small volume, 'Outlines to a Course of Anatomy.'" Green's text, correctly titled *Outlines of a Course of Dissections for the Use of Students at St. Thomas's Hospital*, was published in 1815, the year Keats arrived at the United Hospitals; in 1820 it was enlarged under the title *The Dissector's Manual*.[2] Since Keats entered Guy's Hospital during the transition period between *The London Dissector* and Green's *Outlines*, it is probable that he owned both; he would most certainly have owned the latter, which was recommended by Astley Cooper.[3]

Cooper also recommended two other texts to his students: "Fyfe's Anatomy, and Blumenbach's Physiology";[4] and South claims that "'Innes on the Muscles' and 'Barclay on the Arteries'" were also popular with students.[5] From time to time I quote from these texts with the confidence that even if Keats did not own them he was at least familiar with them, and would have referred to them in the course of his studies. In quoting from Astley Cooper's lectures, I am greatly indebted to Joshua Waddington's excellent notes, "Lectures on Anatomy and the Principal Operations of Surgery . . . by Astley Cooper Esq.," which were made during the same year that Keats attended the lectures and so are exactly what he heard. Waddington's beautifully handwritten notes, now in the Wills Library at Guy's Hospital, were written out after each lecture and so are much fuller than Keats's hasty classroom ones for the same course. The lectures for Cooper's other course, "The Principles and Practice of Surgery," were published by Cooper's student Frederick Tyrrell, with whom Keats lived for a time. Also at the Wills Library are Dr. John Haighton's manuscript "Lectures on the Physiology of the Human Body, Delivered at Guy's Hospital," to which I refer occasionally, although we do not know whether Keats attended this course.

In leaving chemistry and botany to examine anatomy and physiology, we are moving from subjects which, from a medical viewpoint, were primarily concerned with the production of medicines to those dealing with the structure and workings of the human body. As I have observed, however, many of the theories concerning plant anatomy and physiology were applied to human anatomy and physiology. This was particularly true with Linnaeus's elaborate development of analogies between the plant and human realms, and in the theoretical

The Poet-Physician

attempts to discover *the* life force that animates all living matter.[6] Sir Humphry Davy, who proudly acknowledged the connection between physiology and chemistry, warned, however, against the use of such theoretical analogy:

And in pursuing this view of the subject, medicine and physiology, those sciences which connect the preservation of the health of the human being with the abstruse philosophy of organized nature, will be found to have derived from chemistry most of their practical applications, and many of the analogies which have contributed to give to their scattered facts order and systematic arrangement. . . . And if the connection of chemistry with physiology has given rise to some visionary and seductive theories; yet even this circumstance has been useful to the public mind in exciting it by doubt, and in leading it to new investigations. A reproach, to a certain degree just, has been thrown upon those doctrines known by the name of chemical physiology; for in the applications of them, speculative philosophers have been guided rather by the analogies of words than of facts.[7]

In dealing with anatomy and physiology, then, we should bear in mind chemical theories concerning subtle fluids and botanical ideas on organic form, even though this theoretical approach was bitterly attacked by Astley Cooper, who had an inherent distrust of any knowledge not based on experiment and observation. In his *Surigcal Essays,* published with Benjamin Travers, he states:

Young medical men find it so much easier a task to speculate than to observe, that they are too apt to be pleased with some sweeping theory, which saves them the trouble of observing the processes of nature; and they have afterwards, when they embark on their professional practice, not only everything still to learn, but also to abandon those false impressions which hypothesis is sure to create. . . . It is right, therefore, that those who are studying their profession, should be aware that there is no short road to knowledge; that observation on the diseased living, examinations of the dead, and experiments upon living animals, are the only sources of true knowledge, and that deductions from these are the sole basis of legitimate theory.[8]

Cooper had been a pupil of John Hunter, the genius who had almost singlehandedly delivered British surgery from its dependency on theory and had set it up on the solid foundation of empirical proof based on intimate and accurate anatomical knowledge. Such knowledge was to be gained from frequent dissection of, and experimentation on, the human body itself, a lesson that both Cooper and Green instilled in their students. As Green states in his introduction to *The Dissector's Manual*, "Whilst the lectures give a comprehensive view of the subject, with the mutual relation and connexion of all its parts, and their application to practice, it is by dissection alone that such views become esentially our own, or that we dare give them the name of knowledge."[9]

In his introductory surgical lecture, Cooper reiterates again and again the necessity for his students to have sound anatomical and physiological knowledge. He concludes: "In surgical science, hypothesis should be entirely discarded, and sound theory, derived from actual observation and experience, alone encouraged. The first is an *ignus fatuus*, which is sure to mislead; the last a polar-star, a never-failing guide."[10] Although Keats claims that invention is "the Polar Star of Poetry, as Fancy is the Sails, and Imagination the Rudder" (*Letters* 1:170), he never forgot Cooper's insistence that knowledge can be gained only by observation and experience, and as he matured in outlook, he kept hammering home the same lesson to his correspondents. On 31 December 1818 he writes to George and Georgiana: "The more we know the more inadequacy we discover in the world to satisfy us—this is an old observation; but I have made up my Mind never to take any thing for granted—but even to examine the truth of the commonest proverbs" (*Letters* 2:18). Again, on 19 March 1819, while outlining his desire for more knowledge to George and Georgiana, he proclaims, "Nothing ever becomes real till it is experienced—Even a Proverb is no proverb to you till your Life has illustrated it" (*Letters* 2:81). This refusal to accept anything as true, or real, until it has been experienced is a direct echo of Cooper's and Green's approach to medical science.

Lest we think, however, that Keats may have been introduced to such an approach to knowledge elsewhere, two passages in his letters subtly indicate his source. On 8 March 1819, he writes to Haydon:

Conversation is not a search after knowledge, but an endeavour at effect. In this respect two most opposite men, Wordsworth and Hunt, are the same. A friend of mine observed the other day that if Lord Bacon were to make any remark in a party of the present day, the conversation would stop on the sudden. I am convinced of this, and from this I have come to the resolution never to write for the sake of writing, or making a poem, but from running over with any little knowledge and experience which many years of reflection may perhaps give me—otherwise I will be dumb. (*Letters* 2:43)

In this attack on "that most vulgar of all crowds the literary," and in his claim that poetry should be a reflection of "knowledge and experience"—rather than of imagination or beauty— Keats looks to Bacon, the father of modern empirical science often mentioned by Cooper and Haighton, as the man who truly knows how to "search after knowledge." It is with Bacon's scientific interest in "proof" that Keats wishes to approach knowledge and truth; he no longer believes that they can be perceived by flights of the imagination alone. As he writes to Reynolds on 3 May 1818:

In regard to his [Wordsworth's] genius alone—we find what he says true as far as we have experienced and we can judge no further but by larger experience—for axioms in philosophy are not axioms until they are proved upon our pulses: We read fine——things but never feel them to thee full until we have gone the same steps as the Author. (*Letters* 1:279)

The medical image of truth being proved upon the pulses is significant: just as the physician must judge the patient's state of health or disease by examination of the body itself, rather than by resorting to vague hypotheses, so too the poet must judge the validity of his philosophical axioms by experience alone. Cooper and Green had insisted that it is not enough to read about the body; it must be observed, experienced, through dissection.[11] Keats now transfers this scientific principle to his approach to life in general, thus proclaiming that he cannot accept the truth of Wordsworth's discoveries about life until he has himself observed and experienced them. There is no other way of gaining knowledge.

As well as rejecting imaginative hypotheses in science, the new breed of medical practitioners like Hunter and Cooper were also reacting against eighteenth-century rationalism, which constructed elaborate religious, philosophical, and scientific systems on neat, reasoned theories having little or no empirical foundations and very tenuous connections to reality. Cooper was vividly aware that painstaking research would reveal only small facets of truth at a time, and in his introductory lecture he states that he "would not recommend works to young students which lay down *systems* for their guidance; such a plan of reading is bad." In his description of the arteries, Barclay also claims that "by leaving uncertain what is uncertain, and describing as regular only what is regular, we should greatly facilitate the progress of Anatomy."[12]

This distrust of systems seems also to have influenced Keats. It is evident in his attack on Dilke for being a "Godwin-methodist," one of the tribe of "stubborn arguers . . . [who] never begin upon a subject they have not preresolved on" (*Letters* 2:213). Keats abhorred the fact that Dilke could not accept the "uncertainties, Mysteries, doubts" about life, that, like Coleridge, he was "incapable of remaining content with half knowledge" (*Letters* 1:193–94). Of course, Cooper, as a man of science, would claim that the mysteries will eventually be explained by careful empirical research, whereas Keats, as a poet, insists that they are an inherent and valuable aspect of life; but Keats remains very close to his teacher in his distrust of dogmatic systems.

Having discussed Astley Cooper's approach to anatomy and surgery and its influence on Keats's thought, I turn now to more specific aspects of the lectures themselves. Cooper begins with three definitions:[13]

1 Anatomy— Knowledge of Structure
2 Phisiology— — of the Functions of Parts
3 Pathology— — of the Diseases.——

Cooper continues by stating that the body is "Divided into 3 parts 1 Those for Loco Motion 2 Those to support Life 3 Those for the propogation of Species." The second group of parts—"Those to support Life"—are in turn subdivided into three parts—"1 Absorbent 2 Circulating 3 Nervous"—which are defined as:

1 Function of the Stomach and Intestines &c . . .
2 Circulating, Heart, arteries, and Veins . . .
3 Brain Medulla oblongata and Spinalis, & Nerves.[14]

It is these three life-supporting functions that apparently interested Keats most as a student of anatomy, for images and ideas from these areas of the subject later find their way into his poetry and letters. He seems to have been especially fascinated by the brain and the nervous system, perhaps because the brain virtually controls the workings of the rest of the body, as Haighton points out in his lecture on that organ: "The different subjects to which we have lately directed our attention, have led us to speak of the functions of different organs; but as these have no power inherent in themselves, to answer the various purposes nature intended them for, they must have a Communication with the Sensorium commune which is the Brain & Nervous system & the source of all action."[15]

In the previous chapter, I briefly touched upon Keats's use of the brain or skull as a spherical, and hence organic, form as opposed to an angular, mechanical, crystalline form. Philip Ritterbush explains this difference in more detail:

The sphere was the most nearly ideal of the forms [and] . . . its shape served to distinguish living nature from crystal growth. Whatever manifested the spherical form was alive. . . . Oken [*Elements of Physiophilosophy*, 1809–11] had hinted at a globular construction for living matter in saying that the intersection of his three life forces "could only produce the globe." While some animal tissue was made up of points (the nerves), or lines (the muscles), bone would be found to be composed of *globules*, with a tendency to move around the nerves like planets around the sun. Thus arose the spherical shape of the skull because bone was "the obedient planet of the nerve." The primary mucus of life was also thought to be globular in form.[16]

Oken's idea that the sphere is the ideal organic form was widely accepted, and some biologists, convinced by the neatness of the hypothesis, clung to it so tenaciously that when microscopic data at times disagreed with the concept, they claimed that the microscope itself was a primitive instrument and so must be in error. In 1818 Sir Everard Home, the English anatomist, claimed that muscle and nerve fibers are composed of tiny globules joined together in lines.[17]

Astley Cooper was very suspicious of these theories concerning ideal form, and he deliberately attacked the claim that the particles of blood are globular.[18] In doing so, however, he did discuss the theory, and Blumenbach supported the claim of the globular nature of blood particles.[19] Keats was, then, exposed to these controversial hypotheses, and he introduced ideas adapted from them into his poetry.

The first instance of Keats's portrayal of the brain as a spherical, organic, and ultimately creative form appears in the early epistle "To My Brother George," although the image is tentative and somewhat confusing at this stage:

> Full many a dreary hour have I past,
> My brain bewilder'd, and my mind o'ercast
> With heaviness; in seasons when I've thought
> No spherey strains by me could e'er be caught
> From the blue dome, though I to dimness gaze
> On the far depth where sheeted lightning plays;
> Or, on the wavy grass outstretch'd supinely,
> Pry 'mong the stars, to strive to think divinely. (1–8)

Keats compares the clear, blue dome of the sky-sphere, where according to Ptolemaic mythology perfect, divine music originates, with his own mind-brain, which is overcast instead of clear blue as its attempts to be inspired to poetic creativity are thwarted. The comparison is facilitated by the spherical shape of both the sky and his brain, and Keats correlates the mythical creativity represented by the music of the spheres with the literal creativity of the poetic mind.

Keats does not develop this image of the correspondence between the dome of the sky and the creative brain to any extent in the early poems, but he does return to it in a minor poem written on 31 January 1818, between *Endymion* and *Isabella*, "Hence burgundy, claret and port." Here he dismisses conventional liquor as a means of poetic inspiration—foreshadowing the "Ode to a Nightingale"—and claims instead:

The Poet-Physician

My bowl is the sky,
And I drink at my eye,
Till I feel in the brain
A Delphian pain.   (7–10)

The sky, which corresponds to the wine bowl the poet is rejecting, is an inverted bowl, or hemisphere, which provides
inspiration for that human creative sphere, the brain. However, the correspondence between these two forms is still not
abundantly clear.

What is clear is that the image of the mind-brain held a
special interest for Keats during this period. At the same time
as he was writing "Hence burgundy, claret and port," he composed the sonnet "When I have fears that I may cease to be,"
in which the image of the brain is prominent, and in early
March 1818 he wrote another sonnet, "Four seasons fill the
measure of the year," in which he contemplates the "four seasons . . . in the mind of man."

The image of the brain, which Keats keeps on the periphery
of his early poetry, becomes central in his letter to Bailey of 13
March 1818, in which he copies out the "Four seasons" sonnet:
"It is an old maxim of mine and of course must be well known
that evey [sic] point of thought is the centre of an intellectual
world—the two uppermost thoughts in a Man's mind are the
two poles of his World he revolves on them and every thing is
southward or northward to him through their means" (Letters
1:243). The image of the mind of man as a world-globe with
northern and southern hemispheres divided by a pole may
seem odd, vaguely geographical, but it is probably adapted
from Keats's anatomical knowledge.

In his lecture "On the Brain," Cooper says that the organ "is
composed of 3 parts, the Cerebrum, the Cerebellum, and the
Medulla Oblongata. . . . Upon removing the Membranes you
observe the Cerebrum divided into 2 hemispheres by the
falciform process."[20] Green, also writing on the cerebrum,
states:

It is situated in, and fills up the upper part of the cranium. Is of an
Oval rounded figure, and divided by a middle longitudinal section
(fissura longitudinalis) into two equal and similar halves, called its

hemispheres. Their upper and outer surface is rounded, their inner surfaces, which are in apposition to each other, are flattened, and the lower surface is divided in each into three *lobes.*[21]

Although in his letter to Bailey Keats is obviously describing the abstract concept of man's ability to think, to build a speculative world from only two thoughts,[22] he expresses it in very concrete anatomical terms. Even his claim that this "intellectual world" is divided by a pole may owe something to his knowledge that the brain's hemispheres are divided by the falciform process, or falx, as Cooper points out: "The processes of the Dura Mater are first the Falciform, so named for its resemblance to a Scythe, . . . its use is to separate one hemisphere of the Brain from the other."[23]

The cerebellum, like the cerebrum, "is divided behind by the Falx Minor into two Lobes or Hemispheres."[24] Green states that "the *body* of the cerebellum is of a round figure" with its "larger divisions being called *lobes.*"[25] The term "lobes," together with the emphasis in all these passages on the round, oval, or spherical form of the brain, accounts for Keats's description of Moneta's "globed brain" in *The Fall of Hyperion.* In this brief phrase Keats both evokes an intellectual world, or globe, and gives an accurate description of the human organ, using a technique that, as we will see when dealing with the "Ode to Psyche," he finds particularly appealing.

The Fall of Hyperion and *Hyperion* also contain another image of the brain that is influenced by Keats's medical knowledge. In *Hyperion,* Apollo talks of "the wide hollows of my brain" (III, 117), and the image is expanded in *The Fall,* where the narrator relates that

> at the view of sad Moneta's brow,
> I ached to see what things the hollow brain
> Behind enwombed. (I, 275–77)

The image is partially explained by Fyfe's statement that "the *upper* and *inner* Surface of the Cranium is *hollow,*"[26] and Christopher Ricks has noticed Keats's stress on creativity in the image of the brain as a womb in this and two other passages, one from *Otho the Great:*

The Poet-Physician

Thou, Jove-like, struck'dst thy forehead,
And from the teeming marrow of thy brain
I spring complete Minerva!　　　　　(I, i, 95–97)

and the other from the epistle "To My Brother George":

These wonders strange he sees, and many more,
Whose head is pregnant with poetic lore.　　　(53–54)

But Ricks, who believes that creativity is linked to, or a result of, embarrassment on the poet's part, does not recognize that the creativity of the womb, and hence of the poetic brain, is closely connected with its spherical, organic form.[27] As Fyfe points out, the brain, like the womb, is the anatomical shape of a seed or an egg, from which all growth springs:

The *General Figure* of the *upper* part of the Cranium is compared to that of an Egg. . . .
　　Each of the Hemispheres [of the Cerebrum] is of an *oval form*, or they somewhat resemble an Egg cut longitudinal into two equal parts.[28]

Although the idea of a pregnant brain is a common literary metaphor,[29] Keats finds evidence to support the connection between brain and womb in their spheroidal shape, which is an organic, generative form. This idea is most strongly evinced, as I have already illustrated at some length, in *Isabella*, where Lorenzo's head, "the kernel of the grave," by virtue of its resemblance in shape to a seed or egg, becomes the creative source for the basil's luxuriant growth. It is interesting to note that *Isabella*, in which these images of the brain seem to reach their first climax, was written at the same time—February to April 1818—as the "Four seasons" sonnet and the letter to Bailey on "a Man's mind," and immediately following "When I have fears . . . " and "Hence burgundy, claret and port."

Along with his interest in the spherical, creative shape of the brain, Keats has an almost architectural interest in the brain as a chamber or apartment, or even a garden, notions for which he would have found support in the anatomical descriptions of that organ. In *The Fall of Hyperion*, the narrator describes the "high tragedy / In the dark secret chambers of her [Moneta's] skull" (I, 277–78); this image has been developing at various points throughout Keats's poetry and letters.

Before illustrating these architectural metaphors in Keats's references to the brain, however, I should demonstrate their frequent employment in the study of anatomy, often to the chagrin of anatomists, as Green points out:

It is humiliating to the scientific anatomist to reflect, that the dissection of the most important part of the human body [the brain] should yet be that which rewards us with the least satisfying results. The mechanism and the purposes of its several portions are alike obscure; a truth, of which their very names, all fanciful, and not a few deserving a less honourable epithet, may be regarded as an involuntary confession.[30]

That Keats, with his poetic mind, naturally adopted this figurative method of describing the body is attested to by Cowden Clarke:

He once talked to me, upon my complaining of stomachic derangement, with a remarkable decision of opinion, describing the functions and actions of the organ with the clearness and, as I presume, technical precision of an adult practitioner; casually illustrating the comment, in his characteristic way, with poetical imagery: the stomach, he said, being like a brood of callow nestlings (opening his capacious mouth) yearning and gaping for sustenance.[31]

Although Clarke may have been surprised by such figurative analogy—and by Keats's accuracy—Green's comment shows that it was common in anatomy, and Green himself uses the traditional words "arch," "vault," "roof," "floor," "wall," and "pillars" to refer to various parts of the brain. A brief quotation from Fyfe's *Anatomy* on the cerebrum will illustrate how these names were used:

The Centrum Ovale forms an *Arch* or *Roof* over the two Lateral Ventricles; and the under part of this Roof, which is smooth and uniform, constitutes the upper part of these Ventricles. . . .

Under the Septum Lucidum is placed the Substance which has been compared in shape to a *Vault* by the Ancients, and from that has obtained the name of *Fornix*.

The Poet-Physician

The *Fornix* is merely a continuation of the Corpus Callosum, and forms a sort of hollow Ceiling with four *Pillars,* called *Crura,* or *Cornua,* from their winding direction of which there are two anterior, and two posterior.[32]

Other parts of the brain include the "Medullary arch" and the "columnae valvulae."[33]

Given this architectural terminology, it should come as no surprise that Keats visualizes the brain as a "chamber," although the first time he uses this image to any extent the evocation of the brain is indirect. The occasion to which I refer is his now famous letter of 3 May 1818 to Reynolds, on the Mansion of Life:

I compare human life to a large Mansion of Many Apartments, two of which I can only describe, the doors of the rest being as yet shut upon me—The first we step into we call the infant or thoughtless Chamber, in which we remain as long as we do not think—We remain there a long while, and notwithstanding the doors of the second Chamber remain wide open, showing a bright appearance, we care not to hasten to it; but are at length imperceptibly impelled by the awakening of the thinking principle—within us—we no sooner get into the second Chamber, which I shall call the Chamber of Maiden-Thought, than we become intoxicated with the light and the atmosphere, we see nothing but pleasant wonders, and think of delaying there for ever in delight: However among the effects this breathing is father of is that tremendous one of sharpening one's vision into the heart and nature of Man—of convincing ones nerves that the World is full of Misery and Heartbreak, Pain, Sickness and oppression—whereby This Chamber of Maiden Thought becomes gradually darken'd and at the same time on all sides of it many doors are set open—but all dark—all leading to dark passages—We see not the ballance of good and evil. We are in a Mist—*We* are now in that state—We feel the "burden of the Mystery," To this point was Wordsworth come, as far as I can conceive when he wrote 'Tintern Abbey' and it seems to me that his Genius is explorative of those dark Passages.   (*Letters* 1: 280–81)[34]

Though Keats does not refer directly to the brain here, his terms the "thoughtless Chamber" and the "Chamber of Maiden-Thought" suggest that he had that organ in mind; he is, after all, discussing man's mental, rather than physical, development, and it is natural that his anatomist's mind would conceive of that development as the progressive illumination of various chambers of the brain.

This argument would seem to be supported by the fact that Keats originally wrote that one of the effects of being in the Chamber of Maiden-Thought is "that tremendous one of sharpening one's vision into the *head* and nature of Man—of convincing ones nerves that the World is full of Misery and Heartbreak." He can see into his head and manipulate his nerves, which Keats knew from his medical studies originate in the brain.[35] He spoils the accuracy of the passage, however, when he replaces "head" with "heart"—probably to stress emotion over thought—since the nerves are not controlled by the heart. This change is even more confusing since, in this passage, he obviously has in mind not only Wordsworth's "Tintern Abbey" but also *The Recluse*, in which the narrator speaks of

> such fear and awe
> As fall upon us often when we look
> Into our Minds, into the Mind of Man—
> My haunt, and the main region of my song. (38–41)

Keats too is exploring "the Mind of Man," and he feels similar fears and awe, "the 'burden of the Mystery,'" as he looks into the dark passages of the brain which contain those experiences he does not yet comprehend. His confusion at the mystery is also directly parallel to the anatomist's admitted inability to understand the functions of the various parts of the brain. As Green says, "The mechanism and the purposes of its several portions are alike obscure."[36]

Keats, either consciously or subconsciously, uses the brain as a structure or model—nothing more but nothing less—around which to organize his ideas about life, although those ideas ultimately develop far beyond the merely physical descriptions he would have learned in the dissecting room into Wordsworthian concerns about human suffering. That he adapts this physical structure of the brain as a metaphor for portraying intellectual development comes as no surprise, since he has just told Reynolds, in the same letter: "I am glad at not having given away my medical Books, which I shall again look over to keep alive the little I know thitherwards" (*Letters* 1:277).[37]

The "Mansion of Life" metaphor is not unique in Keats's thinking: it harks back to the hymn to Pan in Book I of *Endymion*, where the shepherd praises Pan as the "Dread opener of the mysterious doors / Leading to universal knowledge" (288–89). Here the doors are the same as those which lead out of the Chamber of Maiden-Thought into dark passages where lies the "burden of the Mystery" that cannot be understood by "consequitive reasoning." That Keats views these doors in relation to the brain becomes clear when Endymion urges Pan to

> "Be still the unimaginable lodge
> For solitary thinkings; such as dodge
> Conception to the very bourne of heaven,
> Then leave the naked brain." (293–96)

He is, in effect, urging Pan to be the dark passages of the brain—"the unimaginable lodge / For solitary thinkings"—into which he cannot see, of which he cannot yet conceive. Endymion hopes that Pan will be able to open these doors for him, thus allowing him to understand life more fully.

The "Mansion of Life" metaphor also anticipates a later letter, of 19 February 1819, to George and Georgiana, which, although in a much less serious mood, again discusses the brain in the architectural terms to which Keats has become accustomed. Keats praises the worth of good claret and states: "The more ethereal Part of it mounts into the brain, not assaulting the cerebral apartments like a bully in a bad house looking for his trul and hurrying from door to door bouncing against the waistcoat; but rather walks like Aladin about his own enchanted palace so gently that you do not feel his step" (*Letters* 2:64).

In a much more serious vein, the "Mansion of Life" letter foreshadows the transformation of Apollo into a god in *Hyperion*, whereby the "dark Passages" beyond the Chamber of Maiden-Thought are opened to him. He begins his story by complaining to Mnemosyne, as Keats does to Reynolds, that "For me, dark, dark, / And painful vile oblivion seals my eyes: / I strive to search wherefore I am so sad" (III, 86–87). When he looks into Mnemosyne's face, however, the darkness

of ignorance is replaced by enlightenment, so that Apollo can
see into the dark passages which are in his own brain:

> "yet I can read
> A wondrous lesson in thy silent face:
> Knowledge enormous makes a God of me.
> Names, deeds, gray legends, dire events, rebellions,
> Majesties, sovran voices, agonies,
> Creations and destroyings, all at once
> Pour into the wide hollows of my brain,
> And deify me, as if some blithe wine
> Or bright elixir peerless I had drunk,
> And so become immortal."   (III, 111–20)

Apollo becomes a god by virtue of his ability to understand all
aspects of life, the destructive as well as the creative, the
painful as well as the pleasurable, the dark as well as the
light.

Thus far, I have examined Keats's cerebral metaphors from
the standpoint of geographical and architectural terms as used
in anatomy, but anatomists also employed terminology from
horticultural sources—or nature, to put it in a broader sense—
to describe the brain. Just as Keats drew on the geographical
vocabulary to evoke an intellectual world, or globe, and on the
architectural vocabulary to describe the brain as a mansion
with chambers, so too he draws on the horticultural terminology to evoke vivid mental landscapes. In each case his anatomical knowledge enables him to create very concrete, and very
accurate, metaphors.

The most obvious example of Keats's portrayal of a mental
landscape occurs in the "Ode to Psyche"; Henry Pettit and
Charles Hagelman have written articles on Keats's use of his
anatomical knowledge in this poem to which I am indebted.[38]
Because Hagelman's is the fuller treatment—it includes a sum-
mary of Pettit's argument—and since both articles are little
known, I will briefly summarize it and give some additional
information from Keats's medical training that also helps to
illuminate the poem.

First I should point out that the ode opens with the poet's
request for "pardon that thy [Psyche's] secrets should be

sung / Even into thine own soft-conched ear" (3–4). Editors have always glossed "soft-conched" as "shell-like," which is correct; I would add that Keats adapts the terms from the actual anatomy of the ear. In his lecture "On the Organ of Hearing," Cooper defines one part of the external ear as "the Septum Concha, which is dividing the large cavity of the Ear into two," and Fyfe defines the concha as "a large Cavity under the Antihelix."[39]

Pettit and Hagelman focus their attention on the last stanza of the ode:

> Yes, I will be thy priest, and build a fane
>   In some untrodden region of my mind,
> Where branched thoughts, new grown with pleasant pain,
>   Instead of pines shall murmur in the wind:
> Far, far around shall those dark-cluster'd trees
>   Fledge the wild-ridged mountains steep by steep;
> And there by zephyrs, streams, and birds, and bees,
>   The moss-lain Dryads shall be lull'd to sleep;
> And in the midst of this wide quietness
> A rosy sanctuary will I dress
> With the wreath'd trellis of a working brain,
>   With buds, and bells, and stars without a name,
> With all the gardener Fancy e'er could feign,
>   Who breeding flowers, will never breed the same:
> And there shall be for thee all soft delight
>   That shadowy thought can win,
> A bright torch, and a casement ope at night,
>   To let the warm Love in!   (50–67)

Hagelman, using Green's *Dissector's Manual* as his source, points out that the brain was described in geographical metaphors, with words like "ridges," "canal," "cavernous sinuses"; vegetational metaphors, with words like "branches," "twigs," "roots"; and architectural metaphors, with words like "arch," "vault," "roof," and "pillars." He then concludes:

The development of the imagery associated with the "central idea of building a fane for Psyche in some untrodden region of his mind" appears to have depended to a considerable extent upon the language used to teach anatomy to the medical student. The "untrodden region of my mind" suggests that the brain, which houses the mind, is a geographical unit, a hemispherical world. Just as the physical world still had mysterious, undiscovered areas, the brain also had regions which had not yielded all their secrets to the anatomist. Keats reserves for Psyche's temple a virgin territory, which preserves all the excitment, the mystery, and the anticipation of the unknown—that awe which left the "stout Cortez" "Silent, upon a peak in Darien."[40]

Hagelman has not noted, however, Green's statement that the cranium is "DISTRIBUTED INTO REGIONS,"[41] one of which Keats picks—"some untrodden region of my mind"—in which to "build a fane." The landscape will have "wild-ridged mountains," a reference to the numerous ridges in the brain which surround furrows or concavities that would form a perfect sanctuary. As Cooper states, the skull is "divided into 4 parts by the crucial *ridge* of the os occipitis"; Fyfe, in describing "The *Ridges* and *Depressions* of the Orbitar Processes," defines the ossa temporum, or temple, as "the *Rough, Semicircular Ridge,* at the under part of the external Meatus."[42] Other parts of the brain include the "deep depression" in which the medulla oblongata is housed;[43] the "aquaeductus Sylvii, or canalis medius," "a canal which passes under the tubercula quadrigemina into the fourth ventricle"; and the "FISSURA CEREBRI," "a deep narrow sulcus, which ascends obliquely backwards from the temporal ala."[44] In anatomical descriptions of the brain Keats found a ready-made mental landscape that could easily be adapted to his poetic needs.

In Keats's description, the mental mountains will be covered by "dark-cluster'd trees" formed of "branched thoughts," a brilliant metaphorical amalgamation of a literal and a mental landscape that goes a step further than the simile of *The Eve of St. Agnes:* "Sudden a thought came like a full-blown rose, / Flushing his brow" (136–37). Now the thoughts are literally "branched," an adaptation from the anatomical names "trunk," "root," and "branch," which are used constantly to describe the arteries and nerves running through the brain. Barclay explains that "the larger branches of all these Systems [the Arterial, the Venous, the Absorbent, and the Nervous] are sometimes called Trunks, when viewed as the origins of their own particular ramifications; a sort of language which, although incorrect, creates no confusion."[45] Blumenbach states, "The twigs, or, more properly, the radicles, of the veins unite into branches, and these again into six principal trunks"; Green points out that "the larger branches [of blood vessels], derived from the base of the brain, take their course through the pia mater, ramify and divide minutely"; and the author of *The London Dissector* observes that the "ARTERA MENINGEA MEDIA . . . passes through the spinous hole . . . and spread[s] its numerous branches over the dura mater."[46] Keats's "branched thoughts" are, then, a brilliantly concrete image developed out of his medical knowledge. Even the "streams" in the mental landscape find corollaries in the "Streams of Blood" that nourish the brain.[47]

The ode continues with the poet's claim that he will dress "A rosy sanctuary . . . With the wreath'd trellis of a working brain," which, together with the trees of "branched thoughts" and the whole concept of "the grove," probably owes something, as Hagelman points out,[48] to a part of the cerebellum which "when cut form[s] the appearance of a tree, and its branches, and is therefore termed Arbor Vitae."[49] Hagelman also observes that the image of the "wreath'd trellis of a working brain," which implies the growth of vines as well as "buds and bells," is probably based on the microscopic view of the fibers of the brain.[50] Keats leaves the panoramic view of the brain as a landscape and focuses on the sanctuary with its trellis, which may remind him of the controversial theory, put forward by Gall, Reil, and Spurzheim, and supported by Cooper and Green, that the brain is made up of fibers and that "different fasciculi of these fibrils often intersect each other, or are interwoven."[51] Cooper explains that "the Structure of the Reticular Membrane is composed of spaces, having the appearance of fine net-work; indeed it is most like lace-work; thus pores are left within its fibres."[52]

That Keats was aware of this theory is evidenced in his journal letter of March 1819, written to George and Georgiana a month before "Psyche," in which he describes his "temper indolent and supremely careless," using what has become for him a natural mixture of medical terminology and literary allusion:

Anatomy and Physiology

I long after a stanza or two of Thompson's Castle of indolence—My passions are all alseep [sic] from my having slumbered till nearly eleven and weakened the animal fibre all over me to a delighful sensation about three degrees on this side of faintness—if I had teeth of pearl and the breath of lillies I should call it langour—but as I am I must call it Laziness—In this state of effeminacy the fibres of the brain are relaxed in common with the rest of the body, and to such a happy degree that pleasure has no show of enticement and pain no unbearable frown.   (*Letters* 2:78–79)

The last stanza of "Psyche" demonstrates the same mixture of medical terminology and literary allusion. Keats has combined images from his anatomical knowledge of the brain[53] with the traditional Renaissance and neoclassical view of Fancy as a gardener who improves upon nature, to create a mental world with a landscape that is vividly and accurately realized and yet mysterious enough—"all soft delight / That shadowy thought can win"—to be a fitting abode for a goddess. The imagery has developed far beyond Keats's earlier concepts of the brain, for example, the vague image presented in *Endymion* of "some backward corner of the brain" (II, 11). "Psyche" may owe something to Wordsworth's description of the "shadowy ground" of "the Mind of Man" in *The Recluse*, but it owes much more for its muscularity to its anatomical accuracy. Keats adapts the anatomical facts and uses them in his descriptions of the abundant growth, the organic life, that abounds within the pregnant imagination of the poet. As Blackstone has pointed out, Keats is always fascinated by "the 'silent workings' of genius within him" and particularly by "the identity of the life within and the life without."[54] James Bunn has also written at length on Keats's ability to transform external into mental landscape in the last stanza of "Psyche" and concludes that "intellectually conceived, this picture is an enormous conceit, more appropriate to the shock tactics of Donne than to Keats."[55] I would observe that this task was made much easier for the poet by his knowledge of the brain's anatomy; the description comes naturally to him, even if it is a shock to the reader.

If the "Ode to Psyche" unconsciously owes something to *The Recluse*, *The Fall of Hyperion* seems to be a deliberate attempt by

Keats to explore the territory outlined by Wordsworth in that poem:

> For I must tread on shadowy ground, must sink
> Deep—and, aloft ascending, breathe in worlds
> To which the heaven of heavens is but a veil.
> All strength—all terror, single or in bands,
> That ever was put forth in personal form—
> Jehovah—with his thunder, and the choir
> Of shouting Angels, and the empyreal thrones—
> I pass them unalarmed. Not Chaos, not
> The darkest pit of lowest Erebus,
> Nor aught of blinder vacancy, scooped out
> By help of dreams—can breed such fear and awe
> As fall upon us often when we look
> Into our Minds, into the Mind of Man—
> My haunt, and the main region of my song.
>
> (*The Recluse*, 28–41)

Keats too will "sink deep" before Moneta's altar in his dream as he experiences all pain and terror and fear before he can rise above "the heaven of heavens" to see beyond Moneta's "veil" in order to learn the lessons of life that lie in her mind. She may be a goddess, but the lesson is intensely human.

The Fall of Hyperion is also very much a poetic version of the "Mansion of Life" letter I have been examining, in which Keats praises Wordsworth for his ability to "shed a light" in "those dark Passages" of human experience. In *The Fall* Keats tries to emulate Wordsworth's ability as he goes through the various chambers. He begins his journey in the Thoughtless Chamber with its intoxicating atmosphere and "pleasant wonders." It is a world very much like that inhabited by Cupid and Psyche, with its "trees of every clime" (I, 19), its "fountains" (I, 22), and its "arbour with a drooping roof / Of trellis vines, and bells" (I, 25–26), a place of the calm passivity that Keats inevitably associates with ripeness, fruition, and health. Yet it is followed by the inevitable darkening of the Chamber—which never occurs in "Psyche," since "Real are the dreams of Gods" (*Lamia*, I, 127)—in which the poet realizes "that the World is full of Misery and Heartbreak, Pain, Sickness and oppression" (*Letters* 1:281).

The poet falls down in a swoon and awakens to find all "the fair trees were gone, / The mossy mound and arbour were no more" (I, 59–60). Instead, he is in a huge temple with an altar and a ministering goddess. He must struggle with all his might to climb the steps to the altar, where he goes through a transition of death into life, as Apollo does in *Hyperion*.[56] It is only then that he is allowed to "see" Moneta's story, which is an allegorical equivalent of his own fall from the Chamber of Maiden-Thought—the fall is similar to a loss of virginity—into the suffering and woe of life's "dark Passages." In a Chinese-box effect, as we watch the narrator-poet go through the chambers of life, he watches the Titans work through the same experience. The fact that he sees this drama played out in Moneta's brain emphasizes the idea that the process is mental and spiritual, rather than physical; it also supports my claim that Keats has the architecture of the brain in mind when he describes the Mansion of Life.

The dream-vision of *The Fall*, which focuses more clearly on the mental than did *Hyperion,* is a better vehicle for the subjects with which Keats wishes to come to terms than was the traditional epic, which demanded acceptance of events as the physical, "realistic" level of consistent, sequential narrative. As we watch the poet's dream-vision, he watches Moneta's vision, literally through her eyes:

> "My power, which to me is still a curse,
> Shall be to thee a wonder; for the scenes
> Still swooning vivid through my globed brain
> With an electral changing misery
> Thou shalt with those dull mortal eyes behold,
> Free from all pain, if wonder pain thee not." (I, 243–48)

> As I had found
> A grain of gold upon a mountain's side,
> And twing'd with avarice strain'd out my eyes
> To search its sullen entrails rich with ore,
> So at the view of sad Moneta's brow,
> I ached to see what things the hollow brain
> Behind enwombed: what high tragedy
> In the dark secret chambers of her skull
> Was acting, that could give so dread a stress

To her cold lips, and fill with such a light
Her planetary eyes.   (I, 271–81)

Once more Keats compares the spheroidal shape of the seed,
or grain—albeit a "grain of gold" this time—to the brain. The
comparison is apt, for an immortal brain must be compared to
a more permanent grain. Even the description of Moneta's
"planetary eyes" filled with light, which are earlier compared
to "the mild moon" (I, 269), may owe something to Fyfe's
description of the eye: "The *Ball, Globe,* or *Bulb* of the Eye, is of
a spherical form, to collect the rays of light into a proper
focus."[57]

The tragedy of the Titans' defeat by the Olympians, the story
of the original *Hyperion,* is then revealed to the poet, acted out
in Moneta's brain, with the "shady . . . vale" and the "gloomy
boughs" in the landscape perhaps another brief adaptation of
the geographical and vegetational metaphors used to describe
the anatomy of the brain. As the story unfolds, the pain, suffering, and heartbreak of the Titans and Moneta are transferred
to the observing mind of the poet:

> Without stay or prop
> But my own weak mortality, I bore
> The load of this eternal quietude,
> The unchanging gloom, and the three fixed shapes
> Ponderous upon my senses a whole moon.
> For by my burning brain I measured sure
> Her silver seasons shedded on the night,
> And every day by day methought I grew
> More gaunt and ghostly.   (I, 388–96)

Again the brain is depicted as a globe, the earth, upon which
the seasons are measured by the movement of the moon's
light, an image similar to the earlier one of the mind as two
hemispheres balanced on a pole. In experiencing this pain, the
poet "go[es] the same steps" as the Titans, and, like Apollo in
his initiation in *Hyperion,* he experiences or proves the terrible
despair "upon [his] pulses." It is not enough for him to hear or
see the tragedy; he must experience it. This experience will
allow him to enter the "dark Passages" of life and find "a
ballance of good and evil," although at the end of the first

book the poet is still not sure he is ready for that, just as Keats was not sure when he wrote to Reynolds over a year earlier:

> And she spake on,
> As ye may read who can unwearied pass
> Onward from the antichamber of this dream,
> Where even at the open doors awhile
> I must delay, and glean my memory
> Of her high phrase: perhaps no further dare. (I, 463–68)

Dare he enter those "dark Passages," whose open doors lead out of the Chamber of Maiden-Thought? Perhaps the collapse of the poem shortly after this illustrates Keats's continuing inability to find the "ballance of good and evil" that would allow him to comprehend "the 'burden of the Mystery.' " Furthermore, he may have been at a loss as to what to do with Apollo, since the poet-narrator seems to have usurped the god's position.

Before leaving the subject of the brain, I should comment on Pettit's and Hagelman's suggestion that Cooper, and thus Keats, had been influenced by the subject of phrenology, which claimed that every part of the brain has a specialized function and that a person's intelligence could be measured by feeling the shape of his skull.[58] This doctrine was put forward by two German physicians, F. J. Gall and J. G. Spurzheim, and created intense controversy in the early nineteenth century. Whereas Cooper was obviously aware of the so-called science of phrenology, he had no faith in it, as Waddington's notes attest:

The form of the head has been said to make a great difference in the powers of the mind, —and thus Gaul, & Spurgen [*for* Gall and Spurzheim] tell us that every part of the Brain has its particular function, & that by feeling they can tell the particular propensities of any Person; —what then would they say to this head of a Caribbee Chief, who was remarkable for his learning, especially in Botany, you observe that by artificial means the forehead is rendered quite flat, thus forcing the important organs to the back part; —this practice is very common with the Inhabitants of that Country, —they do it by means of a board, when the child is very young. We find little difference in the Scull of an Inhabitant of New Holland, and that of an European.[59]

Keats apparently held a similar opinion, for in the only reference to phrenology in his poetry, in the comic stanzas "On Some Skulls in Beauley Abbey," written with Brown, he treats the subject as a joke. After stating that the records of the abbey's monks were destroyed by the reformer Knox, the narrator claims that he can still learn about the monks' lives by reading their skulls: "Well! I'm a craniologist, / And may do better" (17–18). After this sarcastic claim, humorous and satiric portraits of the monks are given, and in one of the two portraits Woodhouse believes Keats wrote, there is a deliberate pun poking fun at phrenology:

> This lily-colour'd skull, with all
> The teeth complete, so white and small,
> Belong'd to one whose early pall
>   A lover shaded;
> He died ere supersitition's gall
>   His heart invaded.   (55–60)

In his pun Keats suggests that Dr. Gall, one of the founders of phrenological theory, was ruled by a personified superstition rather than by scientific fact. The monk-lover is lucky to have died before Gall invented his theory.

Another humorous reference to phrenology occurs in the account of Haydon's "immortal dinner." When Kingston, the obtuse comptroller of stamps, asked, "Don't you think Newton a great genius?" "Lamb got up, and taking a candle, said: 'Sir, will you allow me to look at your phrenological development?' "[60] This satirical reference illustrates that, although the group was obviously aware of this controversial subject, they apparently only thought it worth joking about.

Thus far I have examined Keats's use of the image of the brain in isolation, but it should be observed that the brain is part of the whole nervous system, as Keats himself knew. Cooper states: "The nervous system is composed of the following parts, *viz.* brain (which is divided into cerebrum, cerebellum, and medulla oblongata), medulla spinalis, and two sets of nerves—one set issuing from the brain, and the other from the medulla spinalis." Fyfe explains that the brain controls the nervous system: *"The BRAIN is the GRAND AND PRIMARY ORGAN OF SENSE with which the mind is supposed to be most immediately connected, and from which the Nervous Influence is found by experiment, to be communicated to all the other parts of the Body."*[61] The brain receives and sends impulses along "the nerves [which] are freely distributed to every part of the human frame, and are the means by which all voluntary and involuntary motions are maintained."[62] The nerves thus "support the organization of the Body" in order to produce "1 Sensation 2 Volition 3 Involuntary Motion 4 Sympathy."[63]

But Keats does not seem to use the words "nerve" and "nervous" with their medical meanings in his early poetry. Instead, he uses "nervous" and "nervy" with the more consciously literary meanings of "sinewy, muscular," even "vigorous," as can be seen in his descriptions of "Homer with his nervous arms" ("Ode to Apollo," 7), Endymion with "his nervy knees" (*Endymion*, I, 174), and Cybele's lions with their "nervy tails" (*Endymion*, II, 646).

In *Hyperion*, however, the poem in which Keats seems to return again and again to his medical knowledge for choice of words and images, he deliberately uses the anatomical meaning of "nerve." He describes Hyperion's feelings of insecurity after the rest of the Titans have fallen: "But horrors, portion'd to a giant nerve, / Oft made Hyperion ache" (I, 175–76; *The Fall*, II, 23–24). Keats originally wrote "but warnings portioned to a giant sense"; he changed "sense" to "nerve" to create a more accurate, vividly physical description, since the sensation of pain is transmitted to the brain along the nerves. It is this ability to receive sensation and to transmit his will or volition to his domain that Saturn has lost, so that "Upon the sodden ground / His old right hand lay nerveless, listless, dead, / Unsceptred" (I, 17–19; *The Fall*, I, 322–24). Keats knew that once the nerves were severed, once one was "nerveless," the functions of sensation and volition ceased;[64] one was left with an inability to feel, to experience life, which was akin to death. Here Saturn's physical collapse mirrors his mental depression;

he has lost the "nervous grasp" with which he once controlled "Fate."

The focus on Saturn's hand in both these images is interesting, for the hand was a part of the body with which Keats seemed almost obsessed. This is particularly apparent in two curious passages, one from the induction to *The Fall of Hyperion*:

> Whether the dream now purposed to rehearse
> Be poet's or fanatic's will be known
> When this warm scribe my hand is in the grave. (I, 16–18)

and the other a fragment, written at about the same time:

> This living hand, now warm and capable
> Of earnest grasping, would, if it were cold
> And in the icy silence of the tomb,
> So haunt thy days and chill thy dreaming nights
> That thou would wish thine own heart dry of blood,
> So in my veins red life might stream again,
> And thou be conscience-calm'd. See, here it is—
> I hold it towards you.

In addition to the forecast of death in both, and the dark, threatening tone of the latter, there is an almost unnatural detachment in these passages as Keats compares the warmth of the living hand, in which the blood flows like a stream, with the coldness of the dead hand, which he would often have observed during his days as a medical student.

Commenting on this detachment, Ian Jack writes: "It is worth remembering that artists often draw their own hands. On the 3rd of July 1808, for example, Haydon had sketched his own hand, and added the date."[65] Although this is a valid observation, it should also be remembered that Keats was a medical student before he ever met artists like Haydon and Severn. It is far more likely, therefore, that his interest in the hand is a result of his training in surgery, the hand being as important for the surgeon as it is for the painter. As South points out, one of Cooper's favorite maxims was "that a surgeon should have 'an eagle's eye, a lady's hand, and a lion's heart' ";[66] in his introductory lecture, Cooper warned his students:

In the *practice* of surgery, also, many essential qualities are requisite on the part of the surgeon. The first of which is neatness in the application of his remedies; awkardness in this respect will frequently injure his professional prospects—the patient and his friends often judge a man's skill by his manner of bleeding, or from the application of a bandage; and it sometimes happens that "the hand spoils the head."[67]

It was exactly this fear of the inability to make his hand obey his head that Keats later told Brown convinced him to give up medicine.

In fairness to Jack, however, it should be noticed that the author of *The London Dissector* stresses the similarity between the writer's, artist's, and surgeon's use of his hand: "The position of the hand in dissecting should be the same, as in writing or drawing; and the knife, held, like the pen or pencil, by the thumb and the first two fingers, should be moved by means of them only; while the hand rests firmly on the two other fingers bent inwards as in writing, and on the wrist."[68] In the fragment "This living hand," however, the stress on the blood from the lover's heart draining "red life" into the veins of the rejected poet to warm his hand reveals a strongly physiological interest and demonstrates that Keats knew only too well the difference in feeling and temperature between a living and a dead hand. Moreover, the detachment noted by Jack is likely that of the anatomist or surgeon as he observes any organ or limb, even his own hand, in this objective fashion.

The final evidence, however, that Keats was viewing his hand as a man of medicine in these two passages is found in a letter of 21 September 1819 to George and Georgiana, written shortly after Keats had begun *The Fall of Hyperion* and just before he wrote "This living hand." In trying to explain to his brother and sister-in-law the psychological changes he has undergone since he last saw them, Keats lapses into a description of physiological change:

From the time you left me, our friends say I have altered completely—am not the same person—perhaps in this letter I am for in a letter one takes up one's existence from the time we last met—I dare say you have altered also—every man does—Our bodies every seven years are completely fresh-materiald—seven years ago it was not this hand that clench'd itself against Hammond— . . . This is the reason why men who had been bosom friends, on being separated for any number of years, afterwards meet coldly, neither of them knowing why—The fact is they are both altered— . . . 'T is an uneasy thought that in seven years the same hands cannot greet each other again.

(*Letters* 2:208–09)

The attempt to define psychological change in physiological terms is perhaps Keats's way of coping with his personality changes, by trying to understand them in an objective, scientific fashion. He apparently feels uncomfortable with the fact that he has grown away from certain friends and must find a justification in medical terms.

Keats's interest in the hand, like his interest in the brain, reveals the anatomist's fascination with form and structure. As Blackstone observes: "Keats would not have become a medical student if he felt no interest in the structure of the human body. . . . His profound humanism as well as his technical interest in structures, his curious detachment mingled with an unreserved giving of that part of himself that was not detached, mark the true physician."[69] Evidence of Keats's obsession with his hand can also be found in external sources. Leigh Hunt comments: "Keats was sensible of the disporportion above noticed, between his upper and lower extremities and he would look at his hand, which was faded, and swollen in the veins, and say it was the hand of a man of fifty."[70]

But, as the description of Saturn's hand indicates, Keats is also interested in its physiological workings, in how it experiences sensations through the nerves; he knew that "the different sensations reside in peculiar structures as the toes & fingers which have papillae through which the sense of feeling" is experienced.[71] Exactly how the brain receives and sends impulses along the nerves, however, was a debatable and important topic in the early nineteenth century. Physiologists generally agreed that, as Blumenbach explains: "The office of the whole nervous system is twofold, —To excite motion in other parts, especially in the voluntary muscles, . . . and to convey impressions made upon the organs of sense to the brain, and there to excite perception or by means of sympathies to give occasion to reaction."⁷² The controversy arose over how this was performed by the nerves. The primary theories are summarized by Dr. Haighton:

Some have considered the Brain as an Organ which secretes the nervous fluids that the Nerves are cylindrical tubes conveying this fluid to the difft. parts of the body giving to them their proper tone & energy: Others have supposed that impressions were communicated to the Brain, by the Nerves being put in a vibratory motion. The last opinion which has prevailed, is that Animals have the power of generating a something analogous to electricity; this opinion has been gaining ground particularly since the experiments on the Torpedo were made by Mr. Walsh. . . . That this Electric power is resident in the Nerves is very probable from what appeared on the dissection of that animal by Mr. Hunter.⁷³

This last view was supported by Cooper and passed on to Keats:

The opinion of late years entertained concerning the Cause of nervous energy was started by Mr. J. Hunter. He examined the Body of a Gymnotus Electricus he found it provided with abundance of Nerves sufficient to account for its electric properties. From this he inferred that the Nerves were conductor of electric fluid. . . . The present opinion therefore is that a fluid, like that of the electric is secreted in the brain which is thence communicated along the Nerves.⁷⁴

It is this nervous energy, akin to electricity, that Keats describes to George and Georgiana in a letter of 19 March 1819. He discusses the energy which gives both men and animals a sense of purpose in their movements: "I go among the Feilds and catch a glimpse of a stoat or a fieldmouse peeping out of the withered grass—the creature hath a purpose and its eyes are bright with it—I go amongst the buildings of a city and I see a Man hurrying along—to what? The Creature has a purpose and his eyes are bright with it. . . . —there is an ellectric fire in human nature tending to purify" (*Letters* 2:80). This "ellectric fire"⁷⁵ enables man to put his will or volition into action, to initiate voluntary motions by transmitting impulses from the brain through the nerves to the muscles. But Keats takes the idea a step further, out of the realm of science and into that of morality, by claiming that this "fire" has the ability to purify, or purge, man and so make him "disinterested." Of course, there is no scientific evidence for this, but it is interesting that Keats develops his moral speculations out of scientific theory, perhaps in an attempt to give them more credibility.

The other reference Keats makes to the electric fluid secreted by the brain comes in *The Fall of Hyperion,* where Moneta describes the changes of scene in her brain: "for the scenes / Still swooning vivid through my globed brain / With an electral changing misery" (I, 244–46). The changes in scene, all involving painful sensations for both the players and the goddess, are brought about by the electric fluid.

There is also a reference to this electric fluid, or "ellectric fire," in a short, humorous, but vulgar poem that Keats gave to Cowden Clarke, but which Clarke believes was written by Charles Brown. The poem concerns a maiden called Curiosity, who encounters a reclusive philosopher; it ends with these two stanzas:

> She told him she came entirely to learn, Sirs,
> The arts, the sciences, all the fine things;
> And, if so dispos'd, she'd show him in return, Sirs,
> How gravity acted on Coblers and Kings.
> But first, she would wish an experiment made
> On air-pumps, electrics; (fine cures for the spleen)
> And if he would only just lend her his aid,
> She'd then take a shock from his electric machine.
>
> The philosopher gave his immediate consent, Sirs,
> His cylinder fix'd, his conductor was brought;
> And about this fair maiden to shock her he went, Sirs,
> And soon with his fire the fair maiden was fraught.
> They studied together, as the neighbours all say,
> And discover'd such things as before were scarce known;
> He found where the centre of gravity lay;
> And she—O, she found the "Philosopher's stone."[76]

Even if Brown, and not Keats, wrote the poem, it is probable that the scientific information, with its obvious comparison of nervous, sexual energy with electricity, came from Keats, who had seen this analogy made, in a serious fashion, many times before.

In discussions of Keats's knowledge of the nerves, the word "sensation" has cropped up frequently. Fyfe points out that "the Nerves . . . constitute the immediate Organs of Sensation, and convey Impressions made upon them to the Mind."[77] Keats uses the term often, but in order to avoid a lengthy digression, I have until now delayed attempting to define it. A definition is necessary, however, in order to understand fully Keats's adaptation of physiological concepts to his ideas about poetry.

Any examination of Keats's use of the word "sensation" must begin with his important letter of 22 November 1817 to Bailey, in which he discusses "the truth of Imagination" and ends with the impassioned cry "O for a Life of Sensations rather than of Thoughts!" (*Letters* 1:184–85). His use of "sensations" in this letter has been interpreted in various ways. Clarence Thorpe, for example, states that "by 'sensations' Keats here means feelings or intuitions, the pure activity of the imagination, as Ernest de Selincourt, and later Sidney Colvin have pointed out."[78] Bate, on the other hand, claims that "Hazlitt's constant use of the word 'sensations' in the traditional empirical sense—as virtually equivalent to concrete experience—added a new term to Keats's own habitual vocabulary (hence the remark at the moment about the 'Life of Sensations')."[79] As contradictory as these two definitions appear—the one sees "sensation" originating in the poet's mind and the other sees it originating in the external world—they both contain elements of truth.

It should first be pointed out, however, that Keats did not need Hazlitt to teach him the empirical meaning of "sensation" as sense impressions received from the material world. He had been taught this definition by Astley Cooper, before he ever met Hazlitt, in his tenth anatomy lecture, "Physiology of the Nervous System": "The 1st office is that of Sensation—it is an impression made on the Extremities of the Nerves conveyed to the Brain. This is proved by the effects of dividing a Nerve. After a time the sensation of a Nerve will return as it unites."[80] Although the strict definition of "sensation" ends here, Cooper also explains to his students, in their very first lecture, that these sensations elicit responses in the brain: "The effect produced by the nerves is Sensation, and Volition, the latter is differing from the former by beginning from within and proceeding outwards, besides these two there are involuntary functions, for example those of the Heart, and Intestines, there is also a Sympathetic function supported by the nervous power. . . . The nervous power is also connecting the Brain with the Body, thus forming Memory, Judgment, and Imagination."[81]

The imagination, then, is intimately connected, through the nervous system, with sensations. What Keats means by "sensation" is not limited to an external or an internal phenomenon; rather, he uses the word to describe a process, a continuum involving sense stimuli that are transported to the brain, where they elicit a response, or feeling, combinations of which help to form a person's imagination. That "sensation" is this kind of process or continuum is evident when, in commenting on one of Fanny Brawne's friends, Keats states that "she plays the Music without one sensation but the feel of the ivory at her fingers" (*Letters* 2:13). This woman has the sensory perception, the touch, but she lacks the sensibility, the imaginative or emotional response, that is also part of the experience.

At times Keats even attributes the properties of a sensory stimulus to literature, which for him is as real as any concrete object, and which, strictly speaking, does stimulate the senses of sight and hearing. But just as important is the imaginative or emotional response the literature elicits from the reader, as is evident when Keats asks George and Georgiana: "With what sensation do you read Fielding?" (*Letters* 2:18); and again when he tells them that *Lamia* has "that sort of fire in it which must take hold of people in some way—give them either pleasant or unpleasant sensation. What they want is a sensation of some sort" (*Letters* 2:189). Keats was disillusioned with the public at this time, but this last comment is not derogatory or sarcastic; for him, good poetry should act as a stimulant that produces a sensation, and then an imaginative response, from the reader; it should not be a coercive, bullying force that hopes to instill a didactic or moral lesson in the reader's mind: "We hate poetry that has a palpable design upon us— . . . Poetry should be great & unobtrusive, a thing which enters into one's soul" (*Letters* 1:224). *Lamia* is this unobtrusive kind of poetry, and the "sort of fire" it contains is akin to the "ellectric fire" or nervous energy with which man experiences sensations.

For Keats, then, "sensation" involves a complex process, sensory, mental, and emotional, that altogether consitutes the poet's consciousness, his overall mode of perception. It involves the imagination which arranges and interprets our sense impressions into our perception of reality. That is why "What the imagination seizes as Beauty must be truth," or concrete reality; hence, too, Keats's cry of "O for a Life of Sensations rather than of Thoughts!" The process of sensation does not involve the rational, analytical part of the mind, that which deals with abstract ideas and theories. Rather, it is a process based on the perception of the concrete realities of the phenomenal world; the sensory aspect can never be ignored. As Keats tells Bailey in the same letter, the heavenly state of having one's "happiness on Earth repeated in a finer tone and so repeated . . . can only befall those who delight in sensation rather than hunger as you do after Truth" (*Letters* 1:185). In keeping with the concept of negative capability, truth cannot be irritably sought after with fact and reason; truth is perceived through an openness to the life of sensations, the process of perception I have been discussing.[82]

Those critics, therefore, like de Selincourt and Colvin, who have stressed only the intuitive aspect of "sensation," claiming that it is somehow an extrasensory or transcendental perception, have at the very least distorted, at worst wholly misinterpreted, Keats's meaning. They have forgotten something that Keats, with his training in physiology, could never forget: that sensation "is an impression made on the Extemities of the Nerves conveyed to the Brain." Keats's perception of the world is always strongly rooted in the sensory, even if sensory experiences lead to wild flights of the imagination.

Although the poet's openness to sensations, which in turn lead to associations and speculations, is an important part of the process of poetic creativity for Keats, another aspect of that creativity is his seemingly unique ability to identify sympathetically with objects and characters, which is closely linked to his idea that the genuine poet has no identity of his own. Keats's capacity for sympathetic identification is evident as early as 22 November 1817, when he writes to Bailey, in the same renowned letter, that "if a Sparrow come before my Window I take part in its existence and pick about the Gravel" (*Letters* 1:186). But he does not mention the subject again until almost a year later, although it must have been in his mind. On 21 September 1818 he writes to Dilke: "I wish I could say Tom was any better. His identity presses upon me so all day that I am obliged to go out" (*Letters* 1:368–69). And in his letter of 27 October 1818, on the Poetical Character, Keats explains to Woodhouse:

It is a wretched thing to confess; but is a very fact that not one word I ever utter can be taken for granted as an opinion growing out of my identical nature—how can it, when I have no nature? When I am in a room with People if I ever am free from speculating on creations of my own brain, then not myself goes home to myself: but the identity of every one in the room begins to to [sic] press upon me that, I am in a very little time anhilated—not only among Men; it would be the same in a Nursery of children.   (*Letters* 1:387)[83]

Keats seems to have had a remarkable ability to participate in the thoughts and feelings, the very life, not only of people but also of animals. At times he achieves this effect of annulling self by imaginatively projecting himself into the character or characters he contemplates. At other times, however, he does not even have to will himself into the identity of other people; his imagination, and its capacity for sympathetic identification, is so intense that their identities seem to press upon him without his active involvement, even to the point that he sometimes dislikes the feelings he gains from such identification: "To have nothing to do, and to be surrounded with unpleasant human identities; who press upon one just enough to prevent one getting into a lazy position; and not enough to interest or rouse one; is a capital punishment of a capital crime" (*Letters* 2:77).

Numerous critics have written on the topic of Keats's sympathetic identification, yet no one to my knowledge has been able to explain why the phenomenon occurs, apart from the claim that Keats had a particularly acute imagination. I cannot pretend to be able to explain this psychological phenomenon, which Freud later named "projection" and which is now known to be associated with parietal lobe affections; but I can illustrate that Keats was taught about this phenomenon as a medical student, probably before he read Hazlitt's *Principles of Human Action*, which Bate believes is the source of his ideas concerning sympathetic identification.[84]

One of the four functions of the nervous system, Keats was taught, is sympathy: "By Sympathy we mean a sensation or an action existing in one part, consequent to a sensation or action pre-existing in another."[85] Cooper explains this function in more detail:

Between all the different parts of the human frame, there exist intimate relations, which correspond with each other, and carry on a reciprocal intercourse of action. The beautiful harmony produced by these concurrent phenomena is called sympathy. Thus impressions not only produce effects on the part to which they are directly applied; but, in consequence of the freedom of communication between the nervous system, parts of the body situated at a distance from those in which the original mischief exists become affected by it: the real nature of sympathy is yet unknown, but we are acquainted with many of its effects.[86]

Cooper goes on to give examples of natural and diseased sympathy, the latter occurring when a sickness in one part of the body produces symptoms in a completely different part. James Curry, who taught Keats at Guy's, points out that in extreme cases, patients feel "sympathy between different persons."[87] These extreme cases of sympathy in which an individual feels that he experiences the sensations and thoughts of other people were of particular interest to the surgeon John Hunter; he documented the cases of two patients who believed that their own thoughts and sensations were really those of bystanders. As Hunter says, "The objects about him were more to him than his own sensations," which sounds remarkably like Keats's claims that he experienced the sensations of a sparrow or billiard ball. Hunter attributed this phenomenon to "a want of connexion between the mind and the body of the patient."[88]

In pointing out that Keats was aware of sympathetic identification between different individuals as a medical phenomenon, I am not denying Hazlitt's influence on Keats's ideas about the sympathetic imagination; but his medical knowledge probably explains why Keats readily accepted experiences that might appear very disturbing to an untutored lay person.

Keats's knowledge of, and interest in, anatomy and physiology did not cease, then, on his departure from Guy's. He retained much of this knowledge and adapted some of it for use in his poetry and letters, where it not only gives a vividness and concreteness to many of his images, but also helps him to understand the workings of the sympathetic imagination, which he considered an important and integral part of the Poetical Character.

Moreover, Keats's knowledge of anatomy would have stood him in good stead within the circle of artists with whom he was friendly, which included Haydon, Hazlitt, Severn, and Hilton, who was "so pale and cadaverous that we used to call him 'The Anatomical Figure.' "[89] Haydon was, in fact, a very able anatomist. He had from the beginning of his career realized the importance of anatomical knowledge to an artist and, at a time when the study of anatomy was in disrepute at the Royal Academy, had set about, on his arrival in London in 1804, to teach himself the subject, using Albinus's *Anatomy*. According to his own, perhaps inflated, view, he became so knowledgeable in the subject that "Northcote said that my anatomical studies would make me a good surgeon, but that they were no use for a painter. Opie said they were capital. Fuseli swore that he learnt by looking at them."[90]

In 1806 Haydon took a formal course in anatomy with the famous anatomist and neurologist Charles Bell,[91] with whom he became very friendly and whom he assisted in the dissection of bodies, both human and animal. Haydon became so concerned with anatomical accuracy in painting that he would never attempt to paint a subject without first making casts of the figures in their required positions; and in the *Annals of Fine Arts* he soundly criticized Anthony Carlisle, the professor of anatomy at the Royal Academy, for being always concerned with "the indelicacy and indecency of anatomical studies and demonstrations in the lecture room." When Carlisle allowed the exhibition of "the naked figure, cloathed only where delicacy required it should be cloathed," the *Annals* hailed the move as progressive.[92]

It was Haydon who introduced Keats to the famed Elgin Marbles which had been brought to England from the Parthenon by Lord Elgin; Haydon, in fact, helped persuade the Royal Academy that the marbles were genuine. As Jack points out, "Haydon took Keats to see the Marbles on the 1st or 2nd of March 1817, and he must have heard endless talk on the subject in Haydon's painting room. This was a favourite meeting-place for Haydon's friends, and we have Haydon's own word for it that Keats visited it 'at all times, and at all times was welcome.' "[93] Exactly what Keats and Haydon discussed in these meetings or why Haydon took Keats to see the marbles we will never know, but critics have usually assumed that Keats's interest in the marbles stemmed from his "intoxication with the ideal of greatness"[94] or from his broader interest in Greek mythology. Even Finney, who claims that "Keats was fully prepared to understand and appreciate the marbles"[95] because he knew their background, and Jack, who has emphasized Keats's borrowings from these figures for the "stationing" of his characters in *Hyperion*, have overlooked the fact that Keats was eminently qualified to appreciate the anatomical and physiological accuracy of the sculptures. It was precisely for their accuracy that Haydon admired the sculptures most, as his account in his *Journal* of the very first time he saw the marbles indicates:

The first thing I fixed my eyes on was the wrist of a figure in one of the female groups, in which were visible, though in a feminine form, the radius and ulna. I was atonished, for I had never seen them hinted at in any female wrist in the antique. I darted my eye to the elbow, and saw the outer condyle visibly affecting the shape as in nature. I saw that the arm was in repose and the soft parts in relaxation. That combination of nature and idea which I had felt was so much wanting in high art was here displayed to midday conviction. . . . [I was] perfectly comprehending the hint at the skin by knowing well what was underneath it! Oh, how I inwardly thanked God I was prepared to understand all this! Now I was rewarded for all the petty harassings I had suffered. Now was I mad for buying Albinus without a penny to pay for it? Now was I mad for lying on the floor hours together, copying its figures? I felt . . . that they would overturn the false beau-ideal, where nature was nothing, and would establish the true beau-ideal, of which nature alone is the basis.[96]

There is no reason to doubt that Keats experienced a similar sense of wonder and awe at the beauty and anatomical accuracy of the marbles, especially as Cooper, while criticizing modern artists for fashioning their figures from imagination rather than from nature, had said that "the ancients modelled from the living subject, and gave accurate representations of nature."[97] Now, in the marbles, Keats saw a perfect example of this, of art truly holding a mirror up to nature, and I would speculate that he was better qualified to appreciate the marbles, by virtue of his anatomical knowledge, than any of the other members of Haydon's group. Even though the statues led him into wild flights of imagination, according to Severn,[98] it is nevertheless the anatomical, sculptured forms of the statues that find their way into the figures of his Titans.

Not everyone accepted the marbles as accurate representations of human bodies, however, and this subject was at the heart of the controversy concerning their authenticity. Many members of the Royal Academy, not trained in anatomy, claimed that the figures were idealized forms, created from the artists' imaginations and not from reality; they were too beautiful to be truthful. Haydon, however, in his article "On the Judgment of Connoisseurs being preferred to that of Professional Men—The Elgin Marbles," defended the marbles as a union of the ideal and the real because in them nature was presented in its most perfect form: "It is this union of nature with ideal beauty—the probabilities and accidents of bone, flesh, and tendon, from extension, flexion, compression, gravitation, action, or repose, that rank at once the Elgin Marbles above all other works of art in the world."[99] Hazlitt, in his article on "The Elgin Marbles," writes: "Art is the imitation of nature; and the Elgin Marbles are in their essence and their perfection casts from nature, —from fine nature, it is true, but from real, living, moving nature; from objects in nature, answering to an idea in the artist's mind, not from an idea in the artist's mind abstracted from all objects in nature."[100] As both articles appeared in *The Examiner* in 1816, Keats would certainly have read them before he actually saw the marbles, and he must have realized the validity of his friends' arguments when he saw the statues in 1817. On seeing the statues, Keats would immediately have recognized that their beauty lay in their anatomical and physiological truth, and that their truth was beauty incarnate: "Beauty is truth, truth beauty." This is the lesson that the Grecian urn, like the marbles a union of the ideal and the real, teaches the poet, one he perhaps knew from the time he recognized that the Indian Maid and Cynthia, the physically real and the imagined ideal of beauty, are one and the same person.

To pursue this subject further, however, would be to stray from the realm of medicine into that of aesthetics, which is beyond the scope of this study. It is nevertheless easy to see how for Keats the two realms, of anatomy and of sculpture, of nature and of art, of truth and of beauty, are integrally related, for he already recognizes that "every department of knowledge we see excellent and calculated towards a great whole. I am so convinced of this, that I am glad at not having given away my medical Books, which I shall again look over to keep alive the little I know thitherwards" (*Letters* 1:277). This is a lesson that he had been taught by Astley Cooper himself, who told his students something similar about literature:

While professional knowledge should undoubtedly be the first object of your pursuit, general literature should not be neglected, and is so far from being incompatible with that primary object, that it cannot fail to enlarge your views, and give efficacy to your professional researches. . . . there is hardly one branch of knowledge which does not in some measure throw light and illustration upon another.[101]

Keats's knowledge of anatomy and physiology provided him with certain images and ideas which he adapted in his poems and letters; our understanding of that knowledge throws "light and illustration" upon his poetry and thought.

CHAPTER V

Pathology and Medicine

As I noted in my first chapter, while Keats was at Guy's Hospital during the 1815–16 academic year, he attended two courses in medicine: "Practice of Medicine," taught by Drs. Babington and Curry, and "Theory of Medicine, and Materia Medica," taught by Drs. Curry and Cholmeley. Although these lectures, unlike those of Astley Cooper, were never printed and are not, as far as we know, extant in manuscript, the syllabus for Babington's and Curry's course, *Outlines of a Course of Lectures on the Practice of Medicine as Delivered in the Medical School of Guy's Hospital* (1811), survives.[1] We also have an early edition of Curry's *Heads of a Course of Lectures on Pathology, Therapeutics, and Materia Medica; Delivered in the Medical School of Guy's Hospital* (1804), which formed the basis for his and Cholmeley's course, "Theory of Medicine, and Materia Medica." Both Babington's and Curry's *Outlines of a Course of Lectures* and Curry's *Heads of a Course of Lectures* are descriptions, in notation form, of what was to be covered in more detail in the lectures themselves, with interleaved blank pages for the students' lecture notes. They are, then, an accurate, if somewhat abbreviated, account of what students heard when they attended these two courses of lectures on pathology and medicine.

Although some of the great advances being made by men like John Hunter and Astley Cooper in anatomy and surgery had a positive influence on pathology, particularly in the new stress on the study of morbid anatomy,[2] progress in the study of diseases and cures generally lagged behind that being made in anatomy and surgery. Some practitioners were still in fact dealing with centuries-old theories of humoral pathology, popularized by Galen, whereby a body is believed to be in a state of health when its four humors, or fluids, are in balance. In their *Outlines*, Babington and Curry still consider, but dismiss, such theories,[3] although in his *Heads* Curry still talks of certain types of humoral temperaments—sanguineous, melancholic, choleric, phlegmatic—being susceptible to certain diseases.[4] In the meantime, germ theories made very little progress because microscopy had been neglected during the latter part of the eighteenth century and people had little faith in microbes they could not see.

One important advance made in the eighteenth century, however, was Albrecht von Haller's description of the functions of the nervous system and its relation to the brain, a topic touched on in the previous chapter. Von Haller's ideas were supported by physicists like Galvani and Volta, who were moving toward an understanding of the electrical nature of the nervous system, and by neurologists like Hoffmann and Charles Bell.[5] As Babington and Curry point out:

The Mechanical System of Physic much weakened by chemical discoveries. —Phenomena of Nervous System became more attended to, — especially by Hoffman, —who referred the healthy or diseased condition of body, primarily to the state of *moving fibre.* —This doctrine strengthened and illustrated by operation of various subtle agents on the living body; —and particularly by the effects of passions and emotions. —The general principle now universally admitted as a fundamental part of pathology.

Fever considered by Hoffman as primarily arising from diminished vigour of nervous system, and particularly of brain and spinal marrow.[6]

In England, "Hoffman's theory [was] adopted by Dr. Cullen, and illustrated with great ingenuity," so that Cullen's arrangement and classification of diseases, or Methodical Nosology, was widely accepted.[7]

The development in understanding of the nervous system had the advantage of persuading many practitioners to accept the nervous, and ultimately psychological, nature of many diseases, but also the disadvantage of allowing the term "nervous disorder" to become a catch phrase for any disease, physical or mental, that doctors could not understand. As Robert Whytt, an Edinburgh professor of medicine, explains, the fact that the term "nervous" was "commonly given to many symptoms seemingly different, and very obscure in their nature, has often made it be said that Physicians have bestowed the character of *nervous* on all those disorders whose nature and causes they were ignorant of."[8] Astley Cooper gave a similar warning to his pupils, and when Keats wrote in his *Anatomical and Physiological Note Book* that "in diseases Medical Men guess, if they cannot ascertain a disease they call it nervous,"[9] he was serious; this is not the joke many commentators, ignorant of the historical context, have taken it to be.

These theories of the nervous nature of diseases are very important, both in Keats's understanding of many mental and physical disorders that he portrays in his poetry, and, in a much more personal and immediate sense, in his understanding, and that of his physicians, of his own disease. It is an aspect of early nineteenth-century medicine that will need more detailed examination as Keats's use of pathological metaphors and images becomes apparent in his poetry and correspondence.

Before one approaches the poems and letters, however, one needs a definition of pathology and medicine to appreciate fully what Keats was studying at Guy's. As Curry outlines in his introductory lecture, pathology is the study

of the *nature* of those *Morbid conditions* that most frequently occur in the human body; —the *Causes,* whether *predisposing* or *exciting,* which give rise to them; —the *Signs* or *Symptoms* by which they are known; and the *functions* or *parts* in which they more especially take place: — and from a comparison of these with the *natural* and *healthy* state, are drawn, the several *Indications* which require to be fulfilled in order to effect a cure.

Therapeutics, or the practice of medicine, involves "an account of the Discovery of remedies," their classification, "and general rules given for their proper administration"; and materia medica is the study of the "history of Individual Articles," usually botanical and mineral, used in medicine. Curry goes on to stress that "true knowledge and successful treatment of disease" involves "a diligent investigation of the *History of Diseases* in general," together with "a knowledge of the patient's constitution, —idiosyncracies, —and mode of life," and "an intimate acquaintance with the *Materia Medica*" used to treat the disease.[10] In this respect, Keats's knowledge of chemistry and botany would be put to good use.

For Keats, even more important than specific scientific knowledge was the grander, altruistic motive behind the medical profession of healing the sick and relieving the suffering. Alexander Marcet, who taught Keats chemistry, states:

But in thus enforcing a salutary discipline, let us never lose sight of the primary object of this, and all other hospitals, which is—the relief of suffering humanity. The Medical Schools which have been grafted upon these establishments, however useful and important, are but secondary objects; we must therefore always consider the comfort and well-doing of our patients as the first and principal aim in all our proceedings.[11]

William Saunders, who taught at Guy's in the late eighteenth century, called medicine "certainly one of the most Liberall proffessions."[12] It was, no doubt, this high ideal that appealed most of all to Keats, and it was the transference of this ideal from medicine to poetry, as we shall see, that allowed him to leave the service of the former discipline for that of the latter.

The identification of the ideals of medicine and poetry was, of course, made easier, even natural, for Keats by the fact that his beloved Apollo, the most dominant figure throughout his poetry, was "the god of all the fine arts, of medicine, music, poetry, and eloquence, of all which he was deemed the inventor."[13] Moreover, Apollo was the original owner of the caduceus, the very symbol of healing, which he gave to Mercury in exchange for the lyre, the symbol of music and poetry. In one of his *Tatler* essays, Joseph Addison points out that "it has been commonly observed in compliment to the ingenious of our profession, that Apollo was god of verse as well as of physic; and in all ages the most celebrated practitioners of our country were the particular favourites of the muses."[14] Only a few critics, however, have commented on this dual nature of Keats's presiding deity, with the result that many readers have missed an important aspect of Keats's understanding of the role of the poet, that of the poet as healer.[15]

This characterization of the poet as healer probably developed, as Evert suggests, out of Keats's own struggle to decide on a career after he passed his apothecary's licentiate examination in July 1816.[16] The concept existed in embryonic form, however, in Keats's earliest poems and is worth tracing as it develops into a more and more dominant image.

"On Receiving a Curious Shell, and a Copy of Verses, from the Same Ladies," written in the summer of 1815, was addressed to George Felton Mathew in the guise of a young knight, Eric. Having posed questions about Eric's knightly trappings which reveal Eric to be a brave and virile warrior, the speaker then turns to his own attributes, which are strangely different from those of Eric:

> Ah! courteous Sir Knight, with large joy thou art crown'd;
> Full many the glories that brighten thy youth!
> I will tell thee my blisses, which richly abound
> In magical powers to bless, and to sooth.
>
> On this scroll thou seest written in characters fair
> A sun-beamy tale of a wreath, and a chain;
> And, warrior, it nurtures the property rare
> Of charming my mind from the trammels of pain.   (17–24)

Instead of portraying himself as a valiant warrior, or even a virtuous Spenserian knight, the poet-Keats depicts himself as one who soothes and relieves pain with a magical scroll, which is, of course, poetry. Poetry, then, is a kind of healing medicine, and the poet a physician. These ideas are extremely vague at this stage, but the metaphor is already germinating in Keats's mind. It is also interesting to note that what has often been viewed as effeminacy in Keats's heroes is really compassion; they are healers rather than warriors.

Keats returns to these ideas in his next poem, "To George Felton Mathew," written in November 1815. He contemplates a dramatic partnership between himself and Mathew along the lines of that of Beaumont and Fletcher:

> The thought of this great partnership diffuses
> Over the genius loving heart, a feeling
> Of all that's high, and great, and good, and healing. (8–10)

Again the poet and poetry are associated with the high ideal of healing, yet ironically Keats cannot at present see the unity between the two aspects of his life—which he calls "contradictions" (34)—and he fears that loyalty to medicine may prevent him from being a poet:

> far different cares
> Beckon me sternly from soft "Lydian airs,"
> And hold my faculties so long in thrall,
> That I am oft in doubt whether at all
> I shall again see Phœbus in the morning:
> Or flush'd Aurora in the roseate dawning! (17–22)

Poetry as a healing balm is momentarily forgotten and becomes instead a series of fantasies, an escape from the harsh realities of the world of medicine.

Having, in "On Receiving a Curious Shell," made a distinction between Mathew as warrior and himself as a more peaceful, healing knight, in "Calidore," written when he was at Guy's in the spring of 1816, Keats unites the two aspects of knighthood in his hero. After a lengthy description of how the young warrior has assisted two ladies, Keats portrays him in a moment of stasis:

> While 'gainst his forehead he devoutly press'd
> A hand heaven made to succour the distress'd;
> A hand that from the world's bleak promontory
> Had lifted Calidore for deeds of glory. (105–08)

Presumably the deeds of glory will be performed on the battlefield, but the knight also has another destiny, "to succour the distress'd"; that he will accomplish this with his hand may be an indirect reference to the surgeon's dexterity. The equation of knight and physician has begun to form in Keats's mind.

Throughout 1816, when he was daily in attendance at Guy's, Keats's poetry continued to be dominated by a wish to escape from the realities of hospital life, as indicated by poems like "O Solitude! if I must with thee dwell," "To one who has been long in city pent," and "Oh! how I love, on a fair summer's eve." This escapism culminates in the first third of *Sleep and Poetry*, written in late 1816, where Keats compares sleep to a number of sensual luxuries and lays out his plans for poetic development in the beautiful and ever peaceful, pleasure-filled realm of "Flora and old Pan." He then comes to a dramatic pause, and a new mood envelops the poem:

> And can I ever bid these joys farewell?
> Yes, I must pass them for a nobler life,
> Where I may find the agonies, the strife
> Of human hearts. (122–25)

Whether Keats is here still contemplating a career, "a nobler life," in medicine as opposed to poetry is debatable, although he was still a dresser at Guy's and was preparing for examinations in surgery. It is more likely that he is rejecting the escapist poetry, the glorification of pleasures he has just described, in favor of a poetry that comes to terms with, and offers relief for, human agony and suffering. This seems to be borne out by the vision that immediately follows, the content of which has never been satisfactorily explained:

> for lo! I see afar,
> O'er sailing the blue craginess, a car
> And steeds with streamy manes—the charioteer
> Looks out upon the winds with glorious fear. (125–28)

Although Keats does not name the charioteer, he is obviously Apollo, and D'Avanzo claims that the steeds symbolize the poetic imagination controlled by the ultimate poet.[17] Blackstone also states that "the charioteer is Apollo: Apollo descending into the circle of courses to regulate, to instruct, and to heal."[18] These are valid observations, but they do not account for the characters Apollo meets:

> and there soon appear
> Shapes of delight, of mystery, and fear,
> Passing along before a dusky space
> Made by some mighty oaks: as they would chase
> Some ever-fleeting music on they sweep.
> Lo! how they murmur, laugh, and smile, and weep:

Some with upholden hand and mouth severe;
Some with their faces muffled to the ear
Between their arms; some, clear in youthful bloom,
Go glad and smilingly athwart the gloom;
Some looking back, and some with upward gaze;
Yes, thousands in a thousand different ways
Flit onward.   (137–49)

This almost surreal description of seemingly mad, irrational people crying and laughing, mumbling and smiling, their bodies in contorted positions, is precisely that: a description of patients in a mental ward. From its inception Guy's Hospital, under the provision of Thomas Guy's will, had had a "lunatic house" for incurables, and in 1783 a resolution was passed by the hospital governors requiring hospital physicians "to attend the Lunatic Patients"; in 1797 a new lunatic ward was opened on the south side of the hospital.[19] As a dresser, Keats would have been in attendance at the mental ward from time to time and would have witnessed such scenes of suffering, although sometimes contented, humanity.

Apollo, in his dual role as god of poetry and of medicine, descends to listen to these "shapes of delight, of mystery, and fear":

Most awfully intent,
The driver of those steeds is forward bent,
And seems to listen: O that I might know
All that he writes with such a hurrying glow.   (151–54)

As a poet, Apollo draws inspiration from these mad, irrational beings, the result of which is poetry written down—it is important to recognize that for Keats, as for most Romantic poets, poetry is associated with madness and the irrational. As a ministering physician, however, Apollo listens to, and sympathizes with, his patients; he has found the "nobler life" by understanding "the agonies, the strife / Of human hearts," the ideal to which Keats aspires but cannot yet grasp. Perhaps the image of Apollo writing as he listens is adapted from Keats's memories of the physician taking down his patients' case histories, which all doctors were required to keep. Once more Keats has fused the poet and the physician, with perhaps a vestige of the traditional knight-warrior in Apollo's chariot stance. It is this fusion of power and sympathy, beauty and healing, richness and understanding, that Keats defines as poetry later in *Sleep and Poetry:*

> A drainless shower
> Of light is poesy; 'tis the supreme of power;
> 'Tis might half slumb'ring on its own right arm.
> The very archings of her eye-lids charm
> A thousand willing agents to obey,
> And still she governs with the mildest sway:
> But strength alone though of the Muses born
> Is like a fallen angel: trees uptorn,
> Darkness, and worms, and shrouds, and sepulchres
> Delight it; for it feeds upon the burrs,
> And thorns of life; forgetting the great end
> Of poesy, that it should be a friend
> To sooth the cares, and lift the thoughts of man.   (235–47)

Power alone in poetry is only sensational and destructive, a claim which is perhaps an attack on the Graveyard School and on Byron; genuine poetry needs to have a soothing effect, to heal.

That this concept of poetry was very much on Keats's mind at the time is seen in "I stood tip-toe . . .," which was also completed in December 1816. The poem is mainly a lengthy natural description of the flora of Hampstead Heath and Edmonton, with a discussion of mythmaking, but it ends with an apostrophe to Cynthia and an attempted description of her wedding night. In keeping with the rest of the poem, this description is full of beauty and joy, yet there is an image of sickness near the end that is incongruous with the tone of the rest of the poem:

> The evening weather was so bright, and clear,
> That men of health were of unusual cheer;
> Stepping like Homer at the trumpet's call,
> Or young Apollo on the pedestal:
> And lovely women were as fair and warm,
> As Venus looking sideways in alarm.
> The breezes were ethereal, and pure,
> And crept through half closed lattices to cure

The languid sick; it cool'd their fever'd sleep,
And soothed them into slumbers full and deep.
Soon they awoke clear eyed: nor burnt with thirsting,
Nor with hot fingers, nor with temples bursting:
And springing up, they met the wond'ring sight
Of their dear friends, nigh foolish with delight;
Who feel their arms, and breasts, and kiss and stare,
And on their placid foreheads part the hair.   (215–30)

The passage is interesting because of the association of "men of health" with "young Apollo," god of healing and of poetry which, by association, takes on healing powers.

In addition, the description of the fevered patients enjoying the healing breeze is taken directly from Keats's firsthand knowledge of the wards at Guy's, complete with their lattice windows. Robert Armstrong-Jones, a Guy's man, observes that "those who have listened to the crickets chirping in the surgical wards on a hot summer night will recognize this picture."[20] It is one that Keats must have seen often while on duty as dresser, and the symptoms of the patients are medically accurate. The symptoms of nervous fever include "general languor and lassitude" ("the languid sick") and "disturbed or unrefreshing sleep" ("their fever'd sleep"), and those of inflammatory fever include "violent and continued dry heat, . . . suffused redness of eyes" ("they awoke clear eyed" after the healing breezes), "acute pain of head" ("with temples bursting"), and "white and dry tongue; —thirst" ("burnt with thirsting").[21] This accuracy raises Keats's description to a level of vividness and muscularity that far surpasses the effeminate, Huntian style that many have claimed is inherent in words like "languid" and "fevered."

In this passage, we also see that the effect of weather on health is important, a topic to which Keats returns periodically. He knew from Babington and Curry that "other causes which predispose to, or actually excite fever" include "certain intemperies of the atmosphere, independent of its sensible qualities." Although an "accurate register of such changes connected with history of the season and prevailing diseases [was] still wanting," Keats knew that "intermittent [fevers] in temperate and cold climates [are] most common in Spring and

Autumn."²² It is therefore natural that clear summer breezes would cure such fevers. The breeze is also the inspirational breeze of poetry, so that this whole passage becomes a celebration of the healing power of poetry. The concept is perhaps incongruous with the rest of the poem, but it is very accurately described.

The importance of the weather as a cause of disease is made manifest in a sonnet written shortly after "I stood tip-toe . . .," on 31 January 1817:

> After dark vapours have oppressed our plains
> For a long dreary season, comes a day
> Born of the gentle south, and clears away
> From the sick heavens all unseemly stains.
> The anxious month, relieving from its pains,
> Takes as a long lost right the feel of May,
> The eyelids with the passing coolness play,
> Like rose-leaves with the drip of summer rains. (1–8)

Instead of detailing the symptoms of human patients, Keats transfers those symptoms to the season itself so that winter metaphorically becomes a disease cured, like the patients in "I stood tip-toe . . .," by breezes from the south, which are again symbolic of poetry. It is a metaphor that apparently appealed to Keats, for he repeats it later in *The Fall of Hyperion:*

> When in mid-May the sickening east wind
> Shifts sudden to the south, the small warm rain
> Melts out the frozen incense from all flowers,
> And fills the air with so much pleasant health
> That even the dying man forgets his shroud. (I, 97–101)

The metaphor of a diseased winter followed by a healthy spring is a literary commonplace; what makes Keats's images novel and powerful is their medical accuracy. In the sonnet, the "dark vapours" that "oppressed our plains" during the dreary wetness of winter are "Phytoseptic Miasmata or the vapour arising from moist soils . . . [which is] the *essential cause* of both Intermitting and Remitting Fevers."²³ One symptom of these fevers is a "suffused redness of eyes and skin," which may account for the pleasure "the eyelids" take in "the passing coolness" of the healing breeze.

Keats's interest in the influence of geographical terrain and atmospheric conditions on health is even more apparent in a long letter he wrote to Taylor on 5 September 1819, where he gives his friend the benefit of his medical knowledge:

> You should live in a dry, gravelly, barren, elevated country open to the currents of air. . . . The neighbourhood of a rich inclosed fulsome manured arrable Land especially in a valley and almost as bad on a flat, would be almost as bad as the smoke of fleetstreet. Such a place as this was shanklin only open to the south east and sorrounded by hills in every other direction—From this south east came the damps from the sea which having no egress the air would for days together take on an unhealthy idiosyncrasy altogether enervating and weakening as a city Smoke—I felt it very much—Since I have been at Winchester I have been improving in health—it is not so confined— and there is on one side of the city a dry chalky down where the air is worth six pence a pint. So if you do not get better at Retford do not impute it to your own weakness before you have well considered the nature of the air and soil—especially as Autumn is encroaching: for the autum fogs over a rich land is like the steam from cabbage water— . . . Our hea[l]th temperament and dispositions are taken more . . . from the air we breathe than is generally imagined.
>
> (*Letters* 2:155–56)

Although this harangue is evoked by Keats's reading of Burton's *Anatomy of Melancholy*, it probably also involves memories of Babington's and Curry's discussion of different fevers being associated with various terrains. After outlining the dangers of the air in fertile valley estuaries, Babington and Curry conclude, as Keats does here, that autumnal air "in marshy districts" is particularly unhealthy as it gives rise to intermitting and remitting fevers, or what are "vulgarly termed agues."[24]

But to return briefly to the "Dark vapours" sonnet and the passage from *The Fall of Hyperion:* in the latter, the reference to "the sickening east wind" is also pathologically accurate, as is evidenced in Curry's enumeration of the "Occasional or Exciting Causes" of fever: "Certain states of the air independantly of thermometric or hygromatic quality; —shewn in the effects of certain winds: —the East wind in England."[25] The temperate south wind, which melts the winter frost and initiates growth and ripeness, is, in contrast, curative; and thus both the sonnet and the passage from *The Fall* end in a return to health with the change of wind from east to south. There is also an interesting mixture of metaphors from pathology and botany in the sonnet when the return to health is symbolized by vernal-autumnal images of "leaves / Budding—fruit ripening in stillness—autumn suns / Smiling at eve upon the quiet sheaves."

It is important to recognize, also, that these images have meaning beyond mere natural description. I have already pointed out, in the chapter on botany, that in Keats's poetry autumnal fruition is a common metaphor for the creative efforts of the poetic imagination; it is also apparent from this point on that, for Keats, states of health and disease often symbolize the imagination in periods of productivity and stagnation respectively. Viewed in this way, the diseased state described in "Dark vapours" becomes psychological, and the tone personal.

Before making such a claim, however, I should note that the most prominent psychological disease of the eighteenth century was melancholia, or the spleen, also known as the vapours ("dark vapours"), which was believed to be caused in part by "the sickening east wind."[26] Bearing this in mind, we recognize that the depressed, diseased state of winter caused by "dark vapours" is at once a physical description of the landscape covered in miasmatic fog and a psychological account of the poet's state of mind as he leaves winter stagnation and moves into spring creativity.

To understand fully Keats's use of melancholy as a metaphor in his poetry and its effect on him personally—the two aspects become more and more closely interwoven as his poetry progresses—one should know something of the background of the disease. Scholars have usually attributed Keats's knowledge of melancholia to the influence of Robert Burton's *Anatomy of Melancholy*, which remains a controversial source in Keats scholarship.[27] Because Burton's influence has already been discussed in detail, because his work is more literary than strictly medical, and finally, because the topic is too large for the focus of my study, I will not reopen the questions surrounding Burton and Keats, although I do from time to time point briefly to certain Burtonian influences. More to my point, however, is the general consensus among scholars that Keats did not read Burton until at least the winter or spring of 1819,[28] yet he obviously knew much about melancholia long before then. I believe, and will attempt to demonstrate, that much of his knowledge about this disease was gained directly from his medical studies.

By the end of the eighteenth century, melancholia had come to be recognized as a type of hypochondria, a nervous disease caused largely by the imagination and emotions. In the early part of the century, Sir Richard Blackmore, the famous physician to William III and Queen Anne, describes the phenomenon in *A Treatise of the Spleen and Vapours: or, Hypocondriacal and Hysterical Affections* (1725), outlining the imaginary nature of the ailment: "As a melancholy Constitution of the Spirits is fruitful of a surprizing and copious Diversity of odd and ridiculous Phantasms, and fills the Imagination with a thousand uncouth Figures, monstrous Appearances and troublesome Illusions; so it is no less fertile in producing disquieting and restless Passions, while they affect the Heart with Anxiety, Sadness, Fear and Terror."[29] By the middle of the century, however, with increased knowledge of the brain and nervous system, Robert Whytt claimed that melancholy and similar diseases were in fact "nervous disorders":

All diseases may, in some sense, be called affections of the nervous system, because, in almost every disease, the nerves are more or less hurt; and, in consequence of this, various sensations, motions, and changes, are produced in the body. —However, those disorders may, perculiarly, deserve the name of *nervous,* which, on account of an unusual delicacy, or unnatural state of the nerves, are produced by causes, which, in people of a sound contitution, would either have no such effects, or at least in a much less degree.[30]

Whytt classified these disorders as "simply nervous," "hysteric," or "hypochondriac," according to the severity of the symptoms.

Babington and Curry also classify these disorders as hysteria and hypochondriasis, formerly called "Spleen, —Vapours, —

Low Spirits." The symptoms of hypochondriasis are "unusual anxiety, depression of spirits, and belief of present or dread of future evil, directed particularly to the state of health; always accompanied with symptoms of indigestion, and other marks of bodily disorder; and generally also with various, irregular, and often unaccountable sensations and affections, referred exclusively to the patient's imagination."[31] The mental, as opposed to corporeal, form of hypochondriasis is melancholia; the predisposing cause is "a peculiarity of constitution with respect to the Brain and Nerves, generally original," and the exciting causes include "indolent inactive life; —intense study . . . —cold, damp, and variable state of the atmosphere, especially that succeeding the Autumnal Equinox; . . . depressing passions, *e.gr.* Grief, Anxiety, and Fear, by whatever cause produced."[32]

That Keats suffered from bouts of melancholia is evident in one of his earliest personal poems, "To Hope," written in a state of grief at the death of his grandmother:

> When by my solitary hearth I sit,
>   And hateful thoughts enwrap my soul in gloom;
> When no fair dreams before my "mind's eye" flit,
>   And the bare heath of life presents no bloom;
> Sweet Hope, ethereal balm upon me shed,
> And wave thy silver pinions o'er my head.   (1–6)

He continues with fears that the "fiend Despondence" and "Disappointment, parent of Despair," personifications adapted from eighteenth-century poets, may seize and destroy him, and he exhibits the exact "dread of future evil" that Babington and Curry describe:

> Whene'er the fate of those I hold most dear
>   Tells to my fearful breast a tale of sorrow,
> O bright-eyed Hope, my morbid fancy cheer;
>   Let me awhile thy sweetest comforts borrow.   (19–22)

It is also important that Keats knew so early in his career that these bouts of melancholy were caused by his "morbid fancy" or diseased imagination, in keeping with medical opinion.

The appeals to Hope are weak, but as Andrew Brink points out, the poem is one of "self-therapy" in which the poet uses "poetic imagination as a means of grace."[33] The poem, the product of the imagination, itself becomes the means of healing the "morbid fancy," a concept that Keats seems to have recognized when he states: "O let me think it is not quite in vain / To sigh out sonnets to the midnight air!" (27–28).

George notes that during the period when "To Hope" was written (1815) Keats suffered from a "nervous morbid temperament" and was "melancholy and complaining . . . some times telling his Brothers & in an agony he feared he never should be a Poet, & if he was not he would destroy himself." George also states that Keats had "many a bitter fit of hypochondriasm, he avoided teazing any one with his miseries but Tom and myself and often asked our forgiveness; venting, and discussing them gave him relief; . . . no one in England understood his character perfectly but poor Tom and he had not the power to divert his frequent melancholy."[34]

Keats discusses these fears that he will never be a poet in his epistle "To My Brother George" (1–18), where he talks of his mind as being "o'ercast / With heaviness," a common metaphor for melancholia and one that shows the connection of the disease with bad weather. Blackmore, for example, talks of "the dark melancholy Clouds that overcast the Brain."[35] It is also significant that Keats once more finds "relief from pain / When some bright thought has darted through [his] brain" (114–15), and he goes on to state: "These things I thought / While, in my face, the freshest breeze I caught" (121–22), again portraying the poetic breeze as a healing power.

While he was absorbed in his medical studies during late 1815 and 1816, Keats seems to have managed to hold his dark moods at bay, but by early 1817 they were hounding him again. His "dread of future evil, directed particularly to the state of health,"[36] becomes evident in a letter of 17 March to Reynolds: "Banish money—Banish sofas—Banish Wine—Banish Music—But right Jack Health—honest Jack Health, true Jack Health—banish health and banish all the world" (*Letters* 1:125). A month later, when he was in the Isle of Wight trying to begin *Endymion*, Keats complains to Reynolds of being "rather *narvus*" (*Letters* 1:132), "nerves" being another term for melancholia, and again he turns to poetry for relief, this time in a sonnet, "On the Sea," in which the sea itself becomes the healing force: "O ye who have your eyeballs vext and tir'd, / Feast them upon the wideness of the sea."[37] Keats knew, as he tells Reynolds the next day, that the sonnet itself acts like a drug to cure his black moods of despondency: "I find that I cannot exist without poetry—without eternal poetry—half the day will not do—the whole of it—I began with a little, but habit has made me a Leviathan—I had become all in a Tremble from not having written any thing of late—the Sonnet over leaf did me some good. I slept the better last night for it—this Morning, however, I am nearly as bad again" (*Letters* 1:133). These are the words of an addict desperately seeking his drug, but the bitterly ironic aspect of this addiction is that the worse the melancholia becomes, the less likely he is to create poetry, so that his cure is withheld while he is caught in a vicious circle.

This is precisely what Keats saw happening by May 1817, when he received some bad financial news from George. He writes to Haydon:

So now I revoke my Promise of finishing my Poem [*Endymion*] by the Autumn which I should have done had I gone on as I have done—but I cannot write while my spirit is fevered in a contrary direction and I am now sure of having plenty of it this Summer—At this moment I am in no enviable Situation—I feel that I am not in a Mood to write any to day; and it appears that the loss of it is the beginning of all sorts of irregularities. I am extremely glad that a time must come when every thing will leave not a wrack behind. You tell me never to despair—I wish it was as easy for me to observe the saying—truth is I have a horrid Morbidity of Temperament which has shown itself at intervals—it is I have no doubt the greatest Enemy and stumbling block I have to fear—I may even say that it is likely to be the cause of my disappointment.   (*Letters* 1:142)

A few days later he tells Taylor and Hessey that he feels "all the effects of a Mental Debauch—lowness of Spirits—anxiety to go on without the Power to do so" (*Letters* 1:146). Anxiety is the very cause of his melancholy, and, as he cannot get his drug, poetry, Keats seems to accept the prognosis that the ailment is difficult to cure "in those who are of the Melancholic Temperament, —and where it has either been caused by, or become intimately associated with, strong Mental Impressions." Such cases "occasionally terminate in fixed Melancholia," which is his own fear. He must have known, however, that the treatment was "to occupy the mind with naturally associated impressions of superior force; and thereby gradually weaken, and finally destroy, the morbid concatenation of ideas which had taken place."[38] Keats attempts to do this with poetry, and it is interesting that the poem he was writing at this time, *Endymion*, deals with a melancholy lover whose problems are often similar to his own.

From *Endymion* onward, it becomes increasingly difficult to separate many of the problems of the heroes in his narrative poems from those of Keats himself, since these heroes usually symbolize the poet and are thus related to Keats's view of himself. This becomes apparent in the preface to *Endymion* where what he says about the health of the imagination applies equally to Endymion and to himself: "The imagination of a boy is healthy, and the mature imagination of a man is healthy; but there is a space of life between, in which the soul is in a ferment, the character undecided, the way of life uncertain, the ambition thick-sighted: thence proceeds mawkishness, and all the thousand bitters which those men I speak of must necessarily taste in going over the following pages." Like the poet's, Endymion's imagination is in an unhealthy state, melancholia being caused by "unaccountable sensations and affections, referred exclusively to the imagination";[39] and like Keats and the reader, Endymion must suffer "a thousand bitters." Yet Keats's choice of the word "bitters" may itelf be a significant pun, for it means, as well as unpleasant tastes, "a bitter medicinal substance: now usually in plural" (*O.E.D.*). Thus the "bitters" can be both the poor taste exhibited in the poem and the cure for an unhealthy imagination; the very writing and reading of the work is a healing process that helps to mature the imagination.[40] Keats hopes that the poem, as "A thing of beauty" (I, 1), will be "Full of sweet dreams, and health, and quiet breathing" (I, 5), will be like "Apollo's upward fire . . .

Of brightness so unsullied, that therein / A melancholy spirit
well might win / Oblivion" (I, 95–99).

That *Endymion* is, at least partially, a study of melancholia
becomes apparent shortly after the opening celebrations of the
hymn to Pan. Endymion, the shepherd prince, tries in vain to
mask his suffering under this disease:

> hourly had he striven
> To hide the cankering venom, that had riven
> His fainting recollections. Now indeed
> His senses had swoon'd off: he did not heed
> The sudden silence, or the whispers low,
> Or the old eyes dissolving at his woe,
> . . . .
> But in the self-same fixed trance he kept,
> Like one who on the earth had never stept. (I, 395–404)

In this state, no one can help him except

> Peona, his sweet sister: of all those,
> His friends, the dearest. Hushing signs she made,
> And breath'd a sister's sorrow to persuade
> A yielding up, a cradling on her care.
> Her eloquence did breathe away the curse:
> She led him, like some midnight spirit nurse
> Of happy changes in emphatic dreams, (I, 408–14)

to a bower, where she lulls him to sleep. She does for Endymion what Keats's brothers apparently did for him: she offers
healing comfort for his melancholic mind.

Many critics have commented on Peona's ability to heal her
"brain-sick" brother with her Delphic song. De Selincourt
notes that "Peona's healing function may have suggested her
name to Keats, since 'wise Paeon' is mentioned in Spenser
(*F.Q.*, III, iv, 41) as the son of Apollo and the healer Liagore;
and Ovid mentions Paeon as the son of Apollo and, with
Diana, a healer of Hippolytus."[41] Miriam Allott cites Homer's
Iliad (V, 401–02, 899–901) as the likely source for Paeon,[42] and
both she and Evert quote Lempriere: "Paeon, . . . A celebrated
physician who cured the wounds which the gods received during the Trojan war. For him, physicians are sometimes called
Paeonii, and herbs serviceable in medicinal processes, *Paeoniae*

herbae.''[43] Evert concludes: "Given so many healing associations with the name, Peona's healing function at her introduction into the story, the association of healing with the physician-god Apollo, and Peona's medicining with Delphic song, the intended association of her name with Apollo seems indubitable."[44] Such characterization is not entirely new in Keats's poetry, however: as the "midnight spirit nurse," Peona stands in the long line of those knight-healers who appear, in less detailed descriptions, in Keats's earliest poetry. As Apollo's associate, she is both healer, in her treatment of her brother, and poet, by virtue of her singing: the poet is once more the healer. What is novel about this characterization is that Keats has made the healer feminine, a trait that continues in much of his later poetry.

One important aspect of this passage not usually noted is that in the original draft Keats made Peona's procedures in curing Endymion even more medically specific than they are in the final version. On finding him faint, she put "her trembling hand against his cheek"[45] and felt him fevered. In fact, Endymion displays the symptoms of nervous fever, an illness sharing many of the symptoms of melancholy and also induced by emotional stress. Babington and Curry point out that the symptoms include "general languor and lassitude; . . . dulness and confusion of thought; —sadness of mind and dejection of countenance; —respiration short, with frequent sighing; . . . disturbed or unrefreshing sleep; . . . dull pain in the head, especially the occiput;—giddiness . . . sense of anxiety and oppression . . . and excessive faintness, especially in the erect posture."[46] As Endymion relates his story of love for a goddess, he tells of having dreams: "Thus on I thought, / Until my head was dizzy and distraught" (I, 564–65). The dreams disturb his sleep and lead to sighs, tears, and clenched hands (I, 681–82); and after Cynthia's vision disappears, he is plagued with "thoughts so sick" (I, 758) that he eventually faints. Keats's description is remarkably accurate.

On discovering Endymion's ailment, Peona

> Ran some swift paces to a dark wells side,
> And in a sighing time return'd, supplied

179

> With spar cold water; in which she did squeeze
> A snowy napkin, and upon her Knees
> Began to cherish her poor Brother's face;
> Damping refreshfully his forehead's space,
> His eyes, his Lips: then in a cupped shell
> She brought him ruby wine.[47]

Both a cold bath and wine were common treatments for fever, the former to reduce the pulse rate and bring down the temperature, the latter "although stimulant gives to the Body great additional Strength."[48] Babington and Curry state that wine is "the most grateful of all remedies as a tonic and stimulant in certain cases of low fever," and they recommend it for nervous fever as does Saunders, who states that "in this fever, wine is one of the best cordials; . . . it renders the pulse slower and fuller, procures sleep, takes off delirium."[49] It should also be observed that it was the publisher Taylor who, for unknown reasons, recommended that Keats delete these lines from the poem.

After Peona's treatment, "in the bower, / Endymion was calm'd to life again. / Opening his eyelids with a healthier brain" (I, 463–65), he promises to involve himself actively in life, a commonly touted cure for melancholia. But he continues to demonstrate the symptoms of the disease, as is evident in his description of his thoughts and feelings after Cynthia has appeared in his dreams:

> all the pleasant hues
> Of heaven and earth had faded: deepest shades
> Were deepest dungeons; heaths and sunny glades
> Were full of pestilent light;
> . . . .
> How sickening, how dark the dreadful leisure
> Of weary days, made deeper exquisite,
> By a fore-knowledge of unslumbrous night!
> Like sorrow came upon me, heavier still,
> Than when I wander'd from the poppy hill:
> And a whole age of lingering moments crept
> Sluggishly by, ere more contentment swept
> Away at once the deadly yellow spleen. (I, 691–94, 910–17)

Fulfillment in love can be the only real cure for the "Brain-sick shepherd prince" (II, 43);[50] thus the second book opens with a hymn to love before Endymion embarks on his journey to find his unknown lover while struggling "to keep off the burr / Of smothering fancies" (II, 138–39). But even though the disease from which Endymion suffers is mental, Keats increasingly describes it in corporeal terms, using the pathological symptoms of fever with which he was familiar from his medical training. Endymion complains:

> Within my breast there lives a choking flame—
> O let me cool it the zephyr-boughs among!
> A homeward fever parches up my tongue—
> O let me slake it at the running springs!
> Upon my ear a noisy nothing rings—
> O let me once more hear the linnet's note!
> Before mine eyes thick films and shadows float—
> O let me 'noint them with the heaven's light!
> Dost thou now lave thy feet and ankles white?
> O think how sweet to me the freshening sluice!
> Dost thou now please thy thirst with berry-juice?
> O think how this dry palate would rejoice!   (II, 317–28)

Endymion pleads with his beloved to heal his fevered mind, vividly depicted here by a fevered body, complete with "dry burning heat all over, with great restlessness, . . . diminished sensation of eye, ear," and thirst, with the "patient's attention absorbed by his general sufferings."[51] Since, as Babington and Curry point out, "every fever . . . shews a sort of common character, as originating from a *certain disturbed* state of the Nervous System," it is easy to recognize how the "effects of passions and emotions" often result in febrile commotion.[52] For Keats, Endymion's physical symptoms are not merely symbolic of a diseased mind: they are a direct result of it.

The controversy surrounding the meaning of Endymion's search for his mysterious lover is well known. Critical interpretations range from claims that the poem is no more than a straightforward narrative to those that it is a Platonic allegory of the soul's search for Ideal Beauty. Most critics would now probably agree that the narrative is symbolic, if not strictly allegorical, although there would be little agreement as to what it symbolizes. But if, as I believe, Endymion symbolizes the poet in search of ideal poetry, then his fever and melancholia must symbolize the imagination in a diseased state, unable to function. That Endymion cannot find or create poetry, symbolized by Cynthia, is a result of his very desire for immortal poetry, which naturally involves escape from the world and all its miseries. In seeking the ideal and rejecting the real, the imagination is in a state of imbalance, and Keats knew from his studies of pathology that imbalance in the human constitution causes disease. Blumenbach states that *"health* . . . depends upon such an harmony and equilibrium of the matter and powers of the system, as is requisite for the due performance of its functions." Babington and Curry also point out that "living differs from dead body in its power of beginning motion, and producing various *changes;* both necessary to its existence and well-being. . . . Certain *degree* and *order* of these motions and changes, productive of HEALTH; —and any *excess, defect,* or *irregularity* of them, beyond a certain degree, causes DISEASE."[53]

The concept of health as a state of balance or harmony is absolutely central to Keats's understanding of physical and mental well-being, and remains an important concern throughout his poetry. By rejecting the real world for the ideal, Endymion upsets this balance and becomes diseased; in order to heal himself, Endymion, the poet, must learn to appreciate the real world in all its pain and suffering, "the agonies, the strife / Of human hearts." Imaginative flight is not enough; the poet must learn to sympathize with the suffering of others, to dwell in the world:

> But this is human life: the war, the deeds,
> The disappointment, the anxiety,
> Imagination's struggles, far and nigh,
> All human; bearing in themselves this good,
> That they are still the air, the subtle food,
> To make us feel existence, and to shew
> How quiet death is.   (II, 153–59)

Yet Endymion rejects this world and so must be taught how to heal his own diseased imagination by learning how to sympathize with, and ultimately cure, the pains of others. This is perhaps the essential lesson in Keats's approach to life, and it is one that Endymion learns by example. The examples are presented in a number of repeated, parallel situations that mirror one another for emphasis, sometimes becoming redundant.

We have already seen the first example of the sympathetic healer in Peona; Endymion meets his second exemplar in the person of Venus, another female healer who foreshadows Mnemosyne in *The Fall of Hyperion*. Venus is the healer of Adonis, who was wounded by the boar. As the cupid explains:

> when our love-sick queen did weep
> Over his waned corse, the tremulous shower
> Heal'd up the wound, and, with a balmy power,
> Medicined death to a lengthy drowsiness:
> The which she fills with visions, and doth dress
> In all this quiet luxury. (II, 481–86)

Dorothy Van Ghent has commented on the similarity between Endymion and Adonis, and she interprets this healing episode from a mythic and psychological perspective, concluding that it is "significant as an early indication of one dramatic motif in Keats's reigning mythical construct: the transformation of his hero into a 'marble man' as a phase of healing from the fever of opposites and from death."[54] I would argue, however, that Adonis's cure is accomplished, not by freeing him from opposites, but rather by imposing a balance between the ideal and the real worlds, symbolized by his spending six months each in the worlds of immortality and mortality.

Endymion learns from this experience, as is demonstrated when he encounters Alpheus and Arethusa who, like him, burn with the fever of unrequited love (II, 961–64). Endymion, sympathizing with their plight as Apollo does with that of his patients, calls upon his mysterious lover "to soothe, to assuage, / If thou art powerful, these lovers' pains" (II, 1015–16). He has learned to have the physician's sympathy for others, which is part of his own healing process, although he does not yet have the power to initiate a cure.

Once Endymion has shown sympathy for the suffering of others, Cynthia does the same for him and sends a moonbeam to the ocean floor, where "he felt the charm / To breathlessness, and suddenly a warm / Of his heart's blood" (III, 105–07).[55] His healing process is not linear, however, but undulates as his ability to sympathize with others' pain increases or decreases. He immediately faces his second test when he meets Glaucus, an old man who also suffers love melancholy as a result of separation from his lover, Scylla. Endymion's "heart 'gan warm / With pity" (III, 282–83) for the old man, and Glaucus's reaction is exactly the same as Endymion's reaction to Cynthia's pity: his "blood no longer cold / Gave mighty pulses" (III, 304–05). In both cases Keats chooses a physiological change to represent spiritual healing, a strong pulse being a common measure of health.

It is important to note that Glaucus's ailment, like Endymion's, stems from a psychological discontentment with the real world: "Why was I not contented? . . . Fool! I began / To feel distemper'd longings" (III, 372–75) to escape mundane reality. Glaucus seeks to escape into the totally sensual, imbalanced world of Circe, who, instead of assuaging his desires, inflicts him with "fever'd parchings up" and "palsy" (III, 636–37) that are external manifestations of his mental state of imbalance. Glaucus, too, can be cured only by learning to help others, which he accomplishes by tending the bodies of the drowned lovers.

In sympathizing with Glaucus, and thus forgetting his own woes, Endymion actually gains the ability to heal with his own power, symbolized here by his gift of bringing the drowned lovers back to life. This is the physician's healing act taken to its impossible extreme of raising the dead:

> And onward [he] went upon his high employ,
> Showering those powerful fragments on the dead.
> And, as he pass'd, each lifted up its head,
> As doth a flower at Apollo's touch.   (III, 783–86)

The image of Apollo reviving the flower with his rays draws attention once more to his role as physician.

Endymion's final test of his abilities to understand the pains and sufferings of the world is presented in his relationship with the Indian Maid in Book IV. Before turning to Endymion, however, I should point out that the narrator has escapist tendencies of his own, as is evident in his pleas at the start of this book:

> Great Muse, thou know'st what prison,
> Of flesh and bone, curbs, and confines, and frets
> Our spirit's wings: despondency besets
> Our pillows; and the fresh to-morrow morn
> Seems to give forth its light in very scorn
> Of our dull, uninspired, snail-paced lives.   (IV, 20–25)

The poet-narrator's despondency and his desire to escape into immortal poetry parallel the poet-Endymion's melancholia and his desire to escape to immortal love. Both must learn to appreciate "the agonies, the strife / Of human hearts," and their parallel experiences emphasize the fact that Endymion's adventure really concerns the role of the poet in society.

The Indian Maid's story is very similar to Glaucus's: she deserted her lover in order to follow Bacchus, god of wine and sensuality, across the world, only to be left in a state of sorrow which robs her of "The natural hue of health" (IV, 148). On realizing that her despondency is akin to his own melancholia, Endymion immediately begins to sympathize with her plight and falls in love with her. He recognizes that he is now caught between the worlds of the ideal and the real, the immortal and the mortal, Cynthia and the Maid, and he must make a choice.

In choosing the Maid and the real world, Endymion makes the right decision, for the poet must concern himself with society. But the dilemma itself leaves him once more in a diseased state so that he calls upon the Maid to be his "nurse" and to heal his "tortur'd brain [which] begins to craze" (IV, 116–17). Again he is thrown back into melancholy madness and self-pity; and once more a female character, acting as nurse, ministers to him. In a canceled draft, which stresses her medical role more emphatically, the Maid cries out:

> "Is there no balm, no cure
> Could not a beckoning Hebe soon allure
> Three into Paradise? What sorrowing
> So weighs thee down what utmost woe could bring
> This madness—Sit thee down by me, and ease

The Poet-Physician

Thine heart in whispers—haply by degrees
I may find out some soothing medicine."[56]

The Maid is, of course, Cynthia, who is closely allied in Keats's mind to her brother Phoebus Apollo, a fact Keats deliberately emphasizes in this section of the poem by calling her Phoebe. Like her brother, she too is a healer, and as such she shows deep concern for Endymion's human suffering. Although he does not yet realize it, the poetry to which Endymion aspires is concerned with real pain and sorrow; Cynthia tries to teach him this in her guise as the Indian Maid.

Once cured, Endymion inherits the steeds that symbolize his role as poet, but he immediately soars upward to escape the world, and another dream-vision of Cynthia leads to yet another change of mind on his part. He again seeks to escape "earth, and sea, / And air, and pains, and care, and suffering" (IV, 431–32), to reject his role as poet-physician. In so doing he once more forfeits both Cynthia and the Indian Maid and relapses into his febrile state. He must then repair to the Cave of Quietude—probably a deliberate antithesis to the Cave of Spleen in Pope's *The Rape of the Lock*—to be cured of his fever and melancholia. It is only after this healing process, the psychological nature of which is emphasized by the cave symbolizing the psyche, that Endymion can accept the real world once and for all:

> to him
> Who lives beyond earth's boundary, grief is dim,
> Sorrow is but a shadow: now I see
> The grass; I feel the solid ground—
> . . . .
> Behold upon this happy earth we are;
> Let us ay love each other;
> . . . .
> O I have been
> Presumptuous against love, against the sky,
> Against all elements, against the tie
> Of mortals each to each, against the blooms
> Of flowers, rush of rivers, and the tombs
> Of heroes gone!   (IV, 619–22, 625–26, 638–43)

186

By accepting his place in the world, Endymion is finally cured, but Keats is still burdened with the narrative problem of resolving the Indian Maid–Cynthia confusion. He solves this by having Endymion seek a life of chastity, which is, ironically, a life devoted to Cynthia as goddess of chastity. For his devotion Cynthia reveals her identity with the Maid and marries the shepherd prince. Thus she too exemplifies a balance between the real and ideal worlds.

Some critics have complained about the rapidity of this conclusion, which they find unsatisfactory after Endymion's long journey. They do not recognize that Keats's desired conclusion has been reached once Endymion accepts his role in society; as he tells Peona: "Through me the shepherd realm shall prosper well; / For to thy tongue will I all health confide" (IV, 863–64). Similarly, the sages predict that on Cynthia's marriage there "will befall, / . . . health perpetual / To shepherds and their flocks" (IV, 830–32). The marriage itself is a mere formality: the important point is that, in marrying Cynthia, Endymion is not escaping this world; rather, he is ministering to its health. Keats's choice of the word "health," rather than "wealth," in these passages is significant, for it emphasizes again the healing nature of Endymion's role in society. He is the culmination of the knight-poet-physician construct—now modulated to the more placid shepherd-poet-physician—Keats has been developing from his earliest poetry.

Before leaving *Endymion*, I should point out a simile in Book IV which, as E. W. Goodall has noted, is medical in origin:

> one gentle squeeze,
> Warm as a dove's nest among summer trees,
> And warm with dew at ooze from living blood!
> (IV, 665–67)

Goodall observes that "the nature of this dew must have puzzled many a reader of 'Endymion.' My interpretation is that Keats had in his mind the serum which separates from the clot when blood is allowed to stand after venesection."[57] Venesection was a common treatment for numerous ailments, and as Keats undoubtedly knew about the separation of blood into red particles and serum, which was dealt with by Cooper,[58] Goodall is on the right track; but Keats's line is, more correctly, a perfect description of the gaseous vapor given off by warm, standing blood before it separates. Blumenbach's description of this phenomenon is remarkably like Keats's simile: "At first, especially while still warm, [the blood] emits a vapour which has of late been denominated an animal gas. . . . This, if collected, forms drops resembling dew, of a *watery* nature."[59] The watery vapor is like the perspiration Keats is describing in this line. I believe that he originally intended to write "And warm *as* dew at ooze from living blood" in order to compare the warmth of the squeeze to that of fresh blood; but, wishing also to describe the Indian Maid's perspiration in this torrid love scene, he substituted "with" for "as" and so spoiled the simile, although the medical source still fits his meaning.

Although Endymion is the shepherd-poet-physician of his society, Keats has doubts about his own ability to assume such a role. In January 1818, when he began revising *Endymion* for publication, he writes three short poems concerning these doubts. In "On Sitting Down to Read *King Lear* Once Again," he rejects "golden-tongued Romance" as "a barren dream," mere escapism; but in "Lines on Seeing a Lock of Milton's Hair," he complains that he has not yet gained the knowledge or "philosophy" necessary to accept reality, so that poetic creativity leaves him fevered and depressed:

> But vain is now the burning, and the strife,
> Pangs are in vain—until I grow high-rife
>   With old philosophy;
> And mad with glimpses at futurity!   (28–31)

In comparison to Milton, whose work did so much to heal his society, Keats feels his own creative effort is mere fevered activity that lacks the usefulness of philosophic thought. Consequently, in "God of the meridian," he prays to Apollo to help him find his own Cave of Quietude, the state of calm necessary to create healing poetry:

> God of Song,
> Thou bearest me along

Through sights I scarce can bear;
O let me, let me share
With the hot lyre and thee
The staid philosophy.
Temper my lonely hours
And let me see thy bowers
More unalarmed!   (17–25)

The genuine poetry Keats is reaching for can come only from a more comprehensive knowledge which will allow him to appreciate and understand the whole of life, as he explains to Taylor on 27 April 1818:

I was purposing to travel over the north this Summer—there is but one thing to prevent me—I know nothing I have read nothing and I mean to follow Solomon's directions of "get Wisdom—get understanding" —I find cavalier days are gone by. I find that I can have no enjoyment in the World but continual drinking of Knowledge. . . . I have been hovering for some time between an exquisite sense of the luxurious and a love for Philosophy—were I calculated for the former I should be glad—but as I am not I shall turn all my soul to the latter.
(*Letters* 1:271)

Only extensive knowledge can save Keats from the fever of an unhealthy imagination in a state of melancholia. Knowledge becomes necessary, not only for personal, psychological health, but also for the health of the society at large, for only he who can understand life's mysteries can act as physician to his society. And, as Keats explains to Reynolds on 3 May 1818, this "knowledge" includes medical science:

Every department of knowledge we see excellent and calculated towards a great whole. I am so convinced of this, that I am glad at not having given away my medical Books, which I shall again look over to keep alive the little I know thitherwards; and moreover intend through you and Rice to become a sort of Pip-civilian. An extensive knowledge is needful to thinking people—it takes away the heat and fever; and helps, by widening speculation, to ease the Burden of the Mystery: a thing I begin to understand a little.   (*Letters* 1:277)

At the same time as Keats was lamenting the lack of philosophic calm in his poetry, with its inherent implication that febrile creativity is unhealthy, he was also complaining to

Bailey about his inability to prevent human suffering, each failure being one side of the same coin since they both depend on "knowledge." He writes:

> How has that unfortunate Family lived through the twelve [days]? One saying of your's I shall never forget . . . merely you said; *"Why should Woman suffer?"* Aye. Why should she? "By heavens I'd coin my very Soul and drop my Blood for Drachmas."! These things are, and he who feels how incompetent the most skyey Knight errantry its [*for* is] to heal this bruised fairness is like a sensitive leaf on the hot hand of thought. (*Letters* 1:209)[60]

The image of the incompetent knight echoes Keats's earliest poems in which he rejected the traditional role of the knight as heroic combatant in favor of the ideal of the knight as compassionate healer. But even this "skyey," idealistic "Knight errantry" cannot prevent all suffering, a lesson the dresser's hospital duty must have taught him only too well.

The passage also emphasizes the abiding strength of Keats's profound concern for suffering humanity, and this altruistic desire becomes an obsession during the summer of 1818. On 9 April he writes to Reynolds that he "would jump down Ætna for any great Public good" (*Letters* 1:267), and on 10 June he discusses with Bailey "the glory of dying for a great human purpose" (*Letters* 1:293). On 27 October, he writes to Woodhouse about "the life I purpose to myself": "I am ambitious of doing the world some good: if I should be spared that may be the work of maturer years—in the interval I will assay to reach as high a summit in Poetry as the nerve bestowed upon me will suffer" (*Letters* 1:387). It is apparent from this statement that poetry is not the highest social good he hopes to accomplish, although he does not state what is higher.

Keats's concern for suffering humanity, in particular the sufferings of women, is revealed again in his letter of 10 June 1818 to Bailey: "How is it that by extreme opposites we have as it were got disconted [*for* discontented] nerves; . . . were it in my choice I would reject a petrarchal coronation—on accou[n]t of my dying day, and because women have Cancers" (*Letters* 1:292). Here Keats associates his melancholia ("nerves") with the diseases of women, a topic he knew well since it was a favorite of Astley Cooper's. As Bransby Cooper states in his biography of his uncle, "It is not a little curious that the subject which Astley Cooper fixed upon for his first professional essay, was malignant disease in the breast, or cancer, a subject which throughout his life continued especially to engage his attention."[61] In his lectures on surgery, Cooper dealt extensively with "Scirrhous Tubercle, or Cancer," with emphasis on breast cancer in women.[62]

During the spring and summer of 1818, Keats's concern for female suffering became so strong that it dominates his next attempt at a narrative poem, *Isabella*, written in March and April of that year. As Hagelman points out, "Keats's medical training apparently provides the basis for part of his approach to the story of Isabella, which in his account is, among other things, a study of madness."[63] I have already outlined that Thomas Guy's will provided for the hospital to "receive and entertain lunatics, adjudged or called, as aforesaid, incurable," and after 1793 the Hospital Committee decided to admit only female lunatics.[64] As Keats was required to treat these women in his capacity as dresser, he had ample opportunity to observe the effects of madness firsthand.

In my chapter on botany, I noted Keats's use of botanical images and metaphors to describe the love between Isabella and Lorenzo, but Hagelman has also observed: "It is significant that Keats, from the very beginning of the poem, presents Isabella and Lorenzo and the relationship between them in terms of death, sickness, and health, and that Keats often describes them and their reactions in general medical terms."[65] As some brief quotations will indicate, many of the symptoms Keats employs to describe the ill health associated with their love, before it is revealed and requited, are the same symptoms of love melancholy he drew on to describe Endymion's diseased state:

> They could not in the self-same mansion dwell
>   Without some stir of heart, some malady;
> They could not sit at meals but feel how well
>   It soothed each to be the other by.   (3–6)

> And with sick longing all the night outwear,
> To hear her morning-step upon the stair.   (23–24)

A whole long month of May in this sad plight
  Made their cheeks paler by the break of June.   (25–26)

Until sweet Isabella's untouch'd cheek
  Fell sick within the rose's just domain,
Fell thin as a young mother's, who doth seek
  By every lull to cool her infant's pain:
"How ill she is," said he, "I may not speak,
  And yet I will, and tell my love all plain."   (33–38)

So said he one fair morning, and all day
  His heart beat awfully against his side;
And to his heart he inwardly did pray
  For power to speak; but still the ruddy tide
Stifled his voice, and puls'd resolve away—
  Fever'd his high conceit of such a bride.   (41–46)

She saw it [Lorenzo's head] waxing very pale and dead,
  And straight all flush'd.   (53–54)

Most of these descriptions of love melancholy are more generalized than those in *Endymion,* but the symptoms of paleness, fever, headache, and restless sleep, for which love is the only cure, are the same and do not need more detailed examination. However, the image of Lorenzo's resolve to speak to Isabella being "puls'd away" by "the ruddy tide" of his pounding blood does warrant comment for its vivid accuracy in depicting a man in a state of such heightened emotion that he cannot speak. It lifts the description of his beating heart beyond mere literary convention and realistically links the organ to the blood and pulse-beat. The physiological effects of the "Violent passions of the Mind"[66] on the body are brilliantly evoked in this brief passage.

The simile comparing the thinness of Isabella's cheek with that of a young mother worried about her infant is also interesting and thematically significant. Not only is the image one that Keats probably saw often at Guy's; it also subtly introduces an aspect of the poem that is often missed: that Isabella's madness is in part a result of thwarted motherhood instincts, a topic to which I will return shortly.[67]

With Lorenzo's and Isabella's revelation of their love for each other, Keats resorts to botanical images to describe the growth of that love; but with Lorenzo's murder he focuses closely on Isabella's gradual decline into insanity and so returns once more to images of disease. After being told that Lorenzo has gone away on business, Isabella "hung / Upon the time with feverish unrest" (243–44) and would have sunk quickly into despondency and death, but her decline is temporarily halted by the appearance of Lorenzo's ghost in a vision:

> And she had died in drowsy ignorance,
>   But for a thing more deadly dark than all;
> It came like a fierce potion, drunk by chance,
>   Which saves a sick man from the feather'd pall
> For some few gasping moments.   (265–69)

Keats compares the effect of the vision on Isabella to that of a powerful drug which gives a terminally sick man a brief reprieve from death. The medicine does not work a cure; it gives only a false hope, which was often the case with drugs in the early nineteenth century, as Keats must have known, both from experience and from the teachings of Astley Cooper, who had a great distrust of many medicines. Some practitioners followed the Italian doctor Giovanni Rasori's much publicized theory of counter-stimuli, which claimed that the larger the dose of medicine, the more successful it will be. When these doctors found, "by chance," a drug that seemed to work, they overdosed the patient and often thus hastened his death through the build-up of poisonous toxins from the drugs themselves, as Howard Haggard points out: "These mineral substances are powerful poisons, and except in the treatment of syphilis their adoption was in reality disadvantageous. Nevertheless, once the physicians began the use of mineral drugs they employed them extensively and in large doses."[68]

Curry also notes that the "Exciting Causes of disease" include "Poisons, —or the effect of violent remedies."[69] The "fierce potion" Keats describes is apparently one of these "violent remedies," and thus the reader knows immediately that Lorenzo's ghost, far from curing Isabella, will lead her further into madness. Once the ghost disappears, her decline begins:

> The Spirit mourn'd "Adieu!"—dissolv'd, and left
>   The atom darkness in a slow turmoil;
> As when of healthful midnight sleep bereft,
>   Thinking on rugged hours and fruitless toil,
> We put out eyes into a pillowy cleft,
>   And see the spangly gloom froth up and boil:
> It made sad Isabella's eyelids ache,
> And in the dawn she started up awake.   (321–28)

This is not only an excellent description of the turmoil of a sleepless night, but also a subtle introduction to the ill health that will plague Isabella, for she immediately awakens and so loses her "healthful midnight sleep." This is in keeping with Keats's knowledge of "all the train of complaints marking Hysteria and Hypochondriasis," which include "headache, . . . temporary absence of mind, —impaired memory; —unrefreshing sleep, —terrific dreams, —unusual timidity, —despondency of mind."[70] Isabella has had just such a "terrific dream" and "unrefreshing sleep," and, once she possesses Lorenzo's head, she slips into a trancelike existence of despondency and weeping in which she forgets everything of normal life (417–24).

At this point in the poem Keats calls upon the goddess "Melancholy" to "linger here awhile" (433), which clarifies finally Isabella's ailment. His use of this rhetorical convention is misleading, however, for what he is describing is not a literary case of fashionable melancholia, but a clinically accurate account of melancholy madness.[71] He was patently aware that Isabella's sighs, despondent breathing, and moans were not due to the influence of the personified figures, Echo, Music, and Melpomene. Rather, her "unusual anxiety, depression of spirits," with its "various, irregular, and often unaccountable sensations and affections," like weeping over a pot of basil and seeing ghosts, is "referred exclusively to the patient's imagination." And as Isabella's melancholia is "caused by . . . strong Mental Impressions," it "terminates in fixed Melancholia,"[72] and finally death.

But what, one may ask, causes Isabella's imagination to become diseased in the first place? Obviously, part of the cause is the "grief, anxiety, and other passions and affections of the mind"[73] that she experiences on discovering Lorenzo's murder. But it is also partly caused by what I have earlier called Isabella's frustrated motherhood instincts. This idea is emphasized by Keats in the image of Lorenzo's head as an egg over which a mother hen broods:

> And when she left, she hurried back, as swift
> As bird on wing to breast its eggs again;
> And, patient as a hen-bird, sat her there
> Beside her basil, weeping through her hair.   (469–72)

It is not a great leap from here to the realization that Isabella's frustrated motherhood is intimately connected with her sexuality, is in fact Keats's decorous way of expressing her sexual frustration. In a similar fashion, he had emphasized the sexual passion of Lorenzo and Isabella through his use of botanical images. With Lorenzo's death, those sexual needs are thwarted, and Keats deliberately links Isabella's frustration to that of motherhood:

> Soon she turn'd up a soiled glove, whereon
> Her silk had play'd in purple phantasies,
> She kiss'd it with a lip more chill than stone,
> And put it in her bosom, where it dries
> And freezes utterly unto the bone
> Those dainties made to still an infant's cries.   (369–74)

Again the language is politely euphemistic, but that does not belie the strong sexual passion—now frustrated—inherent in these images of erotic "phantasies" and maternal breasts. Keats knew very well from his medical training that *"Venus deficiens"*[74] was one of the causes of melancholia, and he obliquely presents it as a contributing factor in Isabella's case. This sexual undertone in the poem, and its relationship to the heroine's madness and death, has not, to my knowledge, been recognized; yet it is apparent that Keats went out of his way to stress it since none of these images is found in Boccaccio's version of the story. Viewed in this light, the poem becomes a very accurate portrayal of a certain kind of madness induced by grief and sexual frustration. If Keats had anything to be ashamed of in the poem, it is the eighteenth-century rhetorical conventions that he has allowed to intrude on his clinical study.

While Keats was writing *Isabella*, he made a trip to Devonshire, where his letters to Reynolds, who had been ill, reveal that he was going through another period of obsession with health. On 14 March 1818 he writes:

> But ah Coward! to talk at this rate to a sick man, or I hope to one that was sick—for I hope by this you stand on your right foot. — If you are not—that's all, —I intend to cut all sick people if they do not make up their minds to cut sickness—a fellow to whom I have a complete aversion, and who strange to say is harboured and countenanced in several houses where I visit.   (*Letters* 1:245)

In the long personification of "sickness" as a personal enemy the tone is jovial, but the passage reveals a serious underlying concern that came to dominate Keats's mind increasingly over the next three years as disease slowly but surely tightened its hold on his life.

The letters from Devon also reveal Keats's concern over the weather and its relationship to health, specifically to moods of melancholia. After complaining to Reynolds about the perpetual rain and mist, Keats continues: "This devonshire is like Lydia Languish, very entertaining when at smiles, but cursedly subject to sympathetic moisture" (*Letters* 1:245). The reference is to the melancholic heroine of Sheridan's *The Rivals*. As Keats knew, two of the exciting causes of hypochondriasis, or melancholia, are an "indolent inactive life," as the name "Languish" implies, and a "cold, damp, and variable state of the atmosphere,"[75] exactly the kind of weather they were having in Devon, in which a person is induced into depression by "sympathetic moisture."

Keats explains this again to Reynolds a month later, on 10 April:

> The Climate here weighs us [down] completely—Tom is quite low spirited—It is impossible to live in a country which is continually under hatches—Who would live in the region of Mists, Game Laws indemnity Bills &c when there is such a place as Italy? It is said this England from its Clime produces a Spleen, able to engender the finest Senti-

ment—and covers the whole face of the Isle with Green—so it aught, I'm sure.   (*Letters* 1:269)[76]

Instead of describing the country as melancholic, Keats now reveals the effects of the weather on himself and Tom. It was a commonly accepted medical opinion that the spleen "is more frequent in England than in any other country,"[77] a result, it was believed, of the climate. Exactly how the weather affects health was not fully understood, however, as Babington and Curry explain: "Perhaps the particular *electric* state of atmosphere, as connected with nervous or Galvanic influence, may have considerable power in occasioning healthy or morbid effects from atmosphere: — . . . Accurate register of such changes connected with history of the season and prevailing diseases, still wanting."[78] This theory was based on the belief that subtle fluids in the atmosphere sympathetically influenced subtle fluids in the nervous system, and since melancholy was a nervous disorder, it was particularly affected by the weather. Keats does not go into the details of this theory, but his refrence to "sympathetic moisture" in discussing Lydia Languish indicates his knowledge of it.

A brief comment at the end of one of these letters to Reynolds illustrates Keats's realization that the weather, by influencing his nervous condition, also influences his poetic creativity: "the Girls over at the Bonnet shop say we shall now have a Month of seasonable Weather. warm, witty, and full of invention" (*Letters* 1:246). Creativity can occur only when the weather is fine, which means that his imagination is in a healthy state, rid of its moods of melancholic depression. As Keats tells his sister the following spring: "O there is nothing like fine weather, and health, and Books, and a fine country, and a contented Mind, and Diligent-habit of reading and thinking, and an amulet against the ennui" (*Letters* 2:56).[79] Later, in February 1819, when he finds difficulty in writing poetry, he tells George and Georgiana that "I must wait for the sp[r]ing to rouse me up a little" (*Letters* 2:62).

Throughout the spring of 1818, however, with the announcement of George and Georgiana's plan to emigrate to America, Keats became increasingly depressed and experienced his black

197

moods of melancholy more often, as he explains to Bailey on 21 and 25 May:

> I have this morning such a Lethargy that I cannot write—the reason of my delaying is oftentimes from this feeling—I wait for a proper temper— . . . I am now so depressed that I have not an Idea to put to paper—my hand feels like lead—and yet it is and [*for* an] unpleasant numbness it does not take away the pain of existence—I don't know what to write—Monday— . . . even now I have but a confused idea of what I should be about my intellect must be in a degen[er]ating state—it must be for when I should be writing about god knows what I am troubling you with Moods of my own Mind or rather body.
>
> (*Letters* 1:287)

Here Keats again describes the symptoms of nervous disorder caused by "depressing passions" of the mind: "general languor and lassitude; —loss of appetite; —dullness and confusion of thought; —sadness of mind, and dejection of countenance; . . . these often continuing for several days without confinement."[80] The direct cause of this debility is the prospect of definitely losing George to America and of possibly losing Tom to tuberculosis. In this diseased state of "uneasy indolence," he cannot create at all, cannot even compose a letter; yet the very act of writing is therapeutic, if unconsiously so, for by the end of the letter he is punning and joking once more.

In order to lift himself out of this depression, during the summer of 1818 Keats accompanied Brown on a walking tour of Scotland, having apparently recognized, like Burton and others before him, that travel is a cure for melancholia. To some extent his plan worked, and he reveled in the beauty of the Lake District and Scotland; but when he visited places associated with Burns his black moods returned, as he explains in a sonnet "On Visiting the Tomb of Burns":

> The town, the churchyard, and the setting sun,
>   The clouds, the trees, the rounded hills all seem,
>   Though beautiful, cold—strange—as in a dream
> I dreamed long ago. Now new begun,
> The short-lived, paly summer is but won
>   From winter's ague, for one hour's gleam;

> Though saphire warm, their stars do never beam;
> All is cold beauty; pain is never done
> For who has mind to relish, Minos-wise,
>   The real of beauty, free from that dead hue
>   Sickly imagination and sick pride
> Cast wan upon it! Burns! with honour due
> I have oft honoured thee. Great shadow, hide
> Thy face—I sin against thy native skies.

"Winter's ague," both the season itself and the horrible moods of depression Keats suffered during the previous winter, are over, and he is desperately trying to lift his spirits in this new season of growth, in this beautiful countryside. But the summer itself is pale and sickly, its beauty "cold." Keats knows, of course, that this metaphorical "Cold Pastoral" is really the creation of his own "Sickly imagination and sick pride," which deadens everything it sees. While it is itself diseased, the imagination cannot serve the creative function of ministering to the health of the poet, and consequently will not allow him to minister to the health of his society.

Keats's depression on seeing the tomb of Burns was not due to the scenery itself, but to the memories it conjured up of Burns's life. In Burns's frustration and misery, Keats envisioned his own fate, that of the unsuccessful poet, and his horror at this prospect debilitated his creative potential. Keats attempts to exorcise his feelings about the late poet in a longer poem, "There is a joy in footing slow across a silent plain," written on 18 July. Even here, however, he cannot stifle his contemplation of melancholy madness:

> Aye, if a madman could have leave to pass a healthful day,
> To tell his forehead's swoon and faint when first began decay,
> He might make tremble many a man whose spirit had gone forth
> To find a bard's low cradle place about the silent north.   (25–28)

As Caldwell observes, the poem is "heavy with a melancholy not toned and modulated to deliberate effect, but welling up through the lines and submerging them in unintended channels of foreboding."[81] As if afraid of what he has created and of his own madness, which looms beneath the surface of the poem, Keats ends with "a prayer / That man may never lose his mind on mountains bleak and bare" (45–46).

At the same time as he was so concerned about his mental health, Keats was also worried about his physical well-being. On 22 July he tells Bailey that "I shall be prudent and more careful of my health than I have beeen [*sic*]," and he advises his friend, "Now you are so well in health do keep it up by never missing your dinner, by not reading hard and by taking proper exercise" (*Letters* 1:343).[82] This is excellent medical advice for, as Keats knew, the "Exciting Causes of disease" include "Sedentary life; —intense study, . . . Improper diet."[83] Unfortunately, Keats did not follow his own advice, and a cold and sore throat forced him to return to London from Scotland only to find Tom gravely ill.

While nursing Tom, Keats could not help but identify with his brother's suffering, and this became so intense that poetry was his only relief, albeit one he describes as a fever:

His [Tom's] identity presses upon me so all day that I am obliged to go out—and although I intended to have given some time to study alone I am obliged to write, and plunge into abstract images to ease myself of his countenance his voice and feebleness—so that I live now in a continual fever—it must be poisonous to life although I feel well. Imagine 'the hateful seige of contraries'—if I think of fame of poetry it seems a crime to me, and yet I must do so or suffer— . . . after all it may be a nervousness proceeding from the Mercury.
(*Letters* 1:369)

This he wrote to Dilke on 21 September; the following day he wrote to Reynolds:

I never was in love—Yet the voice and the shape of a woman has haunted me these two days—at such a time when the relief, the feverous relief of Poetry seems a much less crime—This morning Poetry has conquered—I have relapsed into those abstractions which are my only life—I feel escaped from a new strange and threatening sorrow. —And I am thankful for it—There is an awful warmth about my heart like a load of Immortality.
(*Letters* 1:370)

In these two letters Keats introduces an important medical metaphor that helps him to explain the phenomenon of poetic creativity. He describes the creative act as a frenzied fever, a fit that brings relief from his nervous moods of depression. The fever of creativity is, in fact, the antithesis of that "uneasy indolence" in which his "sensations are sometimes deadened for weeks together" (*Letters* 1:325). In the fever fit he is alert to the point of frenzy, and yet ironically it is a relief as he leaves his present ills and finds refuge in the world of "abstractions."

Whether Keats himself was developing tuberculosis by this time and was experiencing the *spes phthisica* of the consumptive is uncertain.[84] I have little doubt, however, that he believed he had contracted the disease by then. After all, he had been taught by Babington and Curry that the exciting causes of *phthisis pulmonalis* include "sudden variation of temperature; neglect of covering the breast and neck; . . . Frequent over-exertion"; and "inhaling the breath of persons in the advanced stage of phthisis" was discussed as a possible cause. The first sign of the disease is a "cough, either frequent, and teazing, or occasional and severe."[85] During the variable weather in Scotland, Keats had been soaked on numerous occasions, had overexerted himself by very long walks, and had developed a bad cough that forced him to return home, where he nursed the consumptive Tom in stifling, almost claustrophobic, conditions. Moreover, Babington and Curry warned that the "slightest symptoms [are] alarming, where hereditary tendency traceable."[86] Keats had already lost his mother to the disease and now saw his brother dying of it; he must have felt that the possibility of his having contracted it was great. Furthermore, the fact that he was taking mercury for medicinal purposes at this time may have compounded Keats's worries, for he admits that his nervous condition may be a result of the drug.

Exactly why Keats had begun to treat himself with a "little Mercury" from as early as October 1817[87] is a highly debatable topic, concerned with the larger biographical question of whether or not he had contracted venereal disease during or shortly before his stay with Bailey at Oxford in 1817. Lowell was the first to suggest, and refute, the hypothesis that Keats was suffering from syphilis; subsequent refutations come from Hewlett and Bate; but Ward supports the syphilis theory as probable.[88] Gittings, who treats the topic in detail, postulates that Keats was suffering, not from syphilis, but from gonorrhea, founding his argument on the claim that many doctors in the early nineteenth century—including Solomon Sawrey who Gittings believes was Keats's doctor at the time—prescribed mercury only for venereal diseases and then in small doses only for gonorrhea.[89] However, in an excellent article, C. T. Andrews has since shown that we cannot prove Sawrey was treating Keats in late 1817; that although mercury was being used more cautiously by physicians, it was still being prescribed for a variety of diseases, especially by James Curry who wrote an *Examination of the Prejudices Commonly Entertained Against Mercury* (London, 1802) in defense of the drug; and that Astley Cooper was vehemently opposed to the use of mercury as a cure for gonorrhea, although he did prescribe it sparingly for some other ailments, including tonsillitis. Though not entirely ruling out the possibility that Keats had contracted venereal disease, Andrews demonstrates that "the evidence available so far does not support a diagnosis of venereal disease" and sensibly suggests that "judgment on this issue be suspended unless and until new facts emerge."[90]

We cannot be certain why Keats was taking mercury during 1817 and 1818, but we can be sure that he suspected his febrile state might have resulted from the drug, as he tells Dilke. Astley Cooper had warned his pupils, including Keats, not only that mercury was useless in the treatment of gonorrhea, but also that it lowered the patient's resistance, thus exposing him to other ailments. As Waddington notes: "One of the most common cause of Inflammation in the Periosteum, is the injudicious use of Mercury, for instance if a Person silly enough to take Mercury for a Clap [gonorrhea], when no Mercury is required, & after exposes himself to cold, then the result is often an Inflammation of the Periosteum."[91] Moreover, Babington and Curry had in their lectures dealt with "Mercurial Irritation" as an "exciting cause" in the development of *phthisis pulmonalis*.[92] In light of this, Keats must have been suspicious, if not certain, that he had enhanced the possibility of contracting tuberculosis by taking mercury while nursing Tom. Submerged concern—perhaps even guilt—over this situation seems to surface momentarily in his speculation that his "continual fever" "may be a nervousness proceeding from the Mercury." Keats must have suspected that his generally impaired health was a sign of tubercular infection, and that he had perhaps contributed to its cause by an "injudicious use of Mercury."

More to my point, however, is the fact that the fever fits of poetic creativity Keats describes in these two letters, to Dilke and Reynolds, sound remarkably like "the stimulation of mental activity," or *spes phthisica*, that many consumptives experience with "the depletion of physical energy."[93] Dr. Charles Mayo states: "Victims of chronic tuberculosis have learned the significance of unusual vitality and vigor that often precedes increase in cough, slight fever and another bout with the enemy." D. G. Macleod observes that consumptives "live in an atmosphere of feverish eagerness . . . particularly noticeable in those of naturally artistic or literary tastes,"[94] which is a very apt description of Keats's bouts of creativity.

It is probable, then, that this type of tubercular, feverish activity had begun for Keats in late 1818, and it is significant that throughout 1819 and 1820 he continues to describe poetic creativity in terms of the fever metaphor. It is also significant that in the single year 1819, the period in which the disease was progressing, Keats produced his most prodigious outburst of excellent poetry. Novalis, who died of tuberculosis, may well be correct in saying that "the disease consists probably of the most interesting products and stimuli of our thoughts and activities."[95]

There is no doubt that Keats needed these fever fits to create poetry and to relieve him from melancholic depression.[96] As a number of quotations from his letters during 1819 and 1820 illustrate, these periods of frenzied creativity alternated with the dark moods of melancholia in which he felt lifeless, pessimistic, and uncreative.

On 18 December 1818, while nursing Tom, Keats writes to George and Georgiana: "I am passing a Quiet day—which I have not done a long while—and if I do continue so—I feel I must again begin with my poetry—for if I am not in action mind or Body I am in pain" (*Letters* 2:12). He had in fact already begun work on *Hyperion*, but in January 1819 he writes to Haydon, who had been asking him for money:

The Poet-Physician

I have been writing a little now and then lately: but nothing to speak off—being discontented and as it were moulting—yet I do not think I shall ever come to the rope or the Pistol: for after a day or two's melancholy, although I smoke more and more my own insufficiency—I see by little and little more of what is to be done, and how it is to be done, should I ever be able to do it—On my Soul there should be some reward for that continual "agonie ennuiyeuse." (*Letters* 2:32)

Keats is beginning to recognize the value of these noncreative periods as times to brood and reflect even if his thoughts are often morbid. At times, however, they lead to total incapacitation, as he explains to George and Georgiana on 17 March: "There is a great difference between an easy and an uneasy indolence—An indolent day—fill'd with speculations even of an unpleasant colour—is bearable and even pleasant alone— . . . but to have nothing to do, and to be surrounded with unpleasant human identities; who press upon one just enough to prevent one getting into a lazy position; and not enough to interest or rouze one; is a capital punishment of a capital crime" (*Letters* 2:77).

"Easy indolence," or what Keats elsewhere calls "diligent indolence," is a state of passive but alert receptivity to sensations which lead to speculations and associations, and finally to creativity. In contrast, "uneasy indolence" is an unhealthy, depressed state of mental and physical torpor, complete lifelessness, in which no creativity can go forward.

Interestingly, two days later Keats describes what appears to be a third kind of indolence in his journal letter to George and Georgiana. After being hit in the eye with a cricket ball, he was probably given a dose of opium by Brown,[97] and he describes what may be the aftereffects of the drug:

This morning I am in a sort of temper indolent and supremely careless: I long after a stanza or two of Thompson's Castle of indolence— My passions are all alseep from my having slumbered till nearly eleven and weakened the animal fibre all over me to a delightful sensation about three degrees on this side of faintness—if I had teeth of pearl and the breath of lillies I should call it langour—but as I am I must call it Laziness—In this state of effeminacy the fibres of the brain are relaxed in common with the rest of the body, and to such a happy degree that pleasure has no show of enticement and pain no unbearable frown.   (*Letters* 2:78–79)

Keats knew that in cases of "inflammation excited by *external stimulus*," like his injury from the cricket ball, the *"first* effect of over-stimulus on muscular fibre [is] *excessive contraction"*; but the *"second* effect [is] proportional *fatigue,* and *relaxation,"*[98] with the muscle fibers relaxed. This is precisely the effect he describes in this letter, his relaxed brain fibers resulting in pleasant languor or indolence, and he describes it in the medical terms with which he is so familiar. Even when he outlines this mood in the "Ode on Indolence," he defines it in vaguely medical images:

> The blissful cloud of summer-indolence
> Benumb'd my eyes; my pulse grew less and less;
> Pain had no sting, and pleasure's wreath no flower. (16–18)

Salisbury says "a weak languid pulse" is one of the aftereffects of opium, and Ober points out that the slowed motion and the absence of pleasure and pain described in the passage are "similar to the known effects of opium."[99] It would appear, then, that this state of indolence is drug-induced.

Just as there are two—or possibly three—kinds of indolence for Keats, so there are also two types of fever. That he uses the metaphor of fever in a double-edged fashion becomes clear in a letter of 1 May 1819 to Haydon, who was still pestering him for money: "Now you have maimed me again; I was whole I had began reading again—when your note came I was engaged in a Book—I dread as much as a Plague the idle fever of two months more without any fruit" (*Letters* 2:55). As Louisa Camaiora explains in her very perceptive study of Keats's "idle fever": "In this negative aspect the activity is destructive of inspiration and creativity; it is a fever in the literal sense, an illness that burns and consumes and leaves nothing behind except tension, fear and anxiety. . . . Essentially, this negative mood in Keats seems a question of misdirected energy, an energy which is self-consuming and which results in a burning up of resources."[100] This mood of "idle fever" seems to have been a direct result of the nervous tension that built up in

Keats during his brooding periods of melancholia, when dark thoughts led to pessimism, lethargy, and a stifling of creativity. Just as "uneasy indolence" is the opposite of the "diligent indolence" of imaginative activity, so "idle fever" is the antithesis of the fever of intellectual ferment I outlined earlier. By tracing these alternating moods in Keats's letters during 1819 and 1820, we can ascertain the periods of creative thought in which he wrestled with aesthetic and philosophical problems.

By the end of May 1819, Keats had emerged from his "idle fever" and was back into the energetic mood of creative fever. He writes to Sarah Jeffrey on 31 May:

I have the choice as it were of two Poisons (yet I ought not to call this a Poison) the one is voyaging to and from India for a few years; the other is leading a fevrous life alone with Poetry—This latter will suit me best— . . . yes, I would rather conquer my indolence and strain my ne[r]ves at some grand Poem— . . . I must choose between despair & Energy—I choose the latter—though the world has taken on a quakerish look with me, which I once thought was impossible—
   "Nothing can bring back the hour
   Of splendour in the grass and glory in the flower"
I once thought this a Melancholist's dream.   (*Letters* 2:112–13)

Despite his generally melancholic outlook, he is determined to conquer despair and "uneasy indolence" with energy and creative fever; he refuses to sink into depression.

Within the next week, however, Keats was once more contemplating the ill-treatment of English poets by the public—a topic with extremely personal connotations—so that he writes to Sarah Jeffrey on 9 June: "I have been very idle lately, very averse to writing; both from the overpowering idea of our dead poets and from abatement of my love of fame" (*Letters* 2:116). But by the middle of August, after a depressing stay on the Isle of Wight with Rice, who was ill, he tells Fanny Brawne that he is once more "in complete cue—in the fever; and shall in these four Months do an immense deal" (*Letters* 2:141). This ability to rouse himself to the fever pitch of creativity in order to overcome melancholia became his saving grace.

There is no single explanation for Keats's manic swings between melancholic depression and fever-pitch activity. The depression was to some extent related to very real tragedies that occurred between the end of 1818 and his own death in 1821: Tom's illness and death, the illnesses of various friends, his own diseased state, his lack of public success as a poet, and his poor financial situation. Undoubtedly, his medical knowledge of consumption made the lingering horror of the disease ever more real to him, even if, as I have speculated, it helped to stimulate his moods of feverish creativity. Despite his doctors' insistence that his disease was mental and emotional (*Letters* 2:287–88), Keats must have recognized his fever (*Letters* 2:252), his loss of weight (*Letters* 2:271), his overall weakness and debility, and his cough as the symptoms of phthisis outlined by Babington and Curry:

Cough, hectic fever, . . . accompanied with general emaciation and debility, —and succeeded by colliquative sweats ... . Cough, either frequent, and teazing, or occasional and severe . . . with expectoration of tough phlegm, blackish mucus, or of puriform matter, sometimes streaked with blood . . . Skin in general dry and hot, . . . a regular febrile paroxysm morning and evening, . . . decay of the bodily functions shewn by, —gradual loss of flesh and strength.[101]

If Keats needed any further confirmation of his consumption, he got it on 3 February 1820 in the form of a lung hemorrhage that resulted in blood-spitting. According to Brown, who was present at the time, Keats calmly said: "That blood is from my mouth. . . . Bring me the candle, Brown; and let me see this blood. . . . I know the colour of that blood; —it is arterial blood; —I cannot be deceived in that colour; —that drop of blood is my death-warrant; —I must die."[102] This lucid prognosis was to prove only too correct, despite the obtuse insistence by his physicians and friends that his disease was entirely mental.[103]

During 1820 Keats became obsessed with the subject of health, so that medical advice pervades his letters, particularly those to women. He tells his sister to "be careful always to wear warm cloathing not only in frost but in a Thaw— . . . Whenever you have an inflamatory fever never mind about eating" (*Letters* 2:252). He advises Fanny Brawne to "be very careful of open doors and windows and going without your duffle grey" (*Letters* 2:262), tells Dilke to keep Mrs. Dilke indoors as "it is better to run no chance of a supernumery cold in March" (*Letters* 2:271), and gives similar alarming advice to Reynolds (*Letters* 2:267).

As well as his concern for health, Keats's melancholic depressions during 1819–20 were also heavily influenced by his love for Fanny Brawne, which became his absorbing passion. It was a strange relationship between a warm and genuine, if inexperienced, girl and a man torn by his desire to be alone with poetry on the one hand and to marry the woman he loved on the other. Furthermore, Keats's view of love was warped, during 1819, by his reading of Burton who, in *The Anatomy of Melancholy*, took a cynical, moralizing view of human passion,[104] a view that Keats ultimately could not reconcile with his own feelings. Yet, following Burton, he blamed his love of Fanny at least partially for his melancholia. On 1 July 1819 he writes to her: "I have never known any unalloy'd Happiness for many days together: the death or sickness of some one has always spoilt my hours—and now when none such troubles oppress me, it is you must confess very hard that another sort of pain should haunt me. Ask yourself my love whether you are not very cruel to have so entrammelled me, so destroyed my freedom" (*Letters* 2:123). In his most exalted moods of love melancholy, he dreams of possessing Fanny and dying in the same instant, so intense is his morbid desire (*Letters* 2:133). And in the "Ode on a Grecian Urn," he describes human passion as a disease "That leaves a heart high-sorrowful and cloy'd, / A burning forehead, and a parching tongue" (29–30), in what is yet another variation on the fever metaphor, perhaps adapted from observation of Tom's tubercular fever.

Paradoxically, although he viewed love as a fever, Keats came more and more to think of Fanny as the only physician who could cure his disease. On 15 July 1819 he tells her: "Now you could quite effect a cure: What fee my sweet Physician would I not give you to do so" (*Letters* 2:129); in February 1820 he writes, "If well you are the only medicine that can keep me so" (2:264). Caught in his own moods of melancholy, he sees Fanny as both his killer and his physician, his disease and his cure, as he swings between intense jealousy and hopeless love.

Even as late as February 1820, in the ode "To Fanny," Keats harangues her for causing him jealousy, which he portrays in a canceled draft of the ode as "My temples with hot jealous pulses beat."[105] In order to relieve this sanguineous pressure, he cries out: "Physician Nature! let my spirit blood! / O ease my heart of verse and let me rest" (1–2). Benjamin Ward Richardson has pointed out that this appeal is written "in the precise medical tone of a time when 'let the patient blood' was as much a technical command in medicine as 'right about face' is still a command in military drill."[106] Bloodletting by venesection was an extremely common treatment for various ailments, and Keats would have been required to perform this operation from the time he was an apprentice at Hammond's. More recently, venesection had been performed on him after his lung hemorrhage on 3 February,[107] which probably accounts for his using the concept in this poem. The operation was designed to relieve pressure on the cardiovascular system, which is how Keats employs it in these lines, although he makes a neat transition from treating the heart as a physical organ to treating it as the metaphorical seat of love.

The Keats-Fanny relationship need not detain us further, but it does demonstrate that adverse financial circumstances and illness were not the sole causes of the poet's melancholia. As he himself knew, "a horrid Morbidity of Temperament" had always been a part of his personality, and he openly admits to Brown that "imaginary grievances have always been more my torment than real ones. You know this well. Real ones will never have any other effect upon me than to stimulate me to get out of or avoid them. This is easily accounted for. Our imaginary woes are conjured up by our passions, and are fostered by passionate feeling; our real ones come of themselves, and are opposed by an abstract exertion of mind" (*Letters* 2:181). Keats knew from his medical training that the "unaccountable sensations and affections" of melancholia are "referred exclusively to the patient's imagination." It was perhaps his ability to diagnose the source of his own problem that enabled Keats to lift himself out of these bouts of sterility, unrest, worry, and nervous fear of never achieving anything, back into frenzied bouts of creativity. As always, the vitality of the imagination at work remained for him a drug in which to find relief from his diseased moods, even if, ironically, he used the metaphor of "fever," itself a disease, to describe his cure.

The irony of the "fever" metaphor was not missed by Keats himself, however, and he apparently chose his words very carefully. From the first time that he outlines this creative fever, he refers to it as the lesser of two evils, the other being melancholic depression. He claims that he is "obliged to write. . . . Imagine 'the hateful siege of contraries'—if I think of poetry it seems a crime to me, and yet I must do so or suffer" (*Letters* 1:369); he states that "the feverous relief of Poetry seems a much less crime" (*Letters* 1:370) than love for a woman; and he talks of "a fevrous life alone with Poetry" as one of two "Poisons" (*Letters* 2:112–13). The words are those of one who must swallow a bitter medicine in order to cure an even worse disease.

Keats, then, did not enjoy this fevered activity; he always describes it as a "relief" that is in itself painful. As he tells Rice on 14 February 1820: "I may say that for 6 Months before I was taken ill I had not passed a tranquil day—Either that gloom overspred me or I was suffering under some passionate feeling, or if I turn'd to versify that acerbated the poison of either sensation" (*Letters* 2:260). "Fever," then, is a metaphorical expression not only of the heat and frenzy of poetic creativity, but also of the pain inherent in the drug; the drug is a poison that may itself destroy the patient.

This love-hate relationship toward poetry is very similar to his attitude toward Fanny, and it is perhaps significant that he conceives of both in terms of disease metaphors. He ultimately felt that his life was being destroyed by the two things he loved most—poetry and Fanny—a feeling that was strengthened both by his medical training and by the advice of his physicians. As he tells his sister in April 1820: "The Doctor [Bree] assures me that there is nothing the matter with me except nervous irritability and a general weakness of the whole system which has proceeded from my anxiety of mind of late years and the too great excitement of poetry" (*Letters* 2:287). Two months earlier, in a letter advising Fanny Brawne not to visit him, he says, "I am recommended not even to read poetry much less write it" (*Letters* 2:257). Although Bree's diagnosis is wrong by modern standards, and has been vigorously attacked by Hale-White,[108] Keats himself was familiar with the diagnosis of many ailments as hypochondriasis or nervous fever, of which some of the causes are "indolent inactive life, —intense study," and, possibly, excessive passion.[109] Given these beliefs and his melancholic temperament, it is not surprising that in bouts of desperation he clung to the hope that he had not contracted tuberculosis, even though I am convinced that he knew he had the disease and in more stable, lucid moments correctly contradicted his doctors (*Letters* 2:264, 265). The point to be emphasized, however, is that his medical training enabled Keats to conceive of both poetic exertion and venereal passion as causes of nervous disease; he develops these causes into metaphorical equivalents of the disease itself, so that poetry and Fanny become his sickness.

But to return for a moment to the metaphor of creativity as a fever: Keats never enjoyed this kind of febrile fit, as I have illustrated, and throughout 1819 he sought to escape this painful creativity by spending more time on study, thought, and reflection. He believed that this would give him the knowledge and the philosophical calm to compose poems in a peaceful frame of mind, which he appropriately labels "healthful" as opposed to "feverous."[110] He felt that he achieved this kind of composition in the "Ode to Psyche," which he tells George and Georgiana he had "done leisurely—I think it reads the more richly for it and will I hope encourage me to write other thing[s] in even a more peacable and healthy spirit" (*Letters* 2:106).

On 11 July 1819 he explains to Reynolds this new approach to life and poetry:

However I sho^d like to enjoy what the competences of life procure, I am in no wise dashed at a different prospect. I have spent too many thoughtful days & moralized thro' too many nights for that, and fruitless wo^d they be indeed, if they did not by degrees make me look upon the affairs of the world with a healthy deliberation. I have of late been moulting: not for fresh feathers & wings: they are gone, and in their stead I hope to have a pair of patient sublunary legs.

(*Letters* 2:128)

The Poet-Physician

The desire for a new, "healthy deliberation" is not simply a self-centered hope for a calmer life, but also a moral and ethical attempt to leave behind the imaginary world of escapist poetry, symbolized here by wings, and to come to terms with the realities, the pain, the suffering of life in the sublunary world. Keats realizes that, in order to become the poet-physician of society, he must first heal his own spirit of its violent vacillations between depression and fevered poetic trances. He must learn to accept with calm and patience the whole of life if he is to come to terms with it at all.

Keats's desire for "healthy deliberation" is very closely linked to his need for knowledge of every kind, or what he calls "philosophy." He knows that gaining such knowledge will not be easy, but he never loses sight of it as his ultimate goal. On 21 September 1819 he writes to his brother and sister-in-law:

Some think I have lost that poetic ardour and fire 't is said I once had—the fact is perhaps I have: but instead of that I hope I shall substitute a more thoughful and quiet power. I am more frequently, now, contented to read and think—but now & then, haunted with ambitious thoughts. Qui[e]ter in my pulse, improved in my digestion; exerting myself against vexing speculations—scarcely content to write the best verses for the fever they leave behind. I want to compose without this fever. I hope I one day shall.   (*Letters* 2:209)

It is only natural that, as one trained to think of the body in terms of health and disease, Keats should conceive of the mind and spirit in the same way. He is constantly aware of the effect the mind has on the body, so his healthier mental state results in a quieter pulse and improved digestion.[111] He wants to maintain this state of harmony, of balance, and so seeks to compose poetry of a more thoughtful nature, without the fevered fire of wild sensations.

The whole problem of facing life with a "healthy deliberation" born of philosophical "knowledge," and of escaping the extremes of fevered activity or diseased depression, becomes the central theme of the two *Hyperion*s. Thus, although they are not concerned with medical themes in a strict or narrow sense, they do deal with the broad subject of a healthy or balanced life—a concept Keats developed from his medical training—both for the society and for the poet, and so deserve close analysis within the general context of Keats's medical knowledge.

Hyperion was begun in late autumn 1818, when Keats was nursing Tom, and finally abandoned in April 1819, perhaps because Keats himself had failed to achieve, for reasons I have outlined, the state of mental health he intended for his protagonist. From the very opening lines of the poem the metaphor of health strikes a keynote:

> Deep in the shady sadness of a vale
> Far sunken from the healthy breath of morn,
> Far from the fiery noon, and eve's one star,
> Sat gray-hair'd Saturn.   (I, 1–4)

Both the stifling, claustrophobic, "deadened" (I, 11) valley in which Saturn sits and the diseased state of the god himself—"His old right hand lay nerveless, listless, dead" (I, 18)—are external manifestations, reflections, of his spiritual state of sterility. When he speaks, it is "As with a palsied tongue, and while his beard / Shook horrid with such aspen-malady" (I, 93–94). The images of disease are abundant and deliberate, for Keats is describing, with his usual accuracy, a man caught in the throes of an illness that he cannot comprehend.

Saturn is similar to Endymion at the beginning of the earlier narrative, but Keats no longer employs the symptoms of love melancholy to create his metaphor because love melancholy is a specific, personal ailment with a specific, personal cure; consequently, it lends itself to narrative treatment involving the growth and development of an individual. The very ailment necessitates a love story that concludes either in personal tragedy or in fulfillment, as was the case in *Endymion,* even though in the final analysis Keats makes Endymion responsible for the health of his society. In *Hyperion,* he portrays the illness of a whole society that has gone awry, and to this end he uses more generalized pathological images with symptoms adapted from various illnesses. Consequently, the reader cannot identify any specific disease that plagues Saturn and the other Titans; rather, Keats wants us to recognize their fallen state as

213

one of sickness, the psychological nature of which he gradually reveals.

Just as Endymion, in his illness, turned to Peona for help, so Saturn turns to Thea, Hyperion's wife, for comfort, and we are introduced to another variation of Keats's female nurse:

> It seem'd no force could wake him from his place;
> But there came one, who with a kindred hand
> Touch'd his wide shoulders, after bending low
> With reverence, though to one who knew it not.
> . . . .
> One hand she press'd upon that aching spot
> Where beats the human heart, as if just there,
> Though an immortal, she felt cruel pain:
> The other upon Saturn's bended neck
> She laid, and to the level of his ear
> Leaning with parted lips, some words she spake
> In solemn tenour and deep organ tone.   (I, 22–25, 42–48)

Unlike Peona, however, Thea cannot offer Saturn comfort, much less a cure; she can only tell him what he really needs to hear if he is to cure himself, "the monstrous truth" (I, 65):

> heaven is parted from thee, and the earth
> Knows thee not, thus afflicted, for a God;
> And ocean too, with all its solemn noise,
> Has from thy sceptre pass'd; and all the air
> Is emptied of thine hoary majesty.   (I, 55–59)

Thea sees with remarkable clarity the predicament of the Titans: their reign is over, their power lost, and so they must come to terms with reality. But Saturn refuses to acknowledge this, and his response to Thea's statements is a series of questions that reveal his bewilderment at the change that has overcome him, symbolized by his illness. He has lost his identity, but the questions concerning this loss themselves reveal the root of his problem, for instead of accepting his state with a "healthy deliberation" that is akin to negative capability, he insists on "seeking after fact & reason." As he later tells the Titans,

> not in that strife,
> Wherefrom I take strange lore, and read it deep,
> Can I find reason why ye should be thus:

> No, no-where can unriddle, though I search,
> And pore on Nature's universal scroll
> Even to swooning, why ye, Divinities,
> The first-born of all shap'd and palpable Gods,
> Should cower beneath what, in comparison,
> Is untremendous might.   (II, 147–55)

It is significant that the Olympians have "untremendous might," for Keats's new gods will be healers rather than warriors like the Titans.

In searching for "reason," as Oceanus later tells him, Saturn misses the truth—knowledge gained of experience. That Saturn has not understood the truth of Thea's revelations is shown in the descriptions of him after Thea has given her cold comfort:

> This passion lifted him upon his feet,
> And made his hands to struggle in the air,
> His Druid locks to shake and ooze with sweat,
> His eyes to fever out, his voice to cease.
> He stood, and heard not Thea's sobbing deep;
> A little time, and then again he snatch'd
> Utterance thus. —"But cannot I create?
> Cannot I form?"   (I, 135–42)

The images of disease, with the symptoms of chills, sweating, burning eyes, parched tongue, and impaired hearing, adapted from Keats's knowledge of fever,[112] are the metaphorical equivalent of Saturn's mental confusion. As Keats knew only too well, the symptoms of such fever could literally be caused by the mind, which controls the nervous system. Curry points out that not only is mental judgment impaired by fever, but also there are "striking instances of the effects produced by Anger" on the body.[113]

It is also important to recognize that Keats gives precisely the opposite description of Oceanus before he addresses the Titans: Oceanus

> Arose, with locks not oozy, and began,
> In murmurs, which his first-endeavouring tongue
> Caught infant-like from the far-foamed sands. (II, 170–72)

That Oceanus does not sweat, and that his tongue is not parched, indicate that he does not suffer from fever, that in fact he is in a state of mental health which results in his excellent speech. He tells the Titans that they must find their comfort in the acceptance of truth, "for to bear all naked truths, / And to envisage circumstance, all calm, / That is the top of sovereignty" (II, 203–05).

Saturn's impassioned questions—"But cannot I create? / Cannot I form?"—finally bring into focus Keats's adaptation of the god as another variation of the poet figure, similar to Endymion. On a personal level, Saturn cannot create because his mind—in particular, his imagination—is diseased, in a state of fevered turmoil that thwarts creativity. True creativity, Keats now believes, demands calm thought, "healthy deliberation," leading to broad knowledge and understanding of life. On a wider social level, Saturn, like Endymion before him, has lost the ability to administer to the health of his society, which for Keats is the ultimate task of the poet. And where the social drama was vastly overshadowed by the personal drama in *Endymion*, here Keats brings it to the fore so that it dominates the poem, especially Book II.

The description of the rest of the fallen Titans at the beginning of Book II is based, if not on specific morbid symptoms, at least to some extent on what Keats saw in the wards at Guy's Hospital: pain, suffering, anger, and bewilderment in the face of personal tragedy. The description paints a vivid picture of a mixture of physical and mental suffering:

> Dugeon'd in opaque element, to keep
> Their clenched teeth still clench'd, and all their limbs
> Lock'd up like veins of metal, crampt and screw'd;
> Without a motion, save of their big hearts
> Heaving in pain, and horribly convuls'd
> With sanguine feverous boiling gurge of pulse.
> . . . .
> Next Cottus: prone he lay, chin uppermost,
> As though in pain; for still upon the flint
> He ground severe his skull, with open mouth
> And eyes at horrid working.
> . . . .
> As with us mortal men, the laden heart
> Is persecuted more, and fever'd more,

When it is nighing to the mournful house
Where other hearts are sick of the same bruise;
So Saturn, as he walk'd into the midst,
Felt faint.   (II, 23–28, 49–52, 101–06)

This last simile is built, no doubt, on frequent observation.

As Keats points out, the morbid state is a result of mental and emotional strain rather than physical causes. In Saturn's face, Thea saw

the supreme God
At war with all the frailty of grief,
Of rage, of fear, anxiety, revenge,
Remorse, spleen, hope, but most of all despair. (II, 92–95)

Despair, with which Keats was so familiar himself, thwarts all creativity, deadens and destroys. In fact, the Titans as a whole vacillate between the very two extremes, of fevered activity and despairing melancholy—"in alternate uproar and sad peace" (III, 1)—that Keats has been caught between during the months of composition, as I have outlined from his letters. In the arguments of the Titans, Keats is defining the very problems and questions he faces as a poet: How does one create "without the fever"? How does one gain the philosophical calm to see life steadily and whole? And how does one move beyond personal concerns to heal the society at large? The fact that Keats is articulating these problems is evidence that he is moving toward a solution, and in Book III he begins to describe his ideal poet, Apollo.

Before examining the figure of Apollo, however, we should look briefly at his predecessor, Hyperion. Even though he remains the one unfallen Titan, Hyperion does not escape the pain, suffering, and melancholia of the others: "But horrors, portion'd to a giant nerve, / Oft made Hyperion ache" (I, 175–76). Again, mental anguish is described in physiological terms.

Like the rest of the Titans, on discovering what has happened, Hyperion gravitates first toward fiery wrath— manifested in his "flaming robes," his "fiery steeds," his blood-colored palace—and then toward melancholic depression: "Instead of sweets, his ample palate took / Savour of poisonous brass and metal sick" (I, 188–89). He cannot sleep, a symptom of melancholia, because he is plagued with "effigies of pain" (I, 228), which, appropriately, are figments of his own diseased imagination. In his selfish desire to escape the fall, he seeks to banish these figments of pain and horror. Like Endymion before him, he seeks to hold permanently the world of immortal beauty in which he dwells. He cannot balance the worlds of beauty and pain, of immortality and mortality; he cannot appreciate "the agonies, the strife / Of human hearts"; and so, within the context of Keats's mythos, he cannot be a genuine poet. Hyperion appreciates only the beauty and so is lost in a haunted world of despondency when that beauty dies:

> "The blaze, the splendor, and the symmetry,
> I cannot see—but darkness, death and darkness.
> Even here, into my centre of repose,
> The shady visions come to domineer,
> Insult, and blind, and stifle up my pomp."   (I, 241–45)

Hyperion represents the kind of escapist poet Keats had once been, but whom he now rejects in favor of the poet of the real world. It is also interesting that the images he chooses to build his simile concerning the phantoms that haunt Hyperion's mind are adapted from the very real world of the hospital:

> For as in theatres of crowded men
> Hubbub increases more they call out "Hush!"
> So at Hyperion's words the Phantoms pale
> Bestirr'd themselves, thrice horrible and cold;
> And from the mirror'd level where he stood
> A mist arose, as from a scummy marsh.   (I, 253–58)

Here Keats has in mind both a playhouse and an operating theater which, as South explains, during operations and demonstrations was filled with pushing, shouting students.[114] The "Phantoms pale . . . thrice horrible and cold" that bestir themselves and arise are perhaps Keats's surrealistic vision of cadavers rising from demonstrating tables. They are accompanied by a marsh mist which attacks Hyperion like a disease or a poison: "At this, through all his bulk an agony / Crept gradual, from the feet unto the crown" (I, 259–60).

No doubt Keats developed this description of the mist, which he compares to a serpent, from Milton's description of Satan entering the serpent's body in *Paradise Lost,* Book IX. But he also has in mind, as indicated by the "scummy marsh" (which is not found in Milton's passage), the vapor of marsh miasmata that causes fever. Babington and Curry explain its medical significance: "Phytoseptic Miasmata or the vapour arising from moist soils impregnated with a quantity of vegetable matter in a state of *septic* decomposition, —the *essential cause* of both Intermitting and Remitting Fevers."[115] Hyperion tries to clear these "heavy vapours" (I, 267) that bring disease by releasing the sun, but he fails and is left in agony as the marsh mist rises around him. Keats's images are not, then, random imaginings; they allude to a cause of fever. For Keats, Hyperion's febrile state symbolizes his own inability to create, to assist the Titans, and to save his society because he himself is sick.

Just as Hyperion represents Keats's rejected concept of the poet, Apollo, who appears as "the golden theme" (III, 28) in Book III, is his ideal poet. Unlike Hyperion, whose loss of glory leads to selfish petulance, Apollo, on the eve of fulfilling his high destiny which should lead to pomp and celebration, is struck instead with utter grief as he views the world: "He listen'd, and he wept, and his bright tears / Went trickling down the golden bow he held" (III, 42–43).

Apollo then meets the goddess Mnemosyne, whose face of "eternal calm" (III, 60)—a direct contrast to Saturn's and Hyperion's anger—he has seen before in a dream. She asks Apollo why a youth with a gift as beautiful as his music should feel such sorrow, to which he replies:

> "For me, dark, dark,
> And painful vile oblivion seals my eyes:
> I strive to search wherefore I am so sad,
> Until a melancholy numbs my limbs;
> And then upon the grass I sit, and moan,
> Like one who once had wings. —O why should I
> Feel curs'd and thwarted, when the liegeless air
> Yields to my step aspirant?"   (III, 86–93)

The Poet-Physician

Like Hyperion, Apollo feels the painful darkness of melancholia shrouding him, but the difference between the two—an important one—is that Hyperion's melancholy is purely personal, self-pitying, whereas Apollo's sorrow is for others. As he tells Mnemosyne, he has no personal reason to feel this way on the eve of his ascension.

Like Saturn, Apollo at first makes the mistake of trying to find a rational explanation for his sorrow, as his questions indicate; like Apollo, many readers have been equally baffled by the god's melancholy. But years ago Margaret Sherwood hit upon its significance:

Is not the secret of Apollo's sorrow the very secret of Keats' own heart, as suggested in various passages in his poems and letters, . . . the inability to reconcile the poet-singer career, with the first and greatest of all aims, to relieve suffering? It was a dilemma worthy of the tears of a god. . . . He had been watching the suffering of the dispossessed; he suffers; only he who has suffered can attain supreme insight. Was not this suffering intended to be the necessary preparation for the god to become such a poet that his singing would be justified because of its healing and consoling power?[116]

Sherwood's rhetorical questions go to the very heart of the poem's meaning. Apollo "Find[s] the agonies, the strife / Of human hearts," and unlike Hyperion he does not attempt to escape that pain, anguish, and suffering. Instead, he tries to understand it, to gain knowledge or philosophy, not as Saturn does by "seeking after fact & reason," but intuitively, by looking into Mnemosyne's face and letting her knowledge of the world flow into his brain:

> "Mute thou remainest—mute! yet I can read
> A wondrous lesson in thy silent face:
> Knowledge enormous makes a God of me.
> Names, deeds, gray legends, dire events, rebellions,
> Majesties, sovran voices, agonies,
> Creations and destroyings, all at once
> Pour into the wide hollows of my brain,
> And deify me, as if some blithe wine
> Or bright elixir peerless I had drunk,
> And so become immortal."   (III, 111–20)

At this juncture, I should point out that "the word *Mnemosyne* signifies *memory*, and therefore the poets have rightly called memory the mother of the Muses."[117] What Apollo experiences in becoming a poet-physician is a type of primordial remembrance of all the experiences of humanity; he becomes immortal by becoming supremely mortal, not by escaping to a blissful paradise. Knowledge, or philosophy, comes to Apollo because he has experienced the pain as well as the pleasure, the sorrow as well as the joy, the destroyings as well as the creations, of the human condition. This is immediately emphasized by his own exquisite suffering, described in terms of Keats's memories of patients he had seen dying, including Tom:

> Soon wild commotions shook him, and made flush
> All the immortal fairness of his limbs;
> Most like the struggle at the gate of death;
> Or liker still to one who should take leave
> Of pale immortal death, and with a pang
> As hot as death's is chill, with fierce convulse
> Die into life: so young Apollo anguish'd.   (III, 124–30)

Apollo must experience death in order to gain knowledge, for, as Keats had written to Reynolds a year earlier, while praising Wordsworth as a mighty poet of the human heart: "We find what he says true as far as we have experienced and we can judge no further but by larger experience—for axioms in philosophy are not axioms until they are proved upon our pulses: We read fine—things but never feel them to thee full until we have gone the same steps as the Author. . . . Until we are sick, we understand not; —in fine, as Byron says, 'Knowledge is Sorrow'; and I go on to say that 'Sorrow is Wisdom' " (*Letters* 1:279). To know human suffering, Apollo must experience it in its ultimate form, death; only then can he administer to the health of his society; only then can he be the poet-physician. Knowledge, which allows the poet to reach that state of "healthy deliberation" and to create without the fever, is essential to the poet, as it was to the physician; but, as Astley Cooper had taught his students, it must be knowledge gained of experience. Keats reiterates this in a letter to George

221

and Georgiana just before breaking off *Hyperion:* "Nothing ever becomes real till it is experienced—Even a Proverb is no proverb to you till your Life has illustrated it" (*Letters* 2:81).

Keats goes on in this letter to explain that he is still battling the "agony . . . of ignorance," that he has "no thirst of any thing but knowledge," which probably indicates one of the reasons he broke off *Hyperion* during Apollo's immortalization: Keats himself did not yet have the experiential knowledge to articulate his protagonist's actions and thoughts as a poet-physician.

The desire to attain a state of "healthy deliberation," of harmonious balance between the immortal and mortal worlds, between pleasure and pain, joy and sorrow, beauty and truth, is the dominant theme of Keats's major poems during 1819, the *annus mirabilis*. The rage to come to terms with suffering and agony, with sadness and melancholy—as he finally does in the "Ode on Melancholy" and "To Autumn"—will not be put down, and it surfaces in the five great odes, as well as in the long narratives. I must, however, limit my study to those poems in which Keats makes extensive use of images and metaphors of disease and health: "La Belle Dame sans Merci," "Ode to a Nightingale," and *The Fall of Hyperion*.

"La Belle Dame sans Merci" was written in late April 1819, shortly after Keats had abandoned *Hyperion*. The poem deals with a knight, a warrior rather than a poet-physician, who is a vestige from Keats's early world of escapist, "golden-tongued Romance." In "On Sitting Down to Read *King Lear* Once Again," Keats had rejected escapist poetry in favor of "The bitter-sweet of this Shaksperean fruit," poetry that deals with both the pleasure and pain of reality; he had asked the muse, "Let me not wander in a barren dream" of romance. Now, in "La Belle Dame," he portrays a knight who opts for the perfect, pleasure-filled world of fairy romance and so is left finally to "wander in a barren dream" on a cold, lifeless hillside. The earlier poem is a brilliant foreshadowing of the later one.

After being enveloped in the enchanted world of the fairy Belle Dame, the knight dreams of the real world he has escaped and discovers that it is now only a world of disease and pain:

I saw pale kings, and princes too,
Pale warriors, death pale were they all;
. . . .
I saw their starv'd lips in the gloam
With horrid warning gaped wide.   (37–38, 41–42)

The knight awakens from the dream only to find that he has been afflicted with the same ailment, as the speaker's questions and observations indicate:

O what can ail thee, knight at arms,
Alone and palely loitering?
. . . .
O what can ail thee, knight at arms,
So haggard and so woe-begone?
. . . .
I see a lily on thy brow
With anguish moist and fever dew,
And on thy cheeks a fading rose
Fast withereth too.   (1–2, 5–6, 9–12)

The "hectic fever, . . . general emaciation and debility, . . . colliquative sweats,"[118] and paleness of the knight are the early symptoms of tuberculosis that Keats had come to know so well, as has been recognized for some time.[119] Hyatt Williams and Brink have also interpreted the poem in terms of the dependent, tubercular personality and link this construct to Keats's relationships with his mother and Fanny Brawne.[120] Thus, La Belle Dame herself has been viewed as Death, Consumption, Fanny, and Keats's mother.

Although these interpretations are perfectly valid in themselves, I tend to interpret the ballad, and specifically the knight, in the context of Keats's developing view of the poet, which I have been tracing from his earliest poems. Seen in this context, La Belle Dame represents the world of escapist romance in which the poet can enjoy ideal beauty, permanent sensual pleasure, and perfect sexual bliss, free from the pain and ugliness of the real world. If the poet could remain in such a world of oblivion, all would be well, as Keats told Taylor a year earlier: "I have been hovering for some time between an exquisite sense of the luxurious and a love for Philosophy—

223

were I calculated for the former I should be glad—but as I am not I shall turn all my soul to the latter" (*Letters* 1:271).

If the knight could forget reality completely, as Lycius manages to do for a time with Lamia, he could dwell in bliss indefinitely; but once he thinks of reality, as the knight does in his dream and as Lycius does when he hears the distant trumpets (*Lamia*, II, 27–29), the perfect illusion of romance is shattered. Having experienced the ideal world—which Keats sees by this time as "a barren dream"—the knight can no longer be satisfied with reality; and like Endymion, Saturn, and Hyperion before him, he sinks into diseased, morbid depression, symbolized here by the symptoms of tuberculosis. He is left in an unbalanced state, unable to come to terms with reality, which he views in a totally pessimistic fashion. As Keats says in the "Ode to a Nightingale," in the real world "to think is to be full of sorrow / And leaden-eyed despairs" (27–28).

That this is the thrust of his meaning is indicated in a story Keats tells Fanny Brawne:

I have been reading lately an oriental tale of a very beautiful color—It is of a city of melancholy men, all made so by this circumstance. Through a series of adventures each one of them by turns reach some gardens of Paradise where they meet with a most enchanting Lady; and just as they are going to embrace her, she bids them shut their eyes—they shut them—and on opening their eyes again find themselves descending to the earth in a magic basket. The remembrance of this Lady and their delights lost beyond all recovery render them melancholy ever after. (*Letters* 2:130)

Those heroes who, once the dream is shattered, cannot come to terms with reality, cannot see that pain and suffering is as necessary and integral a part of life as pleasure and joy, cannot, as Oceanus says, "Receive the truth, and let it be [their] balm" (*Hyperion*, II, 243), are doomed to failure. They wallow in self-pitying melancholy, their diseased bodies being the external manifestation of their diseased minds as they "wander in a barren dream"; they can never be poet-physicians, for they are too egocentric. This is precisely what befalls the knight, Saturn, Hyperion, and Lycius, although Lycius escapes into death.

The genuine poet, on the other hand, does not drown in his melancholy, as Keats points out in the first stanza of the "Ode on Melancholy"; instead, like Apollo, he seeks the "knowledge enormous," the philosophy, that will allow him to appreciate all the opposites of life, to see that truth is beauty. This is the state that Keats himself has attained by the time he writes the "Ode on Melancholy"; he has learned to see pain and suffering in a larger context and so is healed of his own morbid desire to escape reality. As he tells George and Georgiana in the famous "soul-making" letter, written at this time: "Do you not see how necessary a World of Pains and troubles is to school an Intelligence and make it a soul? A Place where the heart must feel and suffer in a thousand diverse ways" (*Letters* 2:102).

Philosophy, Keats claims, gives the poet the inner calm to "compose without this fever," and once he has healed himself, the poet can concentrate on ministering to the health of his society. In new verse of "thoughtful and quiet power," he becomes the poet-physician, the one who attempts to relieve the suffering of others. Like Apollo, he gains his immortality, the status of true poet, not by transcending the real world, but by healing it, by being supremely concerned with human suffering, the ideal that Keats had been taught at Guy's Hospital.

In the "Ode to a Nightingale," the nightingale, itself a symbol of the poet by virtue of its mellifluous voice, has also gained its immortal status through its ability to appreciate both human joy and suffering: the bird acts as comforter to Ruth and entertainer to the emperor and clown (61–67). The speaker does not realize this, however, and believes instead that the bird has simply transcended the real world and is completely removed from pain and sorrow. He hopes to achieve a similar escape and thus tries a number of intoxicants in his attempts to fly to an identification with the nightingale.

The ode opens with the speaker's description of the pain he feels after a momentary, imagined identification with the bird, from "being too happy in [the nightingale's] happiness" (6):

> My heart aches, and a drowsy numbness pains
> My sense, as though of hemlock I had drunk,

225

> Or emptied some dull opiate to the drains
> One minute past, and Lethe-wards had sunk.   (1–4)

Too many sources, ranging from Horace to Burton,[121] have been cited for these lines for me to examine the merits of them all. William Ober, however, after pointing out that Keats had probably taken laudanum for his black eye in March 1819, suggests that Keats is describing the actual effects of opium: "Cruel as it is to paraphrase, Keats tells us that he feels depressed, that his sensorium is obtunded as if he had just taken a drug. He mentions hemlock, which does not produce this effect, . . . and opiates which do. Sinking 'Lethe-wards' implies that he has entered an amnesic, trancelike state."[122] This is an astute observation, although Ober's subsequent interpretation of the whole poem as an opium dream in which the song is a hallucination is forced and unnecessary, since the speaker only says he feels "as though" he had drunk an opiate.

In this respect, it should be pointed out that Keats knew from his training in materia medica that opium is often prescribed for both nervous disorders and phthisis,[123] and he may have been treating himself for one of these; we know for certain, from Brown's account, that he was "secretly taking, at times, a few drops of laudanum to keep up his spirits" in early 1820.[124] He was also told about the effects of the drug by William Salisbury, whose description does bear some resemblance to Keats's lines: "The operation of opium . . . [is] followed by a degree of nausea, a difficulty of respiration, lowness of the spirits, and a weak languid pulse." In addition, Salisbury dealt with "CONIUM *maculatum*, HEMLOCK" as a sedative medicine rather than a poison,[125] just as Keats does in the ode.

Perhaps in these opening lines Keats also has in mind a passage from Astley Cooper's lectures on surgery. In discussing "Injuries of the Head," Cooper states:

A sudden shock will so far disturb the circulation of this organ [the brain], as to produce diminution of the powers of the mind, as well as to impair the functions of the body. I shall have occasion to mention to you a most extraordinary case, in which the functions of the mind were suspended from an interruption of the circulation in the brain, for upwards of thirteen months; the patient having, as it were, drunk of the cup of Lethe during all that period. . . .

. . . from that moment . . . his mind had remained in a state of perfect oblivion. He had drunk, as it were, the cup of Lethe; he had suffered a complete death, as far as regarded his mental, and almost all his bodily powers; but by removing a small portion of the bone with the saw, he was at once resotred to all the functions of his mind, and almost all the powers of his body.[126]

Not only is the reference to drinking from the cup of Lethe similar to Keats's description of drinking an opiate and sinking "Lethe-wards," but the larger idea of the man having virtually dissolved into oblivion, annulled himself, is similar to what the speaker in the poem desires:

> That I might drink, and leave the world unseen,
> And with thee fade away into the forest dim:
>
> Fade far away, dissolve, and quite forget
> What thou among the leaves hast never known.   (19–22)

The man's return to normal after his operation is also similar to the speaker's return to self at the end of the poem. It is possible that Keats remembered Astley Cooper's remarks when he came to write the ode.

But to return to the larger issues being dealt with in the poem: because he cannot gain his entry into the ideal world of the nightingale, "In some melodious plot / Of beechen green" (8–9), the speaker sinks into melancholic despondency in which he sees the real world in terms of morbid, pathological symptoms, which Keats adapted from his knowledge of fevers, palsy, and phthisis:

> The weariness, the fever, and the fret
> Here, where men sit and hear each other groan;
> Where palsy shakes a few, sad, last gray hairs,
> Where youth grows pale, and spectre-thin, and dies;
> Where but to think is to be full of sorrow
> And leaden-eyed despairs.   (23–28)

This is the world of Tom's deathbed and the wards of Guy's Hospital, where Keats saw such symptoms daily for over a year; but unlike the physician, the despairing speaker feels he can do nothing in the face of suffering.

He does, however, learn to appreciate the short-lived beauty of the spring in the real world (stanza V), and he recognizes that simple death has not led to the bird's peculiarly immortal status. If he died in such despair, he would simply become "a sod" and the bird's song a "high requiem" (60). He has made some progress toward accepting reality, although the questions about the validity of his experience at the end of the ode illustrate that he is still confused.

Any confusion over the role of the poet in society is finally resolved in *The Fall of Hyperion*, where Keats drops the mask of the knight-warrior-shepherd-lover construct that he has used previously, and now identifies the protagonist as a poet. It is an extremely personal and painful poem, a working out of the long-fought conflict between the fanatic dreamer, whose visions of ideal, paradisal beauty only leave him lost in melancholy madness, "the sable charm," and the genuine poet, who manages to heal his imagination by the therapeutic act of writing:

> Fanatics have their dreams, wherewith they weave
> A paradise for a sect; the savage too
> From forth the loftiest fashion of his sleep
> Guesses at heaven: pity these have not
> Trac'd upon vellum or wild Indian leaf
> The shadows of melodiuos utterance.
> But bare of laurel they live, dream, and die;
> For Poesy alone can tell her dreams,
> With the fine spell of words alone can save
> Imagination from the sable charm
> And dumb enchantment.   (I, 1–11)

As I outlined in the previous chapter, the poem traces the development of the poet on a spiritual journey through various chambers of the mind. The poet's career begins, as Keats's did, in the world of "golden-tongued Romance," "Of Flora, and old Pan," a world "Of brightness so unsullied, that therein / A melancholy spirit well might win / Oblivion" (*Endymion*, I, 97–99). It is the fanatic's perfect, paradisal world of ideal beauty and sensual bliss, symbolized by the rich, luxurious botanical images and the abundance of food and drink of which the poet partakes. But the drink is a drug, more powerful than "Asian poppy," that causes the poet to collapse in a deathlike swoon that prefigures his subsequent dying into life; each stage in the poet's development involves intense pain and struggle, probably hinting at the very difficulty of poetic progress.

On awaking from the swoon, the poet discovers that the ideal world of romance has vanished: "the fair trees were gone, / The mossy mound and arbour were no more" (I, 59–60). The symbols of that world, of Psyche's heaven which can exist only in the poet's mind, lie scattered on the floor:

> All in a mingled heap confus'd there lay
> Robes, golden tongs, censer, and chafing dish,
> Girdles, and chains, and holy jewelries.   (I, 78–80)

The first stage of the poet's career, in which he delights in romance, is over, the dream shattered.

The poet now finds himself in a gigantic ruined temple, the metaphorical equivalent of Saturn's lifeless vale, as the reference to fallen realms indicates:

> what I had seen
> Of grey cathedrals, buttress'd walls, rent towers,
> The superannuations of sunk realms,
> Or nature's rocks toil'd hard in waves and winds,
> Seem'd but the faulture of decrepit things
> To that eternal domed monument.   (I, 66–71)

Having fallen from his edenic state, the poet finds himself in the same position as Saturn in *Hyperion* and the knight in "La Belle Dame sans Merci." And, like Saturn, he meets a woman, Moneta, who reveals to him the truth of his position: "'If thou canst not ascend / These steps [to the altar], die on that marble where thou art'" (I, 107–08).

Now that the ideal world of romance is banished, the gates of the temple being "shut against the sunrise evermore" (I, 86), the poet faces an important decision: like Saturn and Hyperion, he can refuse to face the real world and instead wallow in morbid, self-pitying melancholia, which is a virtual death of the spirit, as Moneta tells him; or he can face the real world in all its ugliness, pain, and sorrow and learn to accept it by dying into life, a paradoxical process that will return him to health and thus allow him to minister to the health of suffering humanity, to be concerned with social, rather than personal, ills.

The struggle between these two choices begins; like Apollo before him, the poet must experience pain and suffering if he is to learn to understand it:

> suddenly a palsied chill
> Struck from the paved level up my limbs,
> And was ascending quick to put cold grasp
> Upon those streams that pulse beside the throat:
> I shriek'd; and the sharp anguish of my shriek
> Stung my own ears—I strove hard to escape
> The numbness; strove to gain the lowest step.
> Slow, heavy, deadly was my pace: the cold
> Grew stifling, suffocating, at the heart;
> And when I clasp'd my hands I felt them not.
> One minute before death, my iced foot touch'd
> The lowest stair; and as it touch'd, life seem'd
> To pour in at the toes.   (I, 122–34)

Here Keats describes the clinical signs of approaching death: the drop in body temperature; the slowing of the pulse rate, vividly portrayed here in the carotid arteries that take blood from the head to the neck, "those streams that pulse beside the throat"; and the loss of sensation. The medical accuracy of the images adds to the horror of the scene.

Just before death, however, the poet reaches the steps and is immediately cured, a sign that his imagination has reached that state of metaphorical health, of harmonious balance, in which it can appreciate all aspects of life. The poet asks Moneta why he has been saved, and implicit in her answer is Keats's definition of the genuine poet:

> "None can usurp this height," return'd that shade,
> "But those to whom the miseries of the world
> Are misery, and will not let them rest."   (I, 147–49)

Hints of this definition have been surfacing in Keats's verse
from as early as *Sleep and Poetry*, where he says that poetry
"should be a friend / To sooth the cares, and lift the thoughts
of man" (246–47); now the definition is vigorously articulated.
In the earlier poem there was some confusion over Apollo's
role as he descends and listens to the "Shapes of delight, of
mystery, and fear" (138); now there is none, for we recognize
the poet as physician.

Keats, however, feels obliged to reiterate his ideas about
the poet and so has the speaker ask why he is at the altar
alone, for surely there are many others "'Who love their
fellows even to the death; / Who feel the giant agony of the
world' " (I, 156–57). To this Moneta delivers a stinging rebuke:

> "They whom thou spak'st of are no vision'ries,"
> Rejoin'd that voice—"They are no dreamers weak,
> They seek no wonder but the human face;
> No music but a happy-noted voice—
> They come not here, they have no thought to come—
> And thou art here, for thou art less than they.
> What benefit canst thou do, or all thy tribe,
> To the great world? Thou art a dreaming thing;
> A fever of thyself—think of the earth;
> What bliss even in hope is there for thee?
> What haven? Every creature hath its home;
> Every sole man hath days of joy and pain,
> Whether his labours be sublime or low—
> The pain alone; the joy alone; distinct:
> Only the dreamer venoms all his days,
> Bearing more woe than all his sins deserve."   (I, 161–76)

The psychotic dreamer, the visionary, the fanatic who craves
only his imaginary paradise, exists in a fevered state, with
which Keats himself was so familiar. His very craving after his
vision makes him dissatisfied with reality, turns him into a
moping melancholic who selfishly "venoms all his days, / Bearing more woe than all his sins deserve."

The truly great, selfless, altruistic, and "disinterested," the
Astley Coopers, the Benjamin Baileys, the Georgiana Keatses,
accept the real world as it is, with its "joy and pain." They do
not have diseased imaginations that make them hate the world

and force them to retreat into this kind of introspective brooding; that is why they are not at the altar.[127] They are the doers in life, rather than the dreamers, the ones who can relieve human suffering because they themselves have a healthy understanding of life. Moneta claims they are superior to visionaries, and Keats himself told Reynolds in August 1819, when he was writing *The Fall*, that he is "convinced more and more day by day that fine writing is next to fine doing the top thing in the world" (*Letters* 2:146). "Fine doing" is the best man can give, but "fine writing" has its place in the world too, as we shall see.

Through Moneta's inquiry, Keats questions the whole justification for his choice of poetry as a career. Could it be that he now has doubts about his decision to abandon medicine, that truly altruistic profession, in favor of poetry? The self-doubts are there, but the answer to those doubts is present also, and is given in the poet's probing statement:

> "sure not all
> Those melodies sung into the world's ear
> Are useless: sure a poet is a sage;
> A humanist, physician to all men."   (I, 187–90)

Moneta distinguishes then between the poet as healer and as dreamer or visionary:

> "The poet and the dreamer are distinct,
> Diverse, sheer opposite, antipodes.
> The one pours out a balm upon the world,
> The other vexes it."   (I, 199–202)

The genuine poet lives in a state of "healthy deliberation" born of knowledge and so can heal his society, can be disinterested; the dreamer lives between fevered visions of paradise and melancholic depression over reality, caught in his egocentricity, lacking the sympathy of the true poet. As Keats proclaims in a sonnet, "On Fame," written earlier in the year:

> How fever'd is the man who cannot look
> Upon his mortal days with temperate blood,
> Who vexes all the leaves of his life's book,
> And robs his fair name of its maidenhood.   (1–4)

The visionary escapist cannot view life with the "temperate blood" that is a physical manifestation of a healthy mind. In creating his imaginary paradise, the dreamer of necessity transforms his real world into a morbid hell.

Through the distinction between the mere dreamer and the genuine poet, Keats affirms that "fine writing" does have a place in the world, and "To Autumn" is an example of that fine writing, "The bitter-sweet . . . Shaksperean fruit" he wanted to create. In this final ode there are no wild, escapist flights of the imagination, only a celebration of the beauty of the real season at its richest and ripest, even though there is an inherent knowledge that the beauty will die with the ensuing winter. In the final stanza, the passing of autumn and the imminent arrival of winter are adumbrated through the images of the "stubble-plains" (26), which indicate that the harvest is over, the perfection passed; the "full-grown lambs" (30), which were born in the spring and are now ready to face the cold; and the "gathering swallows" (33), who are preparing to migrate. In addition, the sunset scene and the "wailful choir" of gnats who "mourn" (27) for the season are suggestive of the approaching end, although the use of present participles in the description creates a beautifully modulated state of lingering before completion. Throughout, there is a calm, philosophic acceptance of death as an integral part of life, and in this very acceptance the poetry is a healing balm. Keats has come a long way from his desire for a "Life of Sensations" and pure imagination; he has gained knowledge and philosophy through experience, as Astley Cooper said he should. He has fused the ideals of his two careers and become, like Apollo, the poet-physician.

In examining the influence of Keats's knowledge of pathology and medicine on his poetry and thought, I have taken a chronological approach, as far as is possible, in order to trace in detail the development of certain images, metaphors, and ideas. Not being a physician, I have resisted the usual urge to diagnose Keats's illnesses from a modern standpoint; rather, by examining his training, I have attempted to show what Keats thought of his illnesses, both mental and physical, and how those thoughts are reflected in the poetry. I have not dwelt on the final months of his phthisis, or the merits of his various doctors, since by then Keats had ceased writing poetry, so that these are strictly biographical topics, and ones that have been examined in detail elsewhere.[128]

An examination of Keats's poems and letters reveals that certain areas of pathology and medicine held special interest for him, in particular melancholia and other nervous disorders in which the morbid state of the mind affects the body through the nervous system. This obsessive interest in melancholia can be explained by his personal affliction, but at the same time his medical training gave him the requisite knowledge to understand the workings of the disease, which may have saved him from its worst excesses. In addition to melancholia, Keats was also interested in the symptoms and effects of fevers and, later on, of tuberculosis. He drew on his knowledge of these diseases in creating specific images and metaphors, and an understanding of his knowledge of pathology allows us to appreciate the muscularity and accuracy of the images and metaphors he adapted from this area of his medical training.

Even more important, however, is the whole approach Keats adapted from pathology of viewing things in terms of health and disease, and the related states of balance and imbalance, referred to in medicine. When he refers to this dichotomy between health and disease, it is usually in a metaphorical sense, although when he describes states of melancholic mental instability, the distinction between the metaphorical and the literal breaks down, for melancholia *is* a disease caused by the imagination. An additional level of significance is included in the metaphors adapted from pathology; since Keats himself suffered from many of the ailments he describes in the poetry, they take on very personal connotations as he uses certain protagonists and their situations to come to grips with his own problems.

As I have demonstrated, Keats conceived of a number of important aspects of life in terms of a health-disease dichotomy. He viewed both the literary love relationships of his protagonists and his literal love affair with Fanny Brawne in this fashion. He also thought of poetic creativity in these terms, particularly in relation to both fever and melancholia. Ultimately, in poems like the "Ode to a Nightingale" and *The Fall of Hyperion,* he conceived of life in terms of health and sickness, concluding that the true poet must heal his own spirit and then minister to the suffering of humanity at large. In the end, for Keats, the ideals of the poet are the same as those of the physician; "a poet is . . . physician to all men."

Conclusion

In a study such as this, which examines the influence of Keats's medical knowledge on his thought, it is imperative that we not lose sight of Keats the poet, for it is only because of his poetry, and his letters about poetry, that Keats holds his prominent place in our culture. Bearing this in mind, I have dealt at length with specific images, metaphors, and ideas in the poems and letters to illustrate how Keats's knowledge of medical science influenced those images and ideas. Throughout, my object has been to illuminate the poetry. Beyond that, however, I have also examined the influence of his medical training on Keats's broader approach to life—on his attitudes toward sensation, knowledge, and experience, for example—in the firm conviction that such an approach is necessary in dealing with a poet whose art is so integrally connected with his own life in particular and with his thoughts on life in general. From 1817 on, poetry was virtually Keats's life, and thus all the more general ideas I have considered ultimately shed some light on the poems themselves.

By approaching Keats's work through his knowledge of medicine, I have in no way tried to deny or belittle the influence of literary sources on his work; to do so would be obtuse and narrow-minded. But to ignore completely the influence of Keats's medical training, as has usually been done, or to deny it altogether is equally myopic. I hope that this study has gone some way toward finally laying to rest the long-held opinion that Keats—with the Romantics in general—was simply antiscientific and anti-intellectual, and toward enhancing our understanding of an important part of his intellectual milieu.

Throughout, I have focused on specific images and metaphors to demonstrate how accurate and vivid they are when understood in their medical context. Such an approach allows us to appreciate a muscularity in certain aspects of Keats's work that has seldom been recognized. But larger issues have also been my concern. In dealing with chemistry, I have shown that certain terms and concepts, particularly those concerned with distillation and related chemical processes, were adapted by Keats in formulating his thoughts on poetic creativity. Only when we understand such terms and concepts in their chemical context do we truly grasp Keats's meaning. From botany, he gained not only specialized knowledge of plants, trees, flowers, and vegetables, but also an acute appreciation of nature in all its diversity, in its cyclical flux of creations and destroyings, of growth and decay, of life and death. From anatomy and physiology, he gained an understanding of the structure and workings of the body and, even more important, the brain, and of how the mind influences, and is in turn influenced by, the body through the nervous system. Appreciation of such knowledge is useful in comprehending Keats's mental landscapes and his notions of sensation and sympathetic identification. Finally, pathology and medicine provided Keats with knowledge of bodily and mental diseases and cures which enabled him to comprehend his own diseases and to portay accurately those of his protagonists. Moreover, from pathology he adopted the approach of viewing aspects of life, in particular love and poetic creativity, in terms of morbid and healthy states; such an approach is closely linked to his thoughts on imagination and philosophy.

In a more general way, his medical training instilled in Keats a sense of the importance of acute observation, both of nature and of man, which is so strongly evinced in his poetry. It also taught him a distrust of purely abstract hypothesis and instilled in him a confidence in empirical experience as the means of gaining knowledge. Perhaps of most importance, however, was the influence of Keats's medical training in strengthening his profound sympathy for human suffering. Guy's Hospital operated on the principles laid down by its founder, the great philanthropist Thomas Guy, who had built the institution for the express purpose of ministering to the suffering of the poor and the incurable. Consequently, as a pupil and dresser at Guy's, Keats would daily have witnessed and treated some of the worst cases of human suffering in the metropolis of London. He never forgot that pain and suffering, or the stated purpose of medicine, to heal it. Perhaps the greatest legacy he took from his first career to his second was that sympathy for human suffering and the desire to heal it, which was transformed into his ideal of the Apollo-like poet-physician, and which contributed in a major way to his greatness as a poet.

Notes

Bibliography

Index

Notes

Introduction

1. Blake, "The Laocoön," in *Complete Writings*, p. 777; "Preface" (1800), in Wordsworth and Coleridge, *Lyrical Ballads*, p. 164.

2. All quotations from Keats's letters are from *The Letters of John Keats*, ed. Hyder E. Rollins, referred to hereafter as *Letters*; volume and page numbers are given in parentheses. Keats's spelling and punctuation are maintained throughout.

3. Bush, *Science and English Poetry*, pp. 80–82.

4. Ibid., p. 101.

5. Abrams, *The Mirror and the Lamp*, p. 303.

6. Ibid.

7. Unless otherwise noted, all quotations of Keats's poetry are from *The Poems of John Keats*, ed. Jack Stillinger; canto and line numbers are given in parentheses.

8. E.g., Elliott, "The Real Tragedy of Keats." See also Havens, "Unreconciled Opposites in Keats."

9. Individual scholars like Charles Hagelman and Stuart Sperry have elucidated particular aspects of Keats's scientific knowledge, but no comprehensive study of that knowledge, comparable to Carl Grabo's or Desmond King-Hele's work on Shelley, has been undertaken.

10. Such denials are numerous; here are two examples: "Very few indications of his professional training are to be found in Keats's letters; fewer still in his poems. . . . Allusions to or analogies drawn from medical subjects are rare in his letters" (Osler, "John Keats—the Apothecary Poet," *Johns Hopkins Hospital Bulletin*, p. 14). "Keats promptly forgot all the morbid but useful things that he learned. There is not the slighest hint in any of his writings, especially his verse, that he ever knew anything about medicine, anatomy or pathology" (Pitfield, "John Keats: The Reactions of a Genius," p. 532).

11. Brown, *Life of John Keats*, pp. 41–42.

12. Milnes, *Life, Letters, and Literary Remains*, pp. 18, 31–32.

13. Rossetti, *Life of John Keats*, pp. 18–19.

14. Colvin, *John Keats, His Life and Poetry*, pp. 16–33.

15. Lowell, *John Keats*, 1: 74–93. The apprenticeship is covered on pp. 46–49.

16. Hewlett, *A Life of John Keats*, pp. 31–33, 36–43.

17. Doubleday, "John Keats as a Student"; Scarlett, "John Keats: Medical Student." Even Evans's recent article, "Keats—The Man, Medicine and Poetry," summarizes Gittings's findings, as does "John's Other Life."

18. Hale-White, *Keats as Doctor and Patient*.

19. Ward, *John Keats*, pp. 21–26, 47–65.

20. Bate, *John Keats*, pp. 30–32, 42–50, 65–67.

21. Gittings, "Keats and Medicine"; "John Keats, Physician and Poet."

22. Gittings, *John Keats*, pp. 56–62, 79–86, 99–105, 114–19.

23. E.g., Goodall, "Some Examples of the Knowledge of Medicine"; Wycherley, "Keats: The Terminal Disease."

24. This article is taken from Hagelman's dissertation, "John Keats and the Medical Profession."

25. An expanded version of this article appears in Sperry's *Keats the Poet*.

26. E.g., Dell, "Keats's Debt to Robert Burton"; Gittings, *John Keats: The Living Year*, pp. 5–6, 9, passim; Ward, "Keats and Burton"; Sinson, *John Keats and the Anatomy of Melancholy*.

27. Blackstone, *Consecrated Urn*, pp. 2–30, 33, 34, passim.

28. King-Hele, *Doctor of Revolution*, pp. 13, 19, 195, passim.

29. Knight, "The Physical Sciences and the Romantic Movement," deals with Coleridge, Wordsworth, Southey, and Shelley, but passes over Keats as anti-scientific.

30. Quoted in Ritterbush, *Art of Organic Forms*, p. 54.

31. Davy, "Parallels Between Art and Science," in *Collected Works*, 8:307–08.

Chapter I: Biography

1. Ward, *John Keats*, pp. 7–8; Bate, *John Keats*, pp. 9–10; Gittings, *John Keats*, pp. 43–45.

2. Altick, *The Cowden Clarkes*, p. 15.

3. Ward, *John Keats*, p. 7.

4. Lowell, *John Keats*, p. 34.

5. Clarke and Clarke, *Recollections of Writers*, p. 2.

6. Lowell, *John Keats*, pp. 35–36; Ward, *John Keats*, p. 8.

7. Murchie, *Spirit of Place in Keats*, p. 6. Keats relates a similar story in a doggerel rhyme written to Fanny from Scotland in July 1818, although there he claims he kept the various fish in "tubs three" at the home of "his Granny-good" in Edmonton (*Letters* 1:314).

8. Brown, *Life of John Keats*, p. 42.

9. Hewlett, *A Life of John Keats*, p. 31; Bate, *John Keats*, p. 29; Ward, *John Keats*, p. 22; Hagelman, "John Keats and the Medical Profession," p. 5. This date is based on Colvin's argument in *John Keats, His Life and Poetry*, p. 16.

10. Gittings, *John Keats*, pp. 56–57; see also Gittings, "John Keats, Physician and Poet," p. 51. Cowden Clarke says that "at 14 he [Keats] went to Hammond's the summer of 1810" (Rollins, *Keats Circle*, 2:169). In 1792, Warner writes, "it was expected that every pupil should bring with him a certificate from his late

master, signifying that he, the pupil, had served five years with dilligence and sobriety" (Wilks and Bettany, *Biographical History*, p. 89).

11. See Richardson, "An Aesculapian Poet," 1:23; Pitfield, "John Keats: The Reactions of a Genius," p. 531; Hale-White, *Keats as Doctor and Patient*, p. 8; Wells, *A Doctor's Life of John Keats*, p. 46; and Scarlett, "John Keats: Medical Student," p. 536.

12. Colvin states: "With no opposition, so far as we learn, on his own part, he was bound apprentice to a Mr. Thomas Hammond" (*John Keats*, p. 16); Lowell imagines a conclave involving Mrs. Jennings, Abbey, and Keats to decide on his career (*John Keats*, p. 46); Bate cannot decide "whether the decision was made entirely by Abbey or with the encouragement of Mrs. Jennings" (*John Keats*, p. 30); and Ward raises the question and then evades it (*John Keats*, pp. 21–22).

13. Hewlett, *A Life of John Keats*, p. 31. In *Life of John Keats*, Brown seems to agree when he states that "though born to be a poet, Keats was ignorant of his birthright until he had completed his eighteenth year. . . . Other and opposite studies [medicine], pursued with an eager temperament, may partly, but, perhaps, not wholly account for Keats's lack of poetic creativity before he was eighteen" (pp. 41–42).

14. See p. 16.

15. Clarke and Clarke, *Recollections of Writers*, pp. 329–30, 336.

16. Ibid., p. 327. Edward Holmes, a fellow student, says that "Keats was not in childhood attached to books. His *penchant* was for fighting. . . . The point to be chiefly insisted on is that he was *not* literary—*his love of books & poetry manifested itself chiefly about a year before he left school*" (Rollins, *Keats Circle*, 2:163–65).

17. Cowden Clarke, in Rollins, *Keats Circle*, 2:147.

18. Haydon, *Diary*, 2:107.

19. Rollins, *Keats Circle*, 2:165.

20. Clarke and Clarke, *Recollections of Writers*, p. 328; Brown, *Life of John Keats*, p. 63; C. W. Dilke, in Rollins, *Keats Circle*, 1:325.

21. Basing his conjecture on the evidence that there was a family of surgeons called Keate (also "Keats") in Somerset who resembled the poet physically, Gittings suggests that medicine may have been a family tradition ("Keats and Medicine," p. 139).

22. See Ward, *John Keats*, pp. 26–32; Bate, *John Keats*, pp. 32–41. Cowden Clarke's description of these afternoons is given in Rollins, *Keats Circle*, 2:148–49.

23. Quoted in Hake and Compton-Rickett, *Life and Letters of Theodore Watts-Dunton*, 1:152.

24. Rollins, *Keats Circle*, 2:169.

25. Cowden Clarke writes: "It should seem that Hammond had released him from his apprenticeship before his time; and I have some vague recollection that such was the case, for they did not agree." But he continues: "Upon recurring to the dates of his apprenticeship, Keats must have fulfilled his engagement with Hammond" (Rollins, *Keats Circle*, 2:169).

26. Rollins, *Keats Circle*, 1:277. See also Gittings, *John Keats*, p. 67.

27. Rollins, *Keats Circle*, 2:177.

28. Ibid., 1:307.

29. Colvin, *John Keats,* p. 17. Osler gives the same quotation with no source in "John Keats—the Apothecary Poet," in his *Alabama Student,* p. 40. Vincent has expanded this idea into the erroneous statement that "at the end of 4 years, Hammond dismissed him [Keats] as a lazy, idle fellow, always reading and scribbling" ("A Medical Truant," p. 648).

It should be pointed out that there are very few extant poems from this period, although the fellow apprentice may have confused Keats's love of translating with that of writing poetry. Cowden Clarke says that "with the exception of the duty he had to perform in the surgery—by no means an onerous one—his whole leisure hours were employed in indulging his passion for reading and translating" (quoted in Lowell, *John Keats,* p. 49).

30. Brown, *Life of John Keats,* p. 41.

31. Poynter, *Evolution of Medical Education,* p. 80.

32. For a discussion of apothecaries, see South, *Memorials,* pp. 63–65.

33. Cameron, *Mr. Guy's Hospital,* p. 81.

34. Poynter, *Evolution of Medical Education,* p. 81.

35. Gittings, *John Keats,* p. 61.

36. Gittings, "John Keats, Physician and Poet," p. 51.

37. Newman, for example, says that Keats "can have learned but little of the Science of Medicine" from Hammond ("John Keats: Apothecary and Poet," p. 171).

38. James Paget, in the memoirs of his apprenticeship days, which were somewhat later than Keats's, recalls that he was allowed to dissect removed internal organs and amputated limbs after operations. In this way, he learned much practical anatomy and was well prepared when he attended lectures at a London hospital (*Memoirs and Letters,* pp. 20–30).

39. "Fourth Report of the General Committee," p. 512.

40. *Medicine in 1815,* p. 19.

41. "Fourth Report of the General Committee," p. 512.

42. Ibid., p. 513.

43. "Apothecaries Bill," pp. 423–24.

44. See Mann, "John Keats: Further Notes," pp. 23–25; and Gittings, *John Keats,* p. 81.

45. South, *Memorials,* pp. 30–31.

46. Printed in Lowell, *John Keats,* 1:154.

47. Scarlett, "John Keats: Medical Student," p. 53. Vincent states: "At this time Guy's and St. Thomas's were still more or less united, . . . neither attempting organized instruction but merely giving the students opportunities to learn what they could. The young men 'walked the wards' and took notes if they felt like it" ("A Medical Truant," p. 648).

48. "Medical School of St. Thomas's and Guy's," p. 259.

49. "St. Thomas's and Guy's Hospitals."

50. *Medicine in 1815,* p. 20.

51. Doubleday, "Short Biographical History," p. 510.

52. South, *Memorials,* pp. 32–33.

53. Quoted in R. C. Brock, *Life and Works of Astley Cooper,* p. 100.

54. Ibid., pp. 102–03.

55. *Medicine in 1815*, p. 26.
56. R. C. Brock, *Life and Works of Astley Cooper*, p. 108.
57. Cameron, *Mr. Guy's Hospital*, p. 156.
58. South, *Memorials*, pp. 209–16.
59. "Apothecaries' Hall."
60. Gittings, *John Keats*, p. 82.
61. South, *Memorials*, p. 33.
62. Ibid.
63. Ibid., pp. 34–35.
64. Cameron, *Mr. Guy's Hospital*, p. 151.
65. Wilks and Bettany, *Biographical History*, pp. 364, 363. See also Cameron, *Mr. Guy's Hospital*, p. 160.
66. Astley Cooper, *Principles and Practice*, p. 1.
67. On Keats's meeting with Green and Coleridge, see *Letters*, 2:88.
68. South, *Memorials*, p. 37.
69. Green, *Dissector's Manual*, pp. xlvi–xlvii.
70. Wilks and Bettany point out that because bodies were cheaper in Dublin—usually twenty-five shillings, but sometimes as low as ten—"there was a constant traffic between the capitals, the subjects being packed in boxes so that their contents were unknown" (*Biographical History*, pp. 158–59).
71. Gittings, *John Keats*, pp. 83–84; Hewlett, *A Life of John Keats*, p. 39. The most detailed account of the Guy's body-snatchers is given by Hagelman, who builds a convincing argument for his claim that Keats had personal contact with these men ("John Keats and the Medical Profession," pp. 218–34).
72. Bransby Cooper, *Life of Sir Astley Cooper*, 1:407.
73. It should be pointed out, however, that this description of the dissecting room, quoted by Hewlett (*A Life of John Keats*, pp. 37–38), comes from a student at Guy's in 1841, over twenty years after Keats was there.
74. Quoted in Gittings, "John Keats, Physician and Poet," p. 52.
75. Warner states: "The Chymical lectures continue until there has been two courses given, which employs them from the 1st of October until the month of May" (quoted in Wilks and Bettany, *Biographical History*, p. 93).
76. South, *Memorials*, p. 58.
77. Wilks and Bettany, *Biographical History*, pp. 200–01.
78. Ibid., p. 208.
79. Cameron, *Mr. Guy's Hospital*, p. 126.
80. Sperry, *Keats the Poet*, p. 36. Gittings claims Keats was taught chemistry by Marcet, but gives no reason for excluding Babington and Allen (*John Keats*, p. 82).
81. "Apothecaries' Hall."
82. South, *Memorials*, pp. 58–59.
83. Wilks and Bettany, *Biographical History*, p. 206. See also Bransby Cooper, *Life of Sir Astley Cooper*, 1:309.
84. Gittings, *John Keats*, p. 82. Gittings's claim is presumably based on Keats's certificate, which gives these names of courses but no teachers.
85. Cameron, *Mr. Guy's Hospital*, p. 126.

86. See Robert Darwin, *Principia Botanica*, p. vi; and Wilks and Bettany, *Biographical History*, pp. 475–77.

87. "Announcement." Tommy Wheeler, the botanical teacher of the Society of Apothecaries' Company, also gave a series of lectures on botany at the Society's Hall, along with demonstrations at the Chelsea garden and field excurions (South, *Memorials*, pp. 66–67). Whether Keats, like South, attended these we do not know.

88. Salisbury, "To the Editors," *London Medical & Physical Journal*, 35 (1816): 430.

89. Salisbury, "Mr. Salisbury's Botanical Excursions."

90. Ibid., p. 517.

91. The figure of £33.12s. is given by Gittings (*John Keats*, p. 83) without any source. Cameron states that "the charges were ten guineas for the Practice of Medicine, Materia Medica and Chemistry" (*Mr. Guy's Hospital*, p. 148; see also Wilks and Bettany, *Biographical History*, pp. 93–94). South states that "the fee for the anatomical lectures was ten guineas, and the same for dissections" (*Memorials*, p. 31). These amounts, together with a registration fee of £2.3s., give a total of £33.13s. Hagelman believes Keats spent £48.7s. ("John Keats and the Medical Profession," p. 153).

92. Joseph Warner's account (1792) is quoted in full in Wilks and Bettany, *Biographical History*, pp. 88–94.

93. Ibid., p. 476.

94. South, *Memorials*, p. 33.

95. *John Keats's Anatomical and Physiological Note Book.* If Dilke's grandson is correct, other medical note books of Keats's were extant until as late as 1875. Writing of himself in a memoir on his grandfather, he states: "Mr. Dilke's grandson has still in his possession a great number of Keats's letters; —his Ovid, . . . his medical note-books; and Keats' own copy of Endymion" (Dilke, *Papers of a Critic*, 1:2).

96. See, for example, the comments of the following critics:

Lowell: "He worked hard, as is shown by a note-book on his courses of anatomy and surgery. The notes are full and explicit" (*John Keats*, p. 75).
Newman: "Some of the manuscript notes which Keats took down are still extant, and indicate an industrious and accurate student" (*Interpreters of Nature*, p. 174).
Hale-White: "Judging by Keats's notes, these must have been admirable teaching lectures" (*Keats as Doctor and Patient*, p. 23).

See also Murchie, *Spirit of Place in Keats*, p. 33; Scarlett, "John Keats: Medical Student," p. 538; and Gittings, "John Keats, Physician and Poet," p. 53.

97. Hewlett, *A Life of John Keats*, p. 38. Waddington's manuscript notes on Cooper's course of anatomy and surgery are at the Wills Library, Guy's Hospital.

98. See, for example, Lowell, *John Keats*, p. 75; Scarlett, "John Keats: Medical Student," p. 538; and Ward, *John Keats*, p. 51.

99. Stephens gave two accounts of Keats, one to George Felton Mathew in 1847 (Rollins, *Keats Circle*, 2:206–14) and the other to Benjamin Ward Richard-

son, another doctor, in 1858 (*The Asclepiad* [London, 1884], pp. 138–55). The fact that these accounts are written thirty and forty years after the events, and that they differ on certain points, throws some doubt on their accuracy.

100. Rollins, *Keats Circle*, 2:208. Richardson writes: "In the lecture-room he seemed to sit apart—I am retailing Mr. Stephens' recollections—and to be absorbed in something else, as if the subject suggested thoughts to him which were not practically connected with it. He was often in the subject and out of it, in a dreamy way. He never attached much consequence to his own studies in medicine" (*Disciples of Aesculapius*, 1:22).

101. Rollins, *Keats Circle*, 2:207.

102. Ibid., 2:149. Cowden Clarke gives a slightly different account in *Recollections of Writers*: "He at once made no secret of his inability to sympathize with the science of anatomy, as a main pursuit in life; for one of the expressions that he used, in describing his unfitness for its mastery, was perfectly characteristic. He said, in illustration of his argument, 'The other day, for instance, during the lecture, there came a sunbeam into the room, and with it a whole troop of creatures floating in the ray; and I was off with them to Oberon and fairy-land' " (p. 336).

103. Rollins, *Keats Circle*, 2:211.

104. Dendy, *Philosophy of Mystery*, p. 99.

105. Evans, "Keats as a Medical Student." R. W. King replies to Evans in support of Dendy's account in *TLS* (21 June 1934).

106. Finney, *Evolution of Keats's Poetry*, 1:91. Gittings claims that Dendy's account is of Keats during the autumn term of 1816, when he had already decided to give up medicine (*John Keats*, p. 134).

107. See, for example, the comments of the following critics:

Osler: "He doesn't seem to have been a very brilliant student. Poetry rather than surgery was followed as a vocation" ("John Keats—the Apothecary Poet," *Johns Hopkins Hospital Bulletin*, p. 12).

Lowell: "But at the time he lodged in St. Thomas's Street, scientific research was a task to be got through as quickly as possible and then forgotten" (*John Keats*, p. 90).

Pitfield: "Keats did not in any way distinguish himself while in the medical school" ("John Keats:The Reactions of a Genius," p. 531).

108. See Colvin, *John Keats*, p. 28; Newman, *Interpreters of Nature*, p. 175; Noad, "Young Laurels," p. 527. Stephens expresses the same attitude (Rollins, *Keats Circle*, 2:211).

109. Brown, *Life of John Keats*, p. 41.

110. Gittings, *John Keats*, p. 134.

111. Evidence of Keats's appointment as a dresser comes from entries in Guy's Hospital registers in 1815. On 29 October 1815 one entry records that "Mr. Jno. Keats had returned to him £6.6s, he becoming a dresser" (Lowell, *John Keats*, 1:74).

112. Gittings, *John Keats*, p. 82. Gittings points out that Keats's fee was recorded in the volume *Surgeons Pupils of Guy's and St. Thomas's Hospitals from January 1812 to separation March 1825* which has since been lost, although fac-

similes of the pages referring to Keats are in the Keats House Museum, Hampstead. See also Joseph Warner's account in Wilks and Bettany, *Biographical History* p. 91.

113. Wilks and Bettany, *Biographical History*, p. 91.

114. Ibid., p. 90.

115. South, *Memorials*, pp. 25, 125.

116. Ibid., pp. 27, 26, 125.

117. Ibid., pp. 127–29.

118. Ibid., p. 128.

119. Ibid., p. 81.

120. Hagelman, who examines Keats's relationship with George Cooper and Tyrrell at some length, believes it was under their influence that Keats decided to aim for the higher position of surgeon ("John Keats and the Medical Profession," pp. 149–51).

121. Keats's appointment as dresser to Lucas is recorded in the Guy's Hospital volume *Physicians and Surgeons Pupils . . . 1814–1827* and is quoted by Lowell:

> Entered, March 3, 1816, John Keats.
> Under whom: Mr. L. Time: 12 mo.
> Whence they come: From Edmonton.
> S. Office. £1.1s.0d.
>
> (*John Keats*, 1:74)

122. South, *Memorials*, p. 52.

123. Quoted in Gittings, *John Keats*, p. 108.

124. When Keats registered as a dresser on 3 March 1816, he did so for a twelve-month period, which shows that he still intended to take the Royal College of Surgeons examination, one of the requirements for which was surgical practice for a year.

125. R. C. Brock, *Life and Works of Astley Cooper*, p. 44.

126. South, *Memorials*, p. 54.

127. Cameron, *Mr. Guy's Hospital*, p. 138.

128. South, *Memorials*, p. 54.

129. "Extracts from the Act," p. 252.

130. Gittings, *John Keats*, pp. 115–16.

131. Rollins, *Keats Circle*, 2:211.

132. "A Report from the Court of Examiners," p. 342. On the day that Keats sat, the failure rate was one in seven.

133. "Extracts from the Act," p. 251.

134. Stuart Sperry has argued conclusively that John Clarke, his wife, and unmarried daughter settled in Margate after leaving Enfield, and speculates that this is the most likely reason why Keats and Tom, also one of Clarke's old pupils, went to Margate in August 1816 and again in April 1817 ("Isabella Jane Towers," pp. 36–38).

135. All of Keats's letters to Cowden Clarke during this period are addressed to "Mr. C. C. Clarke / Mr. Towers / Warner Street / Clerkenwell" (*Letters* 1:114, 121, 126).

136. Sperry, "Isabella Jane Towers," p. 38.

137. Ibid., p. 48.

138. Hale-White, *Keats as Doctor and Patient*, p. 84.

139. John Flint South admits to fainting frequently while observing operations at Guy's, yet he became a surgeon to the hospital (*Memorials*, p. 36).

140. Brown, *Life of John Keats*, p. 43.

141. Waddington, "Lectures on Anatomy," 2:379.

142. Cooper, *Principles and Practice*, p. 2.

143. Gittings claims that Keats did not take Cooper's "Principles and Practice of Surgery" until the autumn term of 1816, which is when he decided to give up medicine (*John Keats*, p. 124).

144. Cooper, *Principles and Practice*, p. 5.

145. R. C. Brock, *Life and Works of Astley Cooper*, p. 155. Cooper singled out for admonition those students who "will be fluttering in the boxes of another theatre." The London theaters were frequently patronized by Keats and his friends.

146. "Taylor to Woodhouse," Rollins, *Keats Circle*, 1:307.

147. It is interesting to speculate that, although Keats is known to have been cool toward Shelley, they might have discussed medical matters while Shelley was part of the Hunt circle, from 11 December 1816 to 26 February 1817. At the time, Shelley was residing at Marlow, "where he was a blessing to the poor. His charity, though literal, was not weak. He inquired personally into the circumstances of his petitioners, visited the sick in their beds (for he had gone the rounds of the hospitals on purpose to be able to practise on occasion), and kept a regular list of the industrious poor" (Hunt, *Autobiography*, p. 267). Cowden Clarke also acknowledges that Shelley had "gone through a course of medical study in order that he might assist" the poor with advice (*Recollections of Writers*, p. 354). It is difficult to imagine that Shelley would not have discussed his "cases" with Keats, who was by then a qualified apothecary.

148. See, for example, *Letters*, 1:196, 236; 2:271.

149. Clarke and Clarke, *Recollections of Writers*, pp. 336–37.

150. Brown, *Life of John Keats*, p. 64.

151. Ibid., p. 65.

152. Keats writes to George and Georgiana on 3 March 1819: "I have been at different times turning it in my head whether I should go to Edinburgh & study for a physician" (*Letters* 2:70). In July, he wrote to Fanny Keats: "I have enough knowledge of my gallipots to ensure me an employment & maintainance" (*Letters* 2:125).

153. See *Letters*, 2:342, 355.

Chapter II: Chemistry

1. Haighton, "Lectures on Physiology," p. 7.

2. Ibid., p. 168.

3. Davy, *Collected Works*, 2:320–21.

4. Ritterbush, *Art of Organic Forms*, pp. 2–3.

5. Babington and Allen, *Syllabus*, p. iv.

6. Babington, "Lectures on Chemistry," pp. 1–2. The lectures were published before 1816, a second edition appearing at that date, but I have been unable to locate a copy.

7. Sperry, *Keats the Poet*, pp. 30–71.

8. Knight, "Chemistry, Physiology and Materialism," p. 139.

9. Wordsworth, *Prose Works*, 3:46.

10. Mill, *System of Logic*, p. 558.

11. Eliot, "Tradition and the Individual Talent," pp. 26–27.

12. Sperry, *Keats the Poet*, pp. 36–37.

13. Babington and Allen, *Syllabus*, pp. 1–2. Babington gives the same definition in his "Lectures on Chemistry," p. 2.

14. Babington and Allen, *Syllabus*, p. 35.

15. Ibid., p. 4.

16. Babington, "Lectures on Chemistry," p. 27; see also p. 14.

17. Priestley, *Heads of Lectures*, p. 138.

18. Babington and Allen, *Syllabus*, p. 28.

19. Babington, "Lectures on Chemistry," p. 60.

20. Bate, *John Keats*, pp. 243–45.

21. Hazlitt, *Complete Works*, 18:30–33. It should be observed that no one, to my knowledge, has suggested Keats was influenced by this essay. Ian Jack, in discussing Keats's criticism of West's painting, claims that " 'intensity' was also a favourite term of Haydon's (*Diary*, II, 10)" (*Keats and the Mirror of Art*, p. 96), but does not develop the idea any further. Before either Bate or Jack, however, C. L. Finney had put forward the idea that "the principle of intensity, or gusto, was a chief principle of the poetic system which he [Keats] wrought out of his study of Shakespeare's plays. He owed his understanding of this principle partly to Haydon and partly to Hazlitt" (*Evolution of Keats's Poetry*, 1:244). M. H. Abrams also traces Keats's concept of "intensity" back to Hazlitt's idea of gusto, and both ultimately back to Longinus's treatise on the sublime (*The Mirror and the Lamp*, p. 136). Middleton Murry's explanation of the term is, to my mind, confusing: "The bearing of this particular use of 'intensity' upon our passage is manifest. . . . The work of art is 'intense,' and the man who truly experiences it is also 'intense.' 'Intensity' thus is, as we say, objective and subjective; and it peculiarly belongs both to the objective identity of Beauty and Truth and to the subjective response to it" (*Studies in Keats*, p. 55).

22. Sperry, *Keats the Poet*, p. 45.

23. Babington and Allen, *Syllabus*, pp. 8–9.

24. Babington, "Lectures on Chemistry," p. 65.

25. Ibid., p. 101.

26. Stocker, *Pharmacopoeia Officinalis*, p. 4.

27. Babington and Allen, *Syllabus*, p. 129.

28. Ibid., pp. 145–46.

29. Babington, "Lectures on Chemistry," p. 128.

30. Ibid., p. 134.

31. Stocker, *Pharmacopoeia Officinalis*, pp. 304–05. In the *Pharmacopoeia*, there are numerous other examples of the preparation of drugs by means of distilla-

tion, sublimation, abstraction, and digestion. Since Keats was expected to translate part of this book for this L.S.A. examination, he would certainly have been familiar with it.

32. In this and subsequent letters in this chapter, the italics, unless otherwise indicated, are mine.

33. Weiskel, *Romantic Sublime.*

34. Ende, *Keats and the Sublime.* More recently, W. P. Albrecht, supporting Weiskel, has taken a similar "philosophical" approach ("The Tragic Sublime of Hazlitt and Keats"), while John Watson has examined Keats's concept of the sublime exlusively in relation to landscape ("Keats and the Pursuit of the Sublime").

35. See, for example, Elliott, "The Real Tragedy of Keats"; Havens, "Unreconciled Opposites in Keats."

36. Priestley points out the use of the term "fine" in chemistry: "The fineness of gold is generally estimated by dividing the gold into twenty-four parts, called *carats.* The phrase *twenty-three carats fine* means that the mass contains twenty-three parts out of twenty-four of pure gold, the remainder being *alloy,* of some baser metal" (*Heads of Lectures,* p. 89).

37. Sperry, *Keats the Poet,* p. 35.

38. Bonnycastle, *Introduction to Astronomy,* p. 422.

39. See, for example, *Endymion,* I, 360–61; II, 436–38; IV, 420–21; *St. Agnes' Eve,* 318; *Hyperion,* I, 216, 340.

40. Bornstein, "Keats's Concept of the Ethereal," p. 98. Bornstein's argument is an expansion of Earl Wasserman's idea (*Finer Tone,* pp. 15–16), which Wasserman claims is the central principle of Keats's vision: the "mystic oxymoron," or "paradoxical essence," the way in which the poet turns physical matter into ethereal being.

41. Blackstone, *Consecrated Urn,* pp. 112–13.

42. R. T. Davies, "Some Ideas and Usages," p. 136.

43. The best explanation of the theories concerning ether is, to my knowledge, Whittaker's *History of the Theories of Aether and Electricity.* Very briefly, he explains the development of the idea of ether:

> Space is, in Descartes' view, a *plenum,* being occupied by a medium which, though imperceptible to the senses, is capable of transmitting force, and exerting effects on material bodies immersed in it—the *aether,* as it is called. The word had meant originally the blue sky or air, and had been borrowed from the Greek by Latin writers, from whom it had passed into French and English in the Middle Ages. In ancient cosmology it was sometimes used in the sense of that which occupied celestial regions; and when the notion of a medium filling the interplanetary void was introduced, *aether* was the obvious word to use for it. Before Descartes, it had connoted merely the occupancy of some part of space: he was the first to bring the aether into science, by postulating that it had mechanical properties. . . .
>
> [Newton went on to claim that] this aether pervades the pores of all material bodies, and is the cause of their cohesion; its density varies

from one body to another, being greatest in the free interplanetary spaces. It is not necessarily a single uniform substance: but just as air contains aqueous vapour, so the aether may contain various "aethereal spirits," adapted to produce the phenomena of electricity, magnetism and gravitation. (1:5–6, 19)

44. Sperry, *Keats the Poet,* p. 40.
45. Priestley, *Heads of Lectures,* p. 69.
46. Babington, "Lectures on Chemistry," p. 269.
47. Ibid., pp. 265–68; Stocker, *Pharmacopoeia Officinalis,* pp. 98–108.
48. Stocker, *Pharmacopoeia Officinalis,* pp. 98–99.
49. Stocker states that "if it be required very pure, the Ether must be again distilled" (Ibid., p. 100). See also Babington, "Lectures on Chemistry," p. 266.
50. Stocker explains: "Nitric ether appears to be formed by the reciprocal action of nitric acid and alcohol, in which the acid is wholly *decomposed,* and its *decomposition* commences from the very moment the two bodies are mixed. The alcohol also undergoes *decomposition,* part of its elements *combining* with oxygen from the nitric acid *forms* oxalic and acetic acids, while the carbon *separated* . . . is *converted* into carbonic acid gas" (*Pharmacopoeia Officinalis,* pp. 101–02).
51. Bornstein, "Keats's Concept of the Ethereal," p. 99.
52. See p. 60.
53. Davy, *Collected Works,* 4: 140.
54. William Nicholson, *The First Principles of Chemistry,* 2nd ed. (London, 1792), p. 34, quoted in Sperry, *Keats the Poet,* p. 47.
55. Babington, "Lectures on Chemistry," p. 264.
56. Finney, *Evolution of Keats's Poetry,* 1:367. For Sperry's discussion of this passage, see *Keats the Poet,* p. 55.
57. Sperry, *Keats the Poet,* pp. 68–69. For another interpretation of this passage, see Evert, *Aesthetic and Myth,* pp. 190–91.
58. In discussing Bailey's "disinterestedness," his selfless love, Keats describes him as being "real" in a letter to Jane and Mariane Reynolds, written on 14 September 1817: "To your Brother John . . . and to you my dear friends Marrianne and Jane I shall ever feel grateful for having made known to me so *real* a fellow as Bailey. He delights me in the Selfish and (please god) the disenterrested part of my disposition. . . . his Enthusiasm in his own pursuit and for all good things is of an exalted kind" (*Letters* 1:160).
59. Babington, "Lectures on Chemistry," p. 266.
60. Both Evert and D'Avanzo have discussed at length Keats's use of wine as a metaphor for poetry, but neither has mentioned his knowledge of chemistry in this respect. See Evert, *Aesthetic and Myth,* pp. 68–72, and D'Avanzo, *Keats's Metaphors,* pp. 108–12.
61. Priestley explains: "Of liquid inflammable substances the principal is *spirit of wine,* sometimes called *ardent spirit,* and, when highly refined, *alcohol.* It is obtained from vegetable substances by their going through the vinous fermentation" (*Heads of Lectures,* p. 66).
62. Babington, "Lectures on Chemistry," pp. 259–60.

63. Ibid., p. 265.
64. Ibid., p. 262.
65. Ibid., p. 265.
66. Ibid., p. 268.
67. Babington and Allen, *Syllabus*, p. 135.
68. Quoted in Finney, *Evolution of Keats's Poetry*, 1:339, my italics.
69. Ibid., 1:340, my italics.
70. Ibid., 1:297–99. See also Colvin, *John Keats, His Life and Poetry*, p. 205.
71. Ford, *Prefigurative Imagination of John Keats*, pp. 14–15; Pettet, *On the Poetry of Keats*, pp. 126–27.
72. Sperry, *Keats the Poet*, p. 48.
73. The similarity between Keats's ideas concerning art and morality has often gone unnoticed. It is his concept of the selfless Poetical Character that develops into his belief in "disinterestedness" or altruism (*Letters* 2:79). The two are ultimately fused in his idea, presented in *The Fall of Hyperion*, that the poet must feel the woes of all humanity, and must selflessly try to heal those woes, must be a physician-poet.
74. Hagelman, "John Keats and the Medical Profession," p. 255.
75. Babington, "Lectures on Chemistry," p. 39, my italics.
76. Babington points out that "heat promotes the Decomposition of Bodies, and many can not be decomposed without it" (ibid., p. 34). See also Babington and Allen, *Syllabus*, p. 42.
77. Babington, "Lectures on Chemistry," p. 26.
78. Ibid.

Chapter III: Botany

1. Davy, "A Discourse Introductory to a Course of Lectures on Chemistry," in *Collected Works*, 2:312–13.
2. Ritterbush has traced in detail the development of chemical, botanical, and physiological analogy in the eighteenth century; see his *Overtures to Biology*.
3. Robert Darwin, *Principia Botanica*, p. vi.
4. Salisbury, *Botanist's Companion*, 2:43.
5. Curry, *Heads of a Course of Lectures*, p. 23.
6. E.g., Salisbury, "Mr. Salisbury's Botanical Excursions."
7. Towers published *The Domestic Gardener's Manual* in 1830 and followed it with many articles in horticultural journals. See Sperry, "Isabella Jane Towers," pp. 46–47, for a full list of Towers's publications.
8. Hewlett, *A Life of John Keats*, p. 64. Keats mentions Bessy Kent in *Letters* 1:140. See also Tatchell, "Elizabeth Kent and *Flora Domestica*."
9. Rollins, *Keats Circle*, 1:267.
10. Abrams has done this for the Romantics generally in his chapter "Unconscious Genius and Organic Growth" in *The Mirror and the Lamp*, pp. 184–225, but his focus is on Coleridge; Keats gets very minor coverage. Sewell's *Orphic Voice* mentions Keats only very briefly.
11. Blackstone, *Consecrated Urn*, pp. 345–46.

12. *Poems of John Keats,* ed. Allott, p. 88n.

13. Erasmus Darwin, *Loves of the Plants,* 1:57n., in *Botanic Garden.*

14. Thornton, *New Illustration,* unnumbered folio.

15. Robert Darwin, *Principia Botanica,* p. 40 (written by Erasmus Darwin in his son's name). In this image, Keats may also have in mind the claim that in some perennial bulbs, the actual flower may be observed in miniature upon dissection. As Erasmus Darwin explains:

> What is in common language called a bulbous root, is by Linneus termed the Hybernacle, or Winter-lodge of the young plant. As these bulbs in every respect resemble buds, except in their being produced under ground, and include the leaves and flower in miniature, which are to be expanded in the ensuing spring. By cautiously cutting through the concentric coats of a tulip-root, longitudinally from the top to the base, and taking them off successively, the whole flower of the next year's tulip is beautifully seen by the naked eye, with its petals, pistil, and stamens. (*Loves of Plants,* 1:177n., in *Botanic Garden*)

16. Robert Darwin, *Principia Botanica,* p. 42.

17. Thornton, *New Illustration,* unnumbered folio.

18. Robert Darwin, *Principia Botanica,* pp. 29–30. Keats's preference for the form "luxury" rather than the more technically correct "luxuriance" may owe something to his reading of Chapman's *Homer,* where "luxury" is used to mean "luxuriance" (*Illiad,* xxi, 262).

19. E. F. Guy's article on "Keats's Use of 'Luxury' " gives no indication that the word has a scientific meaning.

20. Robert Darwin, *Principia Botanica,* p. 23.

21. Thornton, *New Illustration,* unnumbered folio.

22. E.g., Withering, *Systematic Arrangement,* 1:231, 253. For a similar joke involving his medical knowledge, see Keats's letter of 13 March 1818 to Bailey, where he describes the men of Kent: "The degenerate race about me are Pulvis Ipecac. Simplex a strong dose" (*Letters* 1:241). "Pulvis Ipecac" means "nauseating," and "Simplex" is an emetic.

23. Robert Darwin, *Principia Botanica,* p. 34. For a more detailed discussion of "Vegetable Respiration," specifically the analogy between man's lungs and plants' leaves, see Erasmus Darwin, *Economy of Vegetation,* Additional Note XXXVII, in *Botanic Garden.*

24. D'Avanzo claims that Keats learned about the poetic frenzy induced by eating laurel leaves from Potter's *Archaeologia Graeca: Antiquities of Greece;* see D'Avanzo, *Keats's Metaphors,* pp. 103–05. Keats could just as easily have gained such information from Erasmus Darwin's *Loves of the Plants,* however, where Darwin's footnote on laurel states: "The Pythian priestess is supposed to have been made drunk with infusion of laurel-leaves, when she delivered her oracles. The intoxication or inspiration is finely described by Virgil. Aen. L. vi" (3:40n., in *Botanic Garden*). Keats himself was, of course, very familiar with Virgil.

25. Salisbury, *Botanist's Companion,* 2:62.

26. Thornton, *A Family Herbal,* p. 401.

27. Salisbury, *Botanist's Companion*, 2:135. Erasmus Darwin gives a similar description, as follows: "The distilled water from laurel-leaves is perhaps the most sudden poison, we are acquainted with in this country. I have seen about two spoonfuls of it destroy a large pointer dog, in less than ten minutes. In a smaller dose it is said to produce intoxication; on this account there is reason to believe it acts in the same manner as opium and vinous spirits; but that the dose is not so well ascertained" (*Loves of the Plants*, 3:40n., in *Botanic Garden*).

28. Lowell, *John Keats*, pp. 128–29.

29. Erasmus Darwin, *Loves of the Plants*, 2:425, in *Botanic Garden*.

30. Hunt, *Poetical Works*, p. 352.

31. Bush, *Mythology and the Romantic Tradition*, p. 85.

32. Blackstone, *Consecrated Urn*, p. 375.

33. D'Avanzo, *Keats's Metaphors*, pp. 106–08.

34. Evert, *Aesthetic and Myth*, pp. 107–08.

35. Blackstone, *Consecrated Urn*, pp. 76–78, 129–30, 177. Brown lists *Celtic Researches* among Keats's books at his death (Rollins, *Keats Circle*, 1:254).

36. Plato, *The Timaeus and The Critias or Atlanticus*, p. 204. Keats would have read the *Timaeus* in Taylor's translation, a copy of which was owned by Bailey. Desmond Lee's translation "It [the plant] is always entirely passive" (*Timaeus and Critias*, p. 105) is probably more accurate than Taylor's "it continually suffers all things"; but the sense of passivity is implicit in Taylor's passage. For more on the influence of Plato on Keats, see Blackstone, *Consecrated Urn*, pp. 34, 74, 77, *passim*.

37. Here Keats is also influenced by the classical myth in which Jove and Juno ask Tiresias to judge which sex gets the most pleasure out of sexual intercourse. Keats would have known the story from Ovid's *Metamorphoses*, 3:322–32. See Sandys, *Ovid's Metamorphosis Englished*, pp. 137–38.

38. For a discussion of the image of sensitive plants in Romantic literature, see Maniquis, "The Puzzling *Mimosa*." Maniquis does not include Keats in his study.

39. Quoted in Ritterbush, *Overtures to Biology*, pp. 109–10.

40. D'Avanzo, *Keats's Metaphors*, pp. 202–05.

41. Allott quotes Byron's comment in her note on these lines; see *Poems of John Keats*, p. 157n.

42. Rollins, *Keats Circle*, 1:34–35.

43. Evert, *Aesthetic and Myth*, pp. 30–36, 49–50; and Blackstone, *Consecrated Urn*, pp. 107–09, 384.

44. Blackstone, *Consecrated Urn*, p. 375.

45. For an explanation of this theory, see Erasmus Darwin, *Economy of Vegetation*, 1:463n., in *Botanic Garden*: "The influence of electricity in forwarding the germination of plants and their growth seems to be pretty well established." That Keats was aware of this concept is evidenced in his marginal note on *King Lear*, I, i: "Shakespeare doth scatter abroad on the winds of Passion, where the germs take b[u]oyant root in stormy Air, suck lightning sap, and become voiced dragons" (*Poetical Works and Other Writings*, 3:15). For another interesting botanical note on Shakespeare, this time on *A Midsummer Night's Dream*, see *Poetical Works and Other Writings*, 3:12–13.

46. See Abrams, *The Mirror and the Lamp*, chaps. 7–8; and Ritterbush, *Art of Organic Forms*, chaps. 1–3. Both Abrams and Ritterbush treat Keats as a very minor figure, perhaps because he did not write any formal criticism.

47. See Sandys, *Ovid's Metamorphosis Englished*, 15:199–213. Keats read Sandys's translation in an 1806 version edited by Daniel Chrispin.

48. Evert, *Aesthetic and Myth*, p. 73.

49. Ibid., pp. 74–75.

50. Blackstone, *Consecrated Urn*, pp. 336–38.

51. Ritterbush, *Art of Organic Forms*, p. 27.

52. Erasmus Darwin, *Economy of Vegetation*, 1:278n., in *Botanic Garden*.

53. Ibid.

54. Fyfe, *Compendium of Anatomy*, 1:21.

55. For a discussion of the controversy over the word "death['s]" in this line, see *Poems of John Keats*, ed. Stillinger, p. 634. I have adopted Stillinger's reading.

56. In "To Autumn," there may be an echo from Erasmus Darwin's *Economy of Vegetation* (in *Botanic Garden*); compare Darwin's: "Gay Sylphs attendant beat the fragrant air / On winnowing wings, and waft her golden hair" (1, 75–76) with Keats's: "Thy hair soft-lifted by the winnowing wind" (15). Darwin's influence on Keats may have been stronger than the poet was willing to admit.

57. For descriptions of these plants, see Salisbury, *Botanist's Companion*, 2:51, 137, 139; and Thornton, *A Family Herbal*, pp. 176–77, 549–50.

58. Priestley, *Heads of Lectures*, p. 1.

Chapter IV: Anatomy and Physiology

1. *John Keats's Anatomical and Physiological Note Book,* hereafter referred to as *Note Book.* The actual notebook, in Keats's hand, is now at Keats House, Hampstead.

2. South, *Memorials*, p. 38. As I have failed to locate a copy of Green's *Outlines*, I quote from *Dissector's Manual*, which Green says in the Advertisement "is an enlarged edition of the 'Outlines of a Course of Dissections,' printed some years ago for the use of the Students of Anatomy at St. Thomas's Hospital. The plan therein recommended has been retained, from the conviction of its utility, founded on experience." For a detailed discussion of Green's texts, see Hagelman, "John Keats and the Medical Profession," pp. 106–08.

3. See Waddington, "Lectures on Anatomy," 1:11.

4. Fyfe, *Compendium of Anatomy*; Blumenbach, *Institutions of Physiology*, trans. John Elliotson. Keats would probably have used Blumenbach's *Physiology* in Elliotson's second edition (1810), a copy of which I have been unable to consult, so I have quoted from the third edition (1820). Blumenbach's text is, however, the same in both editions; Elliotson's notes on the text are revised. John Elliotson was assistant physician to St. Thomas's Hospital.

5. South, *Memorials*, p. 38; Innes, *Short Description of the Human Muscles*; Barclay, *Description of the Arteries*.

6. For a detailed consideration of the merits of these theories, see Elliotson's lengthy note in Blumenbach, *Institutions of Physiology*, pp. 46–53.

7. Davy, *Collected Works,* 2:313–14.

8. Quoted in R. C. Brock, *Life and Works of Astley Cooper,* pp. 148–49.

9. J. H. Green, *Dissector's Manual,* p. xlix.

10. Astley Cooper, *Principles and Practice,* p. 1.

11. J. H. Green, *Dissector's Manual,* p. xlvii.

12. Astley Cooper, *Principles and Practice,* p. 7; Barclay, *Description of the Arteries,* p. xx.

13. Keats, *Note Book,* p. 1. Waddington gives the same definitions: "Anatomy consists in the knowledge of the Structure; and relative situation of Organized Bodies; . . . Physiology of the functions of the different parts, and Pathology of their diseased appearances" ("Lectures on Anatomy," 1:1).

14. Keats, *Note Book,* p. 1; cf. Blumenbach, *Institutions of Physiology,* p. 38.

15. Haighton, "Lectures on Physiology," p. 132.

16. Ritterbush, *Art of Organic Forms,* p. 27.

17. Home, "On the Changes the Blood Undergoes."

18. Waddington, "Lectures on Anatomy," 1:21. Babington and Curry are also somewhat suspicious of Boerhaave's and Loewenhoeck's "corpuscularian philosophy" (*Outlines of a Course of Lectures,* p. 18).

19. Blumenbach, *Institutions of Physiology,* p. 6.

20. Waddington, "Lectures on Anatomy," 2:183. *The London Dissector* gives the same information: "The brain is divided into three parts: 1. The cerebrum; 2. The cerebellum; 3. The medulla oblongata. . . . The brain is divided by the falx into two hemispheres and by the pia mater into numerous convolutions. Each hemisphere is divided into three lobes" (p. 130). See also Blumenbach, *Institutions of Physiology,* p. 131.

21. J. H. Green, *Dissector's Manual,* p. 77. See also *London Dissector,* p. 138. Interestingly, Keats would have found a similar concept in the *Timaeus,* where Plato states that "the Gods bound the two divine circulations of the soul in a spherical body, in imitation of the circular figure of the universe: and this part of the body is what we now denominate the head" (*The Timaeus and The Critias,* trans. Taylor, p. 161).

22. Keats describes this concept, in an earlier letter, in terms of a spider that spins a whole web from a few solid points (*Letters,* 1:231–32).

23. Waddington, "Lectures on Anatomy," 2:177. See also J. H. Green, *Dissector's Manual,* p. 74; Fyfe, *Compendium of Anatomy,* 2:16; and Blumenbach, *Institutions of Physiology,* p. 128.

24. Fyfe, *Compendium of Anatomy,* 2:32.

25. J. H. Green, *Dissector's Manual,* p. 87.

26. Fyfe, *Compendium of Anatomy,* 1:22.

27. Ricks, *Keats and Embarrassment,* pp. 162–63.

28. Fyfe, *Compendium of Anatomy,* 1:21; 2:21.

29. See, for example, Sir Philip Sidney's first sonnet in *Astrophel and Stella.*

30. J. H. Green, *Dissector's Manual,* p. 85.

31. Clarke and Clarke, *Recollections of Writers,* p. 132.

32. Fyfe, *Compendium of Anatomy,* 2:23–24, 27; cf. Keats's "wide hollows of my brain."

33. *London Dissector,* p. 131; J. H. Green, *Dissector's Manual,* p. 88.

34. For a discussion of this letter in regard to the types of poetry Keats wants to write, see Thorpe, *Mind of John Keats*, pp. 43–47; Roberts, "Poetry of Sensation"; and Bate, *John Keats*, pp. 328–31.

35. In his *Note Book*, Keats writes: "Nerves are composed of numerous Cords—this is still the Case in the smallest. They take a serpentine direction. They arise by numerous branches from the Substance of ye brain" (p. 54).

36. J. H. Green, *Dissector's Manual*, p. 85.

37. Much critical ink has been spilled explaining the background and meaning of Keats's "Mansion of Life" letter. Critics have argued for its dependence on "Tintern Abbey" and its relationship to *Sleep and Poetry* (Colvin, *John Keats, His Life and Poetry*, pp. 127–28; Robert Bridges, intro. to *Poems of John Keats*, ed. Drury, 1:xxxiii; *Poems of John Keats*, ed. de Selincourt, p. xxxix) and against such dependence (Severs, "Keats's 'Mansion of Many Apartments' "). Gittings has claimed that it is influenced by the preface to *The Excursion* (*John Keats*, pp. 314–15), and Wasserman states that in *The Eve of St. Agnes* "the castle is that Mansion of many Apartments in which human existence plays out its part" (*Finer Tone*, p. 119).

38. Pettit, "Scientific Correlatives"; Hagelman, "Keats's Medical Training."

39. Waddington, "Lectures on Anatomy," 2:225; see also *London Dissector*, pp. 122–23; Fyfe, *Compendium of Anatomy*, 2:80. Keats may also have in mind a part of the internal ear called the cochlea which "has two *Canals* or *Gyri,* called Scalae, from a supposed resemblances [*sic*] to stair-cases; the Gyri or Turns of which are very close to each other, and run in a spiral direction, like the Shell of a Snail, from which the part has obtained its name" (ibid., 2:93).

40. Hagelman, "Keats's Medical Training," pp. 76–77.

41. J. H. Green, *Dissector's Manual*, p. 71.

42. Waddington, "Lectures on Anatomy," 1:269; see also 1:283, 313; Fyfe, *Compendium of Anatomy*, 1:39.

43. J. H. Green, *Dissector's Manual*, p. 87.

44. *London Dissector*, pp. 135–36, 130–31.

45. Barclay, *Description of the Arteries*, p. ii.

46. Blumenbach, *Institutions of Physiology*, p. 64; J. H. Green, *Dissector's Manual*, p. 77; *London Dissector*, p. 127.

47. Keats, *Note Book*, p. 13.

48. Hagelman, "Keats's Medical Training," pp. 77–78.

49. Waddington, "Lectures on Anatomy," 1:93. Fyfe gives a similar definition: "When the Cerebellum is cut in a Vertical direction, the Medullary part is then found to bear a striking resemblance to the branching of the Shrub called *Arbor Vitae:* from which circumstance it has obtained the name of this Shrub" (*Compendium of Anatomy*, 2:33). See also *London Dissector*, p. 139, and J. H. Green, *Dissector's Manual*, p. 88. Hagelman cites only Green, whose definition is the least convincing.

50. Hagelman, "Keats's Medical Training," pp. 79–80.

51. J. H. Green, *Dissector's Manual*, p. 96.

52. Waddington, "Lectures on Anatomy," 1:77. See also Blumenbach, *Institutions of Physiology*, p. 14.

53. Even the final image of Psyche's "casement ope at night" may owe something to Keats's anatomical knowledge. Parts of the inner ear, near the brain, are named the fenestra ovalis and the fenestra rotundum, "both leading into the internal part" of the head (Waddington, "Lectures on Anatomy," 2:233).

54. Blackstone, *Consecrated Urn*, p. 57.

55. Bunn, "Keats's *Ode to Psyche*," p. 584.

56. The poet-narrator's transformation, his dying into life, is described in terms of disease metaphors and will be dealt with in the next chapter. See p. 230.

57. Fyfe, *Compendium of Anatomy*, 2:45.

58. Hagelman, "Keats's Medical Training," pp. 73–74.

59. Waddington, "Lectures on Anatomy," 1:261. See also 1:259, where Cooper points out that inequality between races is the result of sociological events rather than the shape of the skull. His liberal ideas must have been shared by Keats, who believed so strongly in the equality of men. For a much more sympathetic view of Gall's and Spurzheim's theory, see Blumenbach, *Institutions of Physiology*, pp. 32–34.

60. Haydon, *Autobiography and Memoirs*, p. 270.

61. Astley Cooper, *Principles and Practice*, p. 146; see also Waddington, "Lectures on Anatomy," 1:7; Fyfe, *Compendium of Anatomy*, 2:37.

62. Astley Cooper, *Principles and Practice*, p. 146.

63. Keats, *Note Book*, pp. 56, 1.

64. Ibid., p. 55.

65. Jack, *Keats and the Mirror of Art*, p. 226.

66. South, *Memorials*, p. 55.

67. Astley Cooper, *Principles and Practice*, p. 2.

68. *London Dissector*, p. 1.

69. Blackstone, *Consecrated Urn*, pp. xii–xiii; see also pp. 336–37.

70. Hunt, *Autobiography*, p. 279.

71. Keats, *Note Book*, p. 55.

72. Blumenbach, *Institutions of Physiology*, pp. 139–40.

73. Haighton, "Lectures on Physiology," p. 140. Support for the electricity theory came from such important scientists as Joseph Priestley, who claimed that "the influence of the brain and the nerves upon the muscles seems to be of an electric nature" (*Heads of Lectures*, p. 165), and Erasmus Darwin, who states: "The temporary motion of a paralytic limb is likewise caused by passing the electric shock through it; which would seem to indicate some analogy between the electric fluid, and the nervous fluid, which is seperated from the blood by the brain, and thence diffused along the nerves for the purposes of motion and sensation" (*Economy of Vegetation*, 1:367n., in *Botanic Garden*). Marmaduke Berdoe even went so far as to assume that generation was accomplished by "the most active sparks of the electric fluid" (quoted in Ritterbush, *Overtures to Biology*, p. 106); and Charles Bell, the most revolutionary neurologist of the early nineteenth century and a personal friend of Haydon's, rejected all these theories concerning fluids and spirits (*Idea of a New Anatomy*, p. 12).

74. Keats, *Note Book,* p. 58. Waddington gives a slightly expanded version of these same ideas in his notes, "Lectures on Anatomy," 1:115. Blumenbach gives the various theories and tends to support an electric fluid (*Institutions of Physiology,* pp. 140–41); and Fyfe does not support any one theory (*Compendium of Anatomy,* 3:151).

75. Blumenbach points out that some theorists consider nervous energy "analgous to fire, . . . to electricity" (*Institutions of Physiology,* p. 140).

76. The poem appears in Rollins, *Keats Circle,* 1:98–100.

77. Fyfe, *Compendium of Anatomy,* 3:151.

78. Thorpe, *Mind of John Keats,* p. 64.

79. Bate, *John Keats,* p. 240.

80. Keats, *Note Book,* p. 55. Waddington's notes are almost identical ("Lectures on Anatomy," 1:101).

81. Waddington, "Lectures on Anatomy," 1:9. Keats's notes on this lecture are not so clear:

> This [Nervous] System has 4 Function 1 Sensation
> 2 Volition
> 3 Involuntary Motion
> 4 Sympathy.
> The Organs of Sense are 5 Feeling, Sight, Hearing, Smell, Taste.
> The Mind has 3 Functions
> 1 Memory, 2 Judgment 3 Imagination (*Note Book,* pp. 1–2)

82. Although he traced Keats's source for these ideas back to David Hartley rather than to Keats's medical training, James Caldwell long ago recognized the poet's meaning of "sensation":

> What a deal of ink has flown over this wish of Keats for a Life of sensation, rather than thought. It has been cited to convict him of sensuality, and it has been explained and apologized for and said to have nothing to do with sensations of the body. The theory of the association of ideas makes it clear that what Keats means by a life of sensation, is the life of the imagination, a life solidly grounded in bygone events of eye, ear, palate, etc., but modifying, refining, and ramifying them into infinitely complex chains of associates. It is distinguished from thought in that it operates on these directly, preserving and enhancing their color and life and forms, rather than abstracting and generalizing them in systems and relations. (*John Keats' Fancy,* pp. 155–56)

For a detailed discussion of the eighteenth-century theories on "sensation," see also Sperry, *Keats the Poet,* pp. 11–29.

83. For similar complaints about sympathetic identification, see *Letters* 1:392, 395; 2:5, 349.

84. Bate, *John Keats,* pp. 252–62.

85. Haighton, "Lectures on Physiology," p. 140. See also Keats, *Note Book,* pp. 1, 56–57; Waddington, "Lectures on Anatomy," 1:9, 111.

86. Astley Cooper, *Principles and Practice,* p. 10.

87. Curry, *Heads of a Course of Lectures,* p. 8.

88. Quoted in Hunter and Macalpine, *Three Hundred Years of Psychiatry*, pp. 494–95.

89. Haydon, *Autobiography and Memoirs*, p. 29.

90. Ibid., pp. 18, 29–30.

91. Ibid., pp. 32–33.

92. *Annals of Fine Arts*, 2:535, and 3:649; quoted in Jack, *Keats and the Mirror of Art*, pp. 49–50. It is also interesting that Astley Cooper "pointed out the errors of those who paint or chisel from immagination, and not from observation of nature," with specific reference to the breasts and testicles (R. C. Brock, *Life and Works of Astley Cooper*, p. 96).

93. Jack, *Keats and the Mirror of Art*, p. 36.

94. Bate, *John Keats*, p. 146.

95. Finney, *Evolution of Keats's Poetry*, 1:184.

96. Haydon, *Autobiography and Memoirs*, pp. 66–67. Hazlitt, in "On the Elgin Marbles" (*The London Magazine*, February 1822) expresses the same idea:

> We can compare these Marbles to nothing but human figures petrified: they have the appearance of absolute *fac-similes* or casts taken from nature. . . . The utter absence of all setness of appearance proves that they were done as studies from actual models. The separate parts of the human body may be given from scientific knowledge: —their modifications or inflections can only be learnt by seeing them in action. . . . The veins, the wrinkles in the skin, the indications of the muscles under the skin (which appear as plainly to the anatomist as the expert angler knows from an undulation on the surface of the water what fish is playing with his bait beneath it), the finger-joints, the nails, every the smallest part cognisable to the naked eye, is given here with the same ease and exactness, with the same prominence, and the same subordination, that it would be in a cast from nature, i.e. in nature itself. (*Complete Works*, 18:145–47)

97. Quoted in R. C. Brock, *Life and Works of Astley Cooper*, p. 96.

98. Birkenhead, *Against Oblivion*, p. 44.

99. Haydon, *Autobiography and Memoirs*, p. 235.

100. Hazlitt, *Complete Works*, 18:100.

101. Astley Cooper, *Principles and Practice*, pp. 74–75.

Chapter V: Pathology and Medicine

1. Identical *Outlines* were later published under Curry's name alone (London, 1817) when Babington ceased to teach the course, and later still by Cholmeley (London, 1820) when he took over the course.

2. Cooper advised his students "to pay particular attention to Morbid Preparations" (Waddington, "Lectures on Anatomy," 1:11).

3. Babington and Curry, *Outlines of a Course of Lectures*, pp. 119, 148; hereafter referred to as *Outlines*.

4. Curry, *Heads of a Course of Lectures*, pp. 8–9; hereafter referred to as *Heads*.

5. Bell, *Idea of a New Anatomy*.

6. Babington and Curry, *Outlines*, p. 19; cf. Curry, *Heads*, pp. 6–7.

7. Babington and Curry, *Outlines*, p. 20; Curry, *Heads*, p. 19.

8. Whytt, "Nervous Disorders," in Hunter and Macalpine, *Three Hundred Years of Psychiatry*, p. 392.

9. Keats, *Note Book*, p. 57.

10. Curry, *Heads*, pp. 5, 10.

11. Marcet, *Some Remarks on Clinical Lectures*, pp. 18–19.

12. Note by Jane Sutton in her copy of Saunders, *Elements of the Practice of Physic*, p. 42.

13. Lempriere, *Classical Dictionary*, p. 61. Cowden Clarke tells us about Keats's reading: "The books . . . that were his constant recurrent sources of attraction were Tooke's 'Pantheon,' Lempriere's 'Classical Dictionary,' which he appeared to *learn*, and Spence's 'Polymetis.' This was the store whence he acquired his intimacy with the Greek mythology" (Clarke and Clarke, *Recollections of Writers*, p. 329).

14. Addison, *The Tatler*, no. 240; quoted in Blackstone, *Consecrated Urn*, p. 2.

15. Those critics who have commented on the dual nature of Apollo are Evert, whose work I will return to shortly; Blackstone, who quotes the passage from Joseph Addison; and Gittings, who, in commenting on Keats's sympathetic imagination, writes:

> This is the philosophy that Keats puts forward as his way to live as a poet; but it must have occurred to many of you that this description does not in any way apply solely to the life of a poet only. It could well be that Keats is talking about the attitude of the good medical practitioner, the sympathy, the alertness, the judgment and identification at all points that he too needs. . . . The unfinished epic *Hyperion*, has, as its real hero, the newly-made god Apollo; and Apollo, I need not again remind you, was the god of poetry and of healing. He is portrayed everywhere in Keats as learning to be a healer and a poet through his power of sympathetic identification. ("This Living Hand," p. 10)

16. Evert writes:

> I cannot forbear the suggestion that at this crisis in his life the poet might well have been struck by a curious coincidence, namely that his choice lay between two modes of service to the same god. That Apollo was anciently the god of healing, Keats would have known from Spenser and the classical dictionaries, as well as from the Hippocratic Oath (beginning, "By Apollo Physician . . ."), with which he must surely have become acquainted during his just-completed medical studies, though he probably did not have to swear it. (*Aesthetic and Myth*, pp. 95–96)

17. D'Avanzo, *Keats's Metaphors*, pp. 81–82.

18. Blackstone, *Consecrated Urn*, p. 229.

19. "Thomas Guy's Will," in Hunter and Macalpine, *Three Hundred Years of Psychiatry*, p. 330; Cameron, *Mr. Guy's Hospital*, pp. 71–72.

20. Armstrong-Jones, "Some Remarks on Keats and His Friends," *Guy's Hospital Gazette*, p. 520.

21. Babington and Curry, *Outlines*, pp. 58, 48.

22. Ibid., pp. 14, 51.

23. Ibid., p. 50.

24. Ibid., pp. 15–16, 51. On Burton's influence, see Ward, "Keats and Burton," pp. 545–46. Burton's information reinforces Keats's own medical knowledge. Keats's obsession with the atmospheric influence on health is also evidenced in his letter of 6 February 1820 to Fanny Keats: "George has been running great chance of a similar attack [of the cold], but I hope the sea air will be his Physician in case of illness—the air out at sea is always more temperate than on land" (*Letters* 2:251). Again, he draws on his medical knowledge. Babington and Curry state, "All land winds contain more or less miasmata" and go on to prove that sea air is more healthy (*Outlines*, p. 16).

25. Curry, *Heads*, p. 11; cf. Erasmus Darwin, *Economy of Vegetation*, 1:430n., in *Botanic Garden*: "The principal frosts of this country are accompanied or produced by a N.E. wind, and the thaws by a S.W. wind."

26. Babington and Curry, *Outlines*, p. 203. Cf. Pope's description of the Cave of Spleen in *The Rape of the Lock*:

> Swift on his sooty Pinions flitts the *Gnome,*
> And in a Vapour reach'd the dismal Dome.
> No cheerful Breeze this sullen Region knows,
> The dreadful *East* is all the Wind that blows.　　(IV, 17–20)

27. Those critics who have discussed the influence of Burton on Keats include: Colvin, *John Keats, His Life and Poetry*, pp. 354, 396, 405, 412; Dell, "Keats' Debt to Robert Burton"; Gittings, *John Keats: The Living Year*, pp. 5–6, 9, 50–53, *passim;* Gittings, "Keats's Markings"; Ward, "Keats and Burton"; and Sinson, *John Keats and The Anatomy of Melancholy*. Sickels has examined Keats's melancholy in a much more general, and less satisfactory, fashion in her *Gloomy Egotist*, pp. 330–40, 423–25.

28. Ward gives the most comprehensive review of the arguments over this date ("Keats and Burton," pp. 535–42).

29. Hunter and Macalpine, *Three Hundred Years of Psychiatry*, p. 322.

30. Whytt, "Observations on the Nature, Causes and Cure of those Disorders which have been called Nervous, Hypochondriac, or Hysteric" (1765), in Hunter and Macalpine, *Three Hundred Years of Psychiatry*, p. 392. William Cullen, however, disagreed with this use of the term "nervous," claiming that "in a certain view, almost the whole diseases of the human body might be called *nervous,* [although] there would be no use for such a general appellation; it seems improper to limit the term, in the loose inaccurate manner in which it has been hitherto applied, to hysteric and hypochondriacal disorders, which are themselves hardly to be defined with sufficient precision" (*First Lines of the Practice of Physic,* quoted in ibid., p. 475).

31. Babington and Curry, *Outlines*, p. 203. Dugald Stewart also emphasizes the effect of the imagination on bodily symptoms in his *Elements of the Philoso-*

phy of the Human Mind, a book that Joan Coldwell has shown was popular with Cowden Clarke ("Charles Cowden Clarke's Commonplace Book," p. 86).

32. Babington and Curry, *Outlines,* p. 204. Cullen's description of melancholia, with which Keats would also have been familiar, is similar: "Partial insanity, without dyspepsia. It varies according to the various subjects which induce it. [These include] false perception of the state of the patient's health, conceived to be dangerous from slight causes; or from despondence with regard to the state of his affairs . . . vehement love, but without satyriasis or nymphomania . . . superstitious fear of the future . . . weariness of life" (*Nosology* (1772), quoted in Hunter and Macalpine, *Three Hundred Years of Psychiatry,* pp. 478–79).

33. Brink, "Keats's Conflict," pp. 168, 148. Brink's approach to Keats's melancholia from the viewpoint of modern psychology is not entirely compatible with my own approach of viewing the poetry and letters within the context of Keats's medical knowledge, but he does make some valuable observations, one of which is that Haydon also suffered from periods of extreme melancholy, which he may have recognized in Keats.

34. Haydon, *Diary,* 2: 107; Rollins, *Keats Circle,* 1: 284–85.

35. Blackmore, *A Treatise of the Spleen and Vapours: or Hypocondriacal and Hysterical Affections,* quoted in Hunter and Macalpine, *Three Hundred Years of Psychiatry,* p. 322.

36. Babington and Curry, *Outlines,* p. 203.

37. Blackstone comments on this sonnet: "Nature's power is a healing virtue, to be related, insistently, to man's needs—and, let us note, to his immediate psychosomatic imbalance. Nature's restorative virtues are commonplace in Wordsworth too, but the precise therapeutic approach is peculiar to Keats" (*Consecrated Urn,* p. 46).

38. Babington and Curry, *Outlines,* p. 206.

39. Ibid., p. 203.

40. As Keats says: "The Genius of Poetry must work out its own salvation in a man: It cannot be matured by law & precept, but by sensation & watchfulness in itself—That which is creative must create itself—In Endymion, I leaped headlong into the Sea, and thereby have become better acquainted with the Soundings, the quicksands, & the rocks" (*Letters,* 1: 374).

41. De Selincourt's argument is summarized by Evert, *Aesthetic and Myth,* p. 168.

42. *Poems of John Keats,* ed. Allott, p. 138.

43. Lempriere, *Classical Dictionary,* p. 424.

44. Evert, *Aesthetic and Myth,* p. 169.

45. *Poems of John Keats,* ed. Stillinger, p. 114.

46. Babington and Curry, *Outlines,* p. 58; cf. William Saunders: "In this fever, the symptoms of *debility* are chiefly prevalent; dejection and terror of mind, loss of appetite, oppression, watchfulness, sighing, great lassitude" (*Elements of the Practice of Physic,* p. 24).

47. *Poems of John Keats,* ed. Stillinger, p. 115.

48. Keats, *Note Book,* p. 9.

49. Babington and Curry, *Outlines*, p. 45; Saunders, *Elements of the Practice of Physic*, p. 26.

50. Endymion's melancholia is variously called "madness impious" (II, 184), "lonely madness" (II, 748), "Love's madness" (II, 860); and the symptoms of languor, sighing, sorrow, anxiety, restless sleep, and confused thought are repeated many times, e.g., II:43–55, 856–73.

51. Babington and Curry, *Outlines*, pp. 5–6.

52. Ibid., pp. 36, 19.

53. Blumenbach, *Institutions of Physiology*, p. 35; Babington and Curry, *Outlines*, p. 36.

54. Van Ghent, "Keats's Myth of the Hero," p. 11.

55. The phrasing used here is very similar to that which Keats uses to describe his own relief from pain later: "This morning Poetry has conquered. . . . There is an awful warmth about my heart like a load of Immortality" (*Letters* 1:370). Here again poetry is the healer, and the similarity of phrasing suggests that Keats thought of Cynthia as poetry.

56. *Poems of John Keats*, ed. Stillinger, p. 196.

57. Goodall, "Some Examples of the Knowledge of Medicine," p. 239. In addition, Goodall notes the medical accuracy of Ethelbert's speech in *Otho the Great*:

> A young man's heart, by heaven's blessing, is
> A wide world, where a thousand new-born hopes
> Empurple fresh the melancholy blood:
> But an old man's is narrow, tenantless
> Of hopes, and stuff'd with many memories,
> Which, being pleasant, ease the heavy pulse,
> Painful, clogg'd up and stagnate.   (III, ii, 180–86)

He comments: "There are two medical reminiscences in these seven lines. None but a medical man would employ the adjective 'melancholy' in the sense meant here, 'infused with black bile,' a survival of the ancient humoral pathology, which had not quite been discarded in Keats's time. . . . In the last three lines of the passage an idea can be recognised which is prompted by a knowledge of the pathology of arterial obliteration and thrombosis" (p. 239). This instance is particularly interesting, not only for its precision, but also for the fact that in this single speech by Ethelbert (172–91), he uses a metaphor adapted from botany—"Choak not the granary of thy noble mind / With more bad bitter grain"—followed by one from chemistry—"To thee only I appeal, / Not to thy noble son, whose yeasting youth / Will clear itself, and crystal turn again"—and then this one from pathology. The old abbot demonstrates an astute scientific knowledge.

58. Astley Cooper, *Principles and Practice*, pp. 50–51.

59. Blumenbach, *Institutions of Physiology*, pp. 4–5.

60. On the address-fold of this letter Bailey writes: "This letter opens the excellent feelings of an excellent heart. 'The unfortunate family' mentioned was

most kindly treated by poor Keats. B.B." This treatment was presumably medical, but for what ailment we are unaware.

61. Bransby Cooper, *Life of Sir Astley Cooper*, 1:107. See also R. C. Brock, *Life and Works of Astley Cooper*, p. 5.

62. Astley Cooper, *Principles and Practice*, pp. 331–33. Later Cooper published an entire book on breast cancer. Keats's association of his moods with cancer in women may also suggest some personal experience of the disease, and Brink has suggested that Keats's mother may have died of cancer rather than of tuberculosis (*Loss and Symbolic Repair*, p. 164). George said that their mother had a "reumatic" complaint, and "cancerous rheumatism" was a common killer of women (see Cooper, *Principles and Practice*, p. 330). Because both diseases shared many symptoms, they were sometimes confused, but whether Keats ever thought of his mother's symptoms as cancerous is highly debatable.

63. Hagelman, "John Keats and the Medical Profession," p. 255.

64. Wilks and Bettany, *Biographical History*, p. 72; Cameron, *Mr. Guy's Hospital*, p. 72.

65. Hagelman, "John Keats and the Medical Profession," p. 256.

66. Curry, *Heads*, p. 12.

67. Hagelman does not recognize this aspect of the poem, with the result that he claims the simile is "medically precise [but] poetically inappropriate. . . . Keats' medical training has led him astray; he has picked out the superficial likeness in the two situations but has shed a misleading light on Isabella's emotional state" ("John Keats and the Medical Profession," p. 259).

68. Haggard, *Devils, Drugs and Doctors*, p. 366; for my comments on this passage I am indebted to Hagelman, "John Keats and the Medical Profession," p. 261.

69. Curry, *Heads*, p. 7.

70. Babington and Curry, *Outlines*, p. 162.

71. Keats's portrayal of Isabella seems, in fact, to be a nearly perfect case study of the melancholia described by William Saunders when he writes "Of Insantiy": "It is distinguished into the melancholia and mania, the first is insanity with sadness, the mind generally resting on one object. . . . The melancholia is most frequent in the dull and studious, and those who have suffered by repeated misfortunes and disappointments. . . . The remote causes may be referred to the following: 1. The mind too intensely directed to one object, passions of the mind, such as grief, sadness . . . and more especially love" (*Elements of the Practice of Physic*, p. 125).

72. Babington and Curry, *Outlines*, pp. 203, 206. So aware was Keats, at this time, of the effects of the diseased imagination that he wrote to Bailey on 10 June: "Women must want Imagination and they may thank God for it—and so m[a]y we that a delicate being can feel happy without any sense of crime" (*Letters* 1:293). Keats is here discussing his sister-in-law, Georgiana, in what amounts to a rejection of the Isabella type of woman.

73. Babington and Curry, *Outlines*, p. 163.

74. Curry, *Heads*, p. 12. Keats may also be recollecting Babington's and Curry's description "Of Hysteria," a disease which is closely connected to and which shares many of the causes and symptoms of Hypochondriasis, but

which is "almost peculiar to females." Babington and Curry point out that the "origin of the term *Hysteria*" is the Greek word for "uterus" and that its predisposing causes are "often obviously connected with some irregularity of the uterine function." They conclude that it can be treated "sometimes, when practicable, by changing the sexual condition of the patient," a course not open to Isabella who has lost her lover (*Outlines*, pp. 201–03).

75. Babington and Curry, *Outlines*, p. 204.

76. Hyder Rollins claims that the reference to "Green" is to Matthew Green, author of a poem called *The Spleen*. See Smith, "Matthew Green."

77. Babington and Curry, *Outlines*, p. 204.

78. Ibid., p. 14.

79. Again, in August 1819, he writes to Fanny Keats: "The delightful Weather we have had for two Months is the highest gratification I could receive—no chill'd red noses—no shivering—but fair Atmosphere to think in" (*Letters* 2:148).

80. Babington and Curry, *Outlines*, p. 58.

81. Caldwell, *John Keats' Fancy*, p. 43; see also pp. 135–36 for a discussion of Keats's "nerves" in relation to Burns.

82. Keats had given the same advice to Bailey a year earlier: "But do not sacrifice your heal[t]h to Books do take it kindly and not so voraciously. I am certain if you are your own Physician your stomach will resume its proper strength" (*Letters*, 1:170).

83. Curry, *Heads*, p. 12. In their *Outlines*, Babington and Curry list "much study, and consequently sedentary life" as one of the circumstances that render a person vulnerable to fever (p. 47); "sedentary inactive life . . . intense application to study" as causes of dyspepsia (p. 163); and "indolent inactive life; —intense study" as causes of hypochondriasis (p. 204).

84. Ward claims that Keats had contracted tuberculosis by 1818 (*John Keats*, p. 257), but Hale-White claims 1819 as the year of contraction (*Keats as Doctor and Patient*, pp. 68–69). More recently, Lord Brock, himself a respected physician, has argued, "There can be no reasonable doubt that John Keats obtained a lung infection from his brother Tom who died in December 1818" (*John Keats and Joseph Severn*, p. 6).

85. Babington and Curry, *Outlines*, pp. 107, 106.

86. Ibid., p. 108. Keats may also have been worried by Babington's and Curry's description of one tubercular type as of "middle or low stature— opaque skin, —dark hair and eyes, —dilated pupils, —tumid upper lip; — short fingers, with truncated nails" (p. 107). Keats himself was short with dark hair, glowing eyes described as birdlike, which suggests dilated pupils, and a protruding upper lip (see Gittings, *John Keats*, p. 135); he may well have felt that he was physically predisposed to the disease.

87. On 8 October 1817, Keats writes to Bailey: "The little Mercury I have taken has corrected the Poison and improved my Health—though I feel from my employment that I shall never be again secure in Robustness" (*Letters* 1:171).

88. Lowell, *John Keats*, 1:512–13; Hewlett, *A Life of John Keats*, p. 121; Bate, *John Keats*, p. 219; Ward, *John Keats*, p. 134.

89. Gittings, *John Keats*, pp. 643–49. Sawrey published *An Enquiry into some of the Effects of the Venereal Poison on the Human Body* in 1802.

90. Andrews, "Keats and Mercury," pp. 37–42. Andrews quotes Cooper: "In the first place gentleman let me observe to you that no greater folly and indeed cruelty can be committed than that of giving mercury for the cure of this disease [gonorrhea]. A man who gives mercury in gonorrhea really deserves to be flogged out of his profession because he must be quite ignorant of the principles on which this disease is to be cured" (p. 40).

91. Waddington, "Lectures on Anatomy," 1:185.

92. Babington and Curry, *Outlines*, p. 107.

93. Moorman, *Tuberculosis and Genius*, p. xi.

94. Mayo and Macleod, quoted in ibid., pp. xii–xiii.

95. Ibid., p. xiii. I would not go so far as to support Moorman's general contention that we can thank tuberculosis for much great art, but the disease seems to have been a contributing factor in stimulating genius. For other opinions, see Markowitz, "The Role of Tuberculosis," Chalke, "The Impact of Tuberculosis," and Sontag, *Illness as Metaphor*.

96. D'Avanzo has discussed these fevered bouts of creativity and linked them to the frenzy of the Apollonian oracle of Delphi (*Keats's Metaphors*, pp. 92–95).

97. William Ober claims that Keats had taken opium and describes its aftereffects in this letter. He also traces what he believes to be the influence of opium on the "Ode on Indolence" and "Ode to a Nightingale"; see "Drowsed With the Fume of Poppies."

98. Babington and Curry, *Outlines*, p. 63.

99. Salisbury, *Botanist's Companion*, 2:66; Ober, "Drowsed With the Fume of Poppies," p. 872.

100. Camaiora, " 'Idle fever' and 'diligent indolence,' " pp. 168–69.

101. Babington and Curry, *Outlines*, p. 106.

102. Brown, *Life of John Keats*, p. 64. For Keats's more dramatic account of the hemorrhage to Fanny Brawne, see *Letters* 2:254. Lord Brock, following Gittings (*John Keats*, p. 553), argues that Keats suffered two hemorrhages that night, the first a "warning ooze" and the second a massive gush (*John Keats and Joseph Severn*, p. 9). Cooper points out, "The Colour of the Blood is differing in the Arteries, and Veins, in the former it is a florid red, and in the latter, what is called a modena colour" (Waddington, "Lectures on Anatomy," 1:13).

103. On 10 March 1820, only a month after Keats's hemorrhage, Brown writes to Taylor: "I consider him perfectly out of danger, & am happy to tell you that we are now assured there is no pulmonary affection, no organic defect whatever, —the disease is on his *mind*, and there I hope he will soon be cured" (Rollins, *Keats Circle*, 1:104).

104. See Ward, "Keats and Burton," pp. 548–51. For Burton's attitude to love as echoed in Keats's letters, see *Letters* 2:187–88.

105. *Poems of John Keats*, ed. Stillinger, p. 494.

106. Richardson, "An Aesculapian Poet," p. 32.

107. Brown states that after Keats's hemorrhage, "I ran for a surgeon; my friend was bled" (*Life of John Keats*, p. 64). Although this treatment now seems horrifying in view of the already debilitated state of the patient, it was perfectly

normal procedure at the time. Babington and Curry discuss "occassional small bleedings—cupping, —leeches" as treatments for phthisis (*Outlines*, p. 109), and Saunders recommends "small and repeated bleedings" as a proper course of action (*Elements of the Practice of Physic*, p. 57), one that was followed by Keats's physicians at home and in Italy.

108. Hale-White, *Keats as Doctor and Patient*, pp. 54–55.

109. Babington and Curry, *Outlines*, p. 204.

110. See pp. 188–89.

111. This may indicate that he was suffering from "dyspepsia, or indigestion" caused by "anxiety, and other passions and affections of the mind" (Babington and Curry, *Outlines*, pp. 162–63).

112. Babington and Curry (ibid., p. 5) describe "Fever in General": "transient flushings, —beginning in face and neck, and alternating with chills, —but gradually extending, and growing more considerable and universal, and at last becoming dry burning heat all over, with great restlessness, and often violent head-ach. . . . Lastly, moisture begins on face and neck, gradually extending, and becoming general perspiration or sweat. . . . Torpor of brain and nerves . . . shewn by diminished sensation of eye, ear, taste, touch; —by impaired state of recollection and judgment."

113. Curry, *Heads*, p. 12.

114. South in fact draws attention to the similarity between the two types of theater: "The operating theatre was small, and the rush and scuffle to get a place was not unlike that for a seat in the pit or gallery of a dramatic theatre; and when one was lucky enough to get a place, the crowding and squeezing was oftentimes unbearable" (*Memorials,* p. 27).

115. Babington and Curry, *Outlines*, p. 50.

116. Sherwood, "Keats' Imaginative Approach," pp. 256–57.

117. Lempriere, *Classical Dictionary*, p. 378.

118. Babington and Curry, *Outlines*, pp. 105–06.

119. See Graves, *White Goddess*, p. 378; and Wycherley, "Keats: The Terminal Disease."

120. Williams, "Keats' 'La Belle Dame sans Merci' "; Brink, "Keats's Conflict," pp. 186–92. For the influence of Burton's *Anatomy* on the poem, see Sinson, *John Keats and The Anatomy of Melancholy*, pp. 18–19, and Gittings, *John Keats: The Living Year*, p. 117.

121. On the influence of Horace's *Epode* XIV, see Blunden, "Keats and His Predecessors." On the influence of Burton, who recommends opiates for melancholia, see Sinson, *John Keats and The Anatomy of Melancholy*, pp. 22–23, and Gittings, *John Keats: The Living Year*, p. 136.

122. Ober, "Drowsed with the Fume of Poppies," p. 875.

123. See Babington and Curry, *Outlines*, pp. 59, 109; and Saunders, *Elements of the Practice of Physic*, p. 126.

124. Brown, *Life of John Keats*, p. 63.

125. Salisbury, *Botanist's Companion*, 2:66, 54.

126. Astley Cooper, *Principles and Practice*, pp. 151, 173.

127. Keats's description of Georgiana emphasizes these ideas: "She is the most disinterrested woman I ever knew . . . To see an entirely disinterrested Girl quite happy is the most pleasant and extraordinary thing in the

world— . . . Women must want Imagination and they may thank God for it—and so m[a]y we that a delicate being can feel happy without any sense of crime" (*Letters* 1:293). Of Bailey, he writes: "For that sort of probity & disinterestedness which such men as Bailey possess, does hold & grasp the tip top of any spiritual honours, that can be paid to any thing in this world" (*Letters* 1:205).

128. Most of Hale-White's *Keats as Doctor and Patient* deals with the poet's tuberculosis and the treatment he received, and Lord Brock's *John Keats and Joseph Severn* is expressly devoted to carrying Hale-White's contribution further with new material on the disease.

Bibliography

Works by John Keats

John Keats's Anatomical and Physiological Note Book. Edited by Maurice Buxton Forman. New York: Haskell House, 1970.

The Letters of John Keats. Edited by Maurice Buxton Forman. 3rd ed. London: Oxford University Press, 1947.

The Letters of John Keats. Edited by Hyder Edward Rollins. 2 vols. Cambridge, Mass.: Harvard University Press, 1958.

"Note-Book Kept by Keats as a Medical Student." MS. Keats House, Hampstead.

The Poems of John Keats. Edited by G. Thorn Drury. Introduction by Robert Bridges. 2 vols. London: Routledge & Sons, 1896.

The Poems of John Keats. Edited by Ernest de Selincourt. 7th ed. London: Methuen, 1951.

The Poems of John Keats. Edited by Miriam Allott. London: Longman, 1970.

The Poems of John Keats. Edited by Jack Stillinger. Cambridge, Mass.: Harvard University Press, 1978.

Poetical Works. Edited by H. W. Garrod. London: Oxford University Press, 1956.

The Poetical Works and Other Writings of John Keats. Edited by Harry Buxton Forman. 4 vols. London: Reeves & Turner, 1883.

Secondary Materials

Abrams, M. H. *The Mirror and the Lamp: Romantic Theory and the Critical Tradition.* New York: Oxford University Press, 1953.

Albrecht, W. P. "The Tragic Sublime of Hazlitt and Keats." *Studies in Romanticism* 20 (Summer 1981): 185–201.

Allott, Kenneth. "The 'Ode to Psyche.' " In *John Keats: A Reassessment,* edited by Kenneth Muir. 2nd ed. Liverpool: Liverpool University Press, 1969.

Altick, Richard D. *The Cowden Clarkes.* London: Oxford University Press, 1948.

Andrews, C. T. "Keats and Mercury." *Keats Shelley Memorial Bulletin* 20 (1969): 37–43.

Bibliography

"Announcement." *The London Medical and Physical Journal* 34 (1815): 285.

"Apothecaries Bill." *The London Medical and Physical Journal* 33 (1815): 423–24.

"Apothecaries' Hall." *The London Medical and Physical Journal* 34 (1815): 251.

Armstrong-Jones, Robert. "Some Remarks on Keats and His Friends." *Annals of Medical History* 10 (September 1938): 433–44.

———. "Some Remarks on Keats and His Friends." *Guy's Hospital Gazette* 18 (1934): 518–20.

"Atticus Goes to Hospital." *Sunday Times,* 21 February 1960, p. 9.

Babington, William. "Lectures on Chemistry." MS. Wills Library, n.d.

Babington, William, and William Allen. *A Syllabus of a Course of Chemical Lectures Read at Guy's Hospital.* London: W. Phillips, 1802.

Babington, William, and James Curry. *Outlines of a Course of Lectures on the Practice of Medicine as Delivered in the Medical School of Guy's Hospital.* London: M'Creery, 1811.

Babington, William, Alexander Marcet, and William Allen. *A Syllabus of a Course of Chemical Lectures Read at Guy's Hospital.* London: W. Phillips, 1816.

Baldwin, D. L., L. N. Broughton et al., eds. *A Concordance to the Poems of John Keats.* Gloucester: Peter Smith, 1963.

Balslev, Thora. *Keats and Wordsworth: A Comparative Study.* Copenhagen: Munksgaard, 1962.

Barclay, John. *A Description of the Arteries of the Human Body.* Edinburgh: Bryce, 1812.

Bate, Walter Jackson. *John Keats.* New York: Oxford University Press, 1966.

———. *Negative Capability: The Intuitive Approach in Keats.* Cambridge, Mass.: Harvard University Press, 1939.

Bell, Charles. *Idea of a New Anatomy of the Brain.* London: Dawsons, 1966. Facsimile of 1811 edition.

Bell, Charles, and John Bell. *The Anatomy and Physiology of the Human Body.* 3 vols. 7th ed. London: Longman, 1829.

Bergman, Torbern. *Dissertation on Elective Attractions.* Translated by J. A. Schufle. New York: Johnson Reprint Corp., 1968. Facsimile of 1775 edition.

Birkenhead, Sheila. *Against Oblivion: The Life of Joseph Severn.* London: Cassell, 1943.

Blackstone, Bernard. *The Consecrated Urn: An Interpretation of Keats in Terms of Growth and Form.* London: Longmans, 1959.

Blake, William. *Complete Writings.* Edited by Geoffrey Keynes. London: Oxford University Press, 1966.

Bloom, Harold. "To Reason with Later Reason: Romanticism and the Rational." *Midway* 11 (Summer 1970): 97–112.

Blumenbach, Johann Friedrich. *The Institutions of Physiology.* Translated by John Elliotson. 3rd ed. London: Burgess & Hill, 1820.

Blunden, Edmund. "Keats and His Predecessors." *The London Mercury* 20 (July 1929): 290.

———. "Keats' Friend Mathew." *English, the Magazine of the English Association* 1 (1936): 46–55.

Bolitho, Hector. "Doctor Keats." *History of Medicine* 1 (Autumn 1969): 7–9.

Bibliography

Bonnycastle, John. *An Introduction to Astronomy.* 4th ed. London: J. Johnson, 1803.

"A Book that May Have Helped Keats." *The Times* (London), 3 December 1963, p. 14.

Bornstein, George. "Keats's Concept of the Ethereal." *Keats-Shelley Journal* 18 (1969): 97–106.

Bradley, A. C. "Keats and 'Philosophy.' " In his *A Miscellany.* London: Macmillan, 1929.

Brink, Andrew. "Keats's Conflict." In his *Loss and Symbolic Repair: A Psychological Study of Some English Poets.* Hamilton, Ontario: Cromlech Press, 1977.

Brock, Lord. *John Keats and Joseph Severn: The Tragedy of the Last Illness.* London: Keats-Shelley Memorial Association, 1973.

Brock, R. C. *The Life and Works of Astley Cooper.* Edinburgh: Livingstone, 1952.

Brown, Charles Armitage. *Life of John Keats.* Edited by Dorothy Hyde Bodurtha and Willard B. Pope. London: Oxford University Press, 1937.

Bullough, Geoffrey. "Associations, Intuitions, and Immortal Longings in the Nineteenth Century." In his *Mirror of Minds: Changing Psychological Beliefs in English Poetry.* Toronto: University of Toronto Press, 1962.

Bunn, James H. "Keats's *Ode to Psyche* and the Transformation of Mental Landscape." *Journal of English Literary History* 37 (December 1970): 581–94.

Burke, Kenneth. "The Anaesthetic Revelation of Herone Liddell." *Kenyon Review* 19 (Autumn 1957): 505–59.

———. "Symbolic Action in a Poem by Keats." In *John Keats: Odes,* edited by G. S. Fraser. London: Macmillan, 1971.

Burnet, M. *Natural History of Infectious Disease.* London: Cambridge University Press, 1972.

Burton, Robert. *The Anatomy of Melancholy.* Vol. 2. 11th ed. London: Walker, Cuthell, Nunn, Longman, Lackington, 1813. Keats's copy at Keats House, Hampstead.

———. *The Anatomy of Melancholy.* 11th ed. London: Vernor, Hood & Sharpe, 1806. Maurice Buxton Forman's facsimile of Keats's copy at Keats House, Hampstead.

Bush, Douglas. *Mythology and the Romantic Tradition in English Poetry.* New York: Norton, 1963.

———. "Notes on Keats's Reading." *PMLA* 50 (1935): 785–806.

———. *Science and English Poetry.* New York: Oxford University Press, 1950.

Cacciatore, Vera. "A Note from the Keats House in Rome." *Keats-Shelley Journal* 12 (1963): 10.

Caldwell, James Ralston. *John Keats' Fancy: The Effect on Keats of the Psychology of His Day.* Ithaca, N.Y.: Cornell University Press, 1945.

Camaiora, Louisa Conti. " 'Idle Fever' and 'Diligent Indolence.' " *Rivista di Letterature Moderne e Comparate* 28 (1975): 165–84.

Cameron, H. C. *Mr. Guy's Hospital, 1726–1948.* London: Longmans, 1954.

Chalke, H. D. "The Impact of Tuberculosis on History, Literature and Art." *Medical History* 6 (October 1962): 301–18.

Chayes, Irene H. "Dreamer, Poet, and Poem in *The Fall of Hyperion.*" *Philological Quarterly* 46 (October 1967): 499–515.

Bibliography

Cholmeley, Henry James. *Outlines of a Course of Lectures on the Practice of Medicine, Delivered in the Medical School of Guy's Hospital*. London: M'Creery, 1820.

Clarke, Charles Cowden. "Recollections of John Keats." *Gentleman's Magazine*, February 1874, pp. 177–204.

Clarke, Charles Cowden, and Mary Cowden Clarke. *Recollections of Writers*. London: Sampson, Low, Marston, Searle, & Rivington, 1878.

Clarke, Mary Cowden. "A Friend of John Keats." *Illustrated London News*, 15 February 1896, p. 210.

Cleveland, Parker. "Account of the Medical Effects of Electricity." *The London Medical and Physical Journal* 31 (1814): 37–40.

Coldwell, Joan. "Charles Cowden Clarke's Commonplace Book and Its Relationship to Keats." *Keats-Shelley Journal* 29 (1980): 83–95.

Colvin, Sidney. *John Keats, His Life and Poetry, His Friends, Critics, and After-fame*. London: Macmillan, 1917.

———. "Keats and His Friends. Unpublished Poems and Letters." *Times Literary Supplement*, 16 April 1914, pp. 181–82.

Cooper, Astley. *The Lectures of Sir Astley Cooper on the Principles and Practice of Surgery*. Edited by Frederick Tyrrell. 5th American ed. New Orleans: A. Towar, 1839.

———. *The Principles and Practice of Surgery*. Edited by Alexander Lee. London: E. Cox, 1836.

Cooper, Astley, and Benjamin Travers. *Surgical Essays*. 2 vols. London: Cox & Son, 1818.

Cooper, Bransby Blake. *The Life of Sir Astley Cooper, Bart*. 2 vols. London: John Parker, 1843.

Copeman, W. S. C. *The Worshipful Society of Apothecaries of London: A History, 1617–1967*. Oxford: Pergamon, 1968.

Cornelius, Roberta D. "Keats as a Humanist." *Keats-Shelley Journal* 5 (1956): 89–96.

Curry, James. *Heads of a Course of Lectures on Pathology, Therapeutics, and Materia Medica; Delivered in the Medical School of Guy's Hospital*. London: T. Bensley, 1804.

———. *Outlines of a Course of Lectures on the Practice of Medicine, Delivered in the Medical School of Guy's Hospital*. London: M'Creery, 1817.

Dale, Philip Marshall. *Medical Biographies*. Norman: University of Oklahoma Press, 1952.

Darwin, Erasmus. *The Botanic Garden, 1791*. Menston: Scholar Press, 1973. Facsimile of 1791 edition.

Darwin, Robert. *Principia Botanica: A Concise and Easy Introduction to the Sexual Botany of Linnaeus*. Newark: Allin & Ridge, 1793.

D'Avanzo, Mario L. *Keats's Metaphors for the Poetic Imagination*. Durham, N.C.: Duke University Press, 1967.

———. "Keats's 'Ode on Melancholy,' the Cave of Spleen, and Belinda." *Humanities Association Bulletin* (Canada) 22 (Fall 1971): 9–11.

Davies, Edward. *Celtic Researches*. London: Davies, 1804.

Bibliography

Davies, R. T. "Some Ideas and Usages." In *John Keats: A Reassessment*, edited by Kenneth Muir. 2nd ed. Liverpool: Liverpool University Press, 1969.

Davy, Sir Humphry. *The Collected Works of Sir Humphry Davy*. Edited by John Davy. London: Smith, Elder, 1839–40. Vol. 2, *Early Miscellaneous Papers;* vol. 4, *Elements of Chemical Philosophy;* vol. 5, *Bakerian Lectures and Miscellaneous Papers from 1806 to 1815;* vol. 8, *Agricultural Lectures, Part II, and Other Lectures.*

Dell, Floyd. "Keats's Debt to Robert Burton." *Bookman* (New York) 67 (March 1928): 13–17.

Dendy, Walter Cooper. *The Philosophy of Mystery*. London: Longman, 1841.

Dilke, Charles Wentworth. *The Papers of a Critic*. 2 vols. London: Murray, 1875.

Doubleday, F. N. "John Keats and the Borough Hospitals." *Keats Shelley Memorial Bulletin* 13 (1962): 12–17.

———. "John Keats as a Student." *Guy's Hospital Gazette* 66 (August 1952): 312–17.

———. "Keats and the Hammonds." *Times Literary Supplement*, 9 May 1968, p. 484.

———. "A Note on the Operating Theatre in Old St. Thomas's Hospital." *Keats Shelley Memorial Bulletin* 15 (1964): 35–36.

———. "A Short Biographical History of Guy's Hospital." *Medicine Illustrated* 5 (November 1951): 510–16.

Dubos, René, and Jean Dubos. *The White Plague: Tuberculosis, Man and Society.* Boston: Little, Brown, 1952.

Eliot, T. S. "Tradition and the Individual Talent." In his *Selected Prose*, edited by John Hayward. Harmondsworth: Penguin, 1953..

Elliott, G. R. "The Real Tragedy of Keats." *PMLA* 36 (1921): 315–31.

Ende, Stuart A. *Keats and the Sublime*. New Haven, Conn.: Yale University Press, 1976.

Evans, B. Ifor. "Keats as a Medical Student." *Times Literary Supplement* 31 May 1934, p. 391.

———. "Keats—The Man, Medicine and Poetry." *British Medical Journal* 3 (5 July 1969): 7–11.

Evans, David S. "Homage to Herschel." *Contemporary Review* 219 (December 1971): 299–306.

Evert, Walter H. *Aesthetic and Myth in the Poetry of Keats*. Princeton, N.J.: Princeton University Press, 1965.

"Extracts from the Act 'For Better Regulating the Practice of Apothecaries Throughout England and Wales.' " *The London Medical and Physical Journal* 34 (1815): 251–52.

Ferguson, Oliver W. "Warton and Keats: Two Views of Melancholy." *Keats-Shelley Journal* 18 (1969): 12–15.

Finney, Claude Lee. *The Evolution of Keats's Poetry*. 2 vols. Cambridge, Mass.: Harvard University Press, 1936.

Flesch-Brunningen, H. "The Physician and the Pen. John Keats—Physician and Patient." *CIBA Symposium* 10 (1962): 33–37.

Bibliography

Fogle, Richard Harter. *The Imagery of Keats and Shelley: A Comparative Study.* Chapel Hill: University of North Carolina Press, 1949.

Ford, Newell F. *The Prefigurative Imagination of John Keats: A Study in the Beauty-Truth Identification and Its Implications.* Hamden, Conn.: Shoe String Press, 1966.

"Fourth Report of the General Committee of Associated Apothecaries of England and Wales." *The London Medical and Physical Journal* 31 (1814): 512–13.

Fyfe, Andrew. *A Compendium of the Anatomy of the Human Body.* 3 vols. 3rd ed. Edinburgh: Pillans & Sons, 1807.

Garrod, H. W. *Keats.* Oxford: Clarendon Press, 1926.

Gittings, Robert. *John Keats.* Harmondsworth: Penguin, 1971.

―――. "John Keats, Physician and Poet." *Journal of the American Medical Association* 224 (2 April 1973): 51–55.

―――. *John Keats: The Living Year.* London: Heinemann, 1954.

―――. "Keats and Medicine." *Contemporary Review* 219 (September 1971): 138–42.

―――. "Keats and the Hammonds." *Times Literary Supplement,* 4 April 1968, p. 357.

―――. "Keats's Markings." *The Times* (London), 6 December 1963, p. 13.

―――. *The Odes of Keats and Their Earliest Known Manuscripts.* Kent, Ohio: Kent State University Press, 1970.

―――. "A Schoolfellow of Keats." *Times Literary Supplement,* 17 January 1958, p. 36.

―――. "This Living Hand." *Medical History* 16 (January 1972): 1–10.

Goldberg, M. A. *The Poetics of Romanticism: Toward a Reading of John Keats.* Yellow Springs, Ohio: Antioch Press, 1969.

Goodall, E. W. "Some Examples of the Knowledge of Medicine Exhibited in the Poems of John Keats." *Guy's Hospital Gazette* 40 (1936): 238–40.

Graves, Robert. *The White Goddess: A Historical Grammar of Poetic Myth.* London: Faber & Faber, 1948.

Green, Joseph Henry. *The Dissector's Manual.* London: E. Cox, 1820.

―――. *Outlines of a Course of Dissections for the Use of Students of Anatomy at St. Thomas's Hospital.* London: E. Cox, 1815.

Green, Matthew. *The Spleen.* 2nd ed. London: A. Dodd, 1737.

―――. *The Spleen.* Edited by W. H. Williams. London: Methuen, 1936.

Guy, E. F. "Keats's Use of 'Luxury': A Note on Meaning." *Keats-Shelley Journal* 13 (1964): 87–95.

Hagelman, Charles W. "John Keats and the Medical Profession." Ph. D. diss. University of Texas, Austin, 1956.

―――. "Keats's Medical Training and the Last Stanza of the 'Ode to Psyche.' " *Keats-Shelley Journal* 11 (1962): 73–82.

Haggard, Howard W. *Devils, Drugs and Doctors.* New York: Pocket Books, 1953.

Haight, Elizabeth H. *Apuleius and His Influence.* New York: Longmans, 1927.

Haighton, John. "Lectures on the Physiology of the Human Body. Delivered at Guy's Hospital." MS. Wills Library, 1796.

―――. *A Syllabus of the Lectures on Midwifery Delivered at Guy's Hospital.* London: E. Cox, 1814.

Bibliography

Hake, Thomas, and Arthur Compton-Rickett. *The Life and Letters of Theodore Watts-Dunton.* 2 vols. London: Jack, 1916.

Hale-White, Sir William. *Keats as Doctor and Patient.* London: Oxford University Press, 1938.

Hamilton, James W. "Object Loss, Dreaming, and Creativity: The Poetry of John Keats." *The Psychoanalytic Study of the Child* 24 (1969): 488–531.

Hamilton-Edwards, Gerald. "Keats and the Hammonds." *Times Literary Supplement,* 28 March 1968, p. 325.

Hassler, D. M. *Erasmus Darwin.* New York: Twayne, 1973.

Havens, R. D. "Unreconciled Opposites in Keats." *Philological Quarterly* 14 (October 1935): 289–300.

Haydon, Benjamin Robert. *The Autobiography and Memoirs of Benjamin Robert Haydon.* Edited by Tom Taylor. London: Davies, 1926.

_____. *Correspondence and Table Talk.* Edited by F. W. Haydon. 2 vols. London: Chatto & Windus, 1876.

_____. *The Diary of Benjamin Robert Haydon.* Edited by Willard B. Pope. 5 vols. Cambridge, Mass.: Harvard University Press, 1960–63.

Haynes, Jean. "Keats's Paternal Relatives." *Keats Shelley Memorial Bulletin* 15 (1964): 27–28.

Hazlitt, William. *The Complete Works of William Hazlitt.* Edited by P. P. Howe. Vols. 10, 18. London: Dent, 1930–34.

Hewlett, Dorothy. *A Life of John Keats.* 2nd ed. London: Hurst & Blackett, n.d.

Holloway, John. "The Odes of Keats." In his *The Charted Mirror.* London: Routledge & Kegan Paul, 1960.

_____. "A Reply to Sir Peter Medawar." *Encounter* 33 (July 1969): 81–85.

Home, Everard. "On the Changes the Blood Undergoes in the Act of Coagulation." *Philosophical Transactions* 108 (1818): 172–98.

Hulton, Paul. "A Little-Known Cache of English Drawings." *Apollo* 89 (January 1969): 52–55.

Hunt, Leigh. *The Autobiography of Leigh Hunt.* Edited by J. E. Morpurgo. London: Cresset Press, 1949.

_____. *Lord Byron and Some of His Contemporaries.* New York: AMS Press, 1966. Facsimile of 1828 edition.

_____. *The Poetical Works of Leigh Hunt.* Edited by H. S. Milford. London: Oxford University Press, 1923.

Hunter, R. and I. Macalpine, eds. *Three Hundred Years of Psychiatry, 1535–1860.* London: Oxford University Press, 1963.

Innes, John. *A Short Description of the Human Muscles, Arranged as they Appear on Dissection.* London: E. Cox, 1815 .

J. W. C. "Remarks on the Condition of Apothecaries, with Suggestions for a New Bill." *The London Medical and Physical Journal* 31 (1814): 229–30.

Jack, Ian. *Keats and the Mirror of Art.* Oxford: Oxford University Press, 1967.

Jackson, H. J. "Coleridge's Collaborator, Joseph Henry Green." *Studies in Romanticism* 21 (Summer 1982): 161–79.

Jarcho, Saul. "Auenbrugger, Laennec, and John Keats: Some Notes on the Early History of Percussion and Auscultation." *Medical History* 5 (1961): 167–72.

Bibliography

"John's Other Life." *Scientific American* 228 (June 1973): 40.

Jones, Leonidas. "Reynolds and Keats." *Keats-Shelley Journal* 7 (1958): 47–59.

Kauffman, C. H. *The Dictionary of Merchandize and Nomenclature in All Languages: For the Use of Counting-Houses.* 2nd ed. London: T. Boosey, 1805.

King-Hele, Desmond. *Doctor of Revolution: The Life and Genius of Erasmus Darwin.* London: Faber & Faber, 1977.

Kirkpatrick, T. P. C. "The Apothecary and Poet." *British Medical Journal* 1 (1933): 348.

Knight, D. M. "Chemistry, Physiology and Materialism in the Romantic Period." *Durham University Journal* 64 (March 1972): 139–45.

———. "The Physical Sciences and the Romantic Movement." *History of Science* 9 (1970): 54–75.

Larrabee, Stephen. *English Bards and Grecian Marbles.* New York: Columbia University Press, 1943.

Leavy, Stanley A. "John Keats's Psychology of Creative Imagination." *Psychoanalytic Quarterly* 39 (April 1970): 173–97.

Lefanu, W. R. A. *A List of Medical Libraries in the British Isles.* London: A.S.L.I.B., 1946.

Lempriere, J. *A Classical Dictionary.* London: Routledge & Sons, n.d.

"A List of Certified Apothecaries." *London Medical Repository* 6 (1816): 345.

The London Dissector. 3rd ed. London: J. Murray, 1811.

Lowell, Amy. *John Keats.* 2 vols. London: Jonathan Cape, 1925.

MacGillivray, J. R. *Keats: A Bibliography and Reference Guide with an Essay on Keats' Reputation.* Toronto: University of Toronto Press, 1949.

Madden, J. S. "Melancholy in Medicine and Literature: Some Historical Considerations." *British Journal of Medical Psychology* 39 (June 1966): 125–30.

Maniquis, Robert M. "The Puzzling Mimosa: Sensitivity and Plant Symbols in Romanticism." *Studies in Romanticism* 8 (Spring 1969): 129–55.

Mann, Phyllis G. "John Keats: Further Notes." *Keats Shelley Memorial Bulletin* 12 (1961): 21–27.

———. "Keats's Maternal Relations." *Keats Shelley Memorial Bulletin* 15 (1964): 32–34.

———. "New Light on Keats and His Family." *Keats Shelley Memorial Bulletin* 11 (1960): 33–38.

Marcet, Alexander. *A Case of Hydrophobia.* London: Woodfall, 1809.

———. *Some Remarks on Clinical Lectures, Being the Substance of an Introductory Lecture Delivered at Guy's Hospital. On the 27th of January, 1818.* London: Woodfall, 1818.

Margolis, John D. "Keats's 'Men of Genius' and 'Men of Power.' " *Texas School of Literature and Language* 11 (1970): 1333–47.

Markowitz, Jacob. "The Role of Tuberculosis in Literary Genius." *Canadian Forum* 34 (May 1954): 34–37.

Medawar, Sir Peter B. "Science and Literature." *Encounter* 32 (January 1969): 15–23.

"Medical School of St. Thomas's and Guy's." *The London Medical and Physical Journal* 34 (1815): 259.

Bibliography

"Medical School of St. Thomas's and Guy's Hospitals." *The London Medical and Physical Journal* 33 (1815): 75.

Medicine in 1815. London: Wellcome Historical Medical Library, 1965.

Mill, John Stuart. *A System of Logic Ratiocinative and Inductive*. New York: Longmans, Green, 1919. First published 1843.

Milnes, Richard Monckton. *Life, Letters, and Literary Remains of John Keats*. New York: Putnam, 1848.

Moorman, Lewis J. "John Keats, 1795–1821." *New England Journal of Medicine* 249 (July 1953): 26–28.

———. *Tuberculosis and Genius*. Chicago: University of Chicago Press, 1940.

Muir, Kenneth. "Keats and Hazlitt" and "The Meaning of the Odes." In *John Keats: A Reassessment*, edited by Kenneth Muir. 2nd ed. Liverpool: Liverpool University Press, 1969.

Murchie, Guy. *The Spirit of Place in Keats*. Toronto: Ryerson, 1955.

Murry, John Middleton. *Studies in Keats*. London: Oxford University Press, 1930.

Newman, George. "John Hunter: The Private Practitioner as Pioneer in Preventive Medicine," and "John Keats: Apothecary and Poet." In his *Interpreters of Nature*. Freeport, N.Y.:Books for Libraries Press, 1968.

Noad, K. B. "Young Laurels: The Brief Lives of John Irvine Hunter, Rene Laennec and John Keats." *Medical Journal of Australia* 47 (April 1960): 521–27.

Ober, William B. "Drowsed with the Fume of Poppies: Opium and John Keats." *Bulletin of the New York Academy of Medicine* 44 (July 1968): 862–81.

Osler, William. "John Keats—the Apothecary Poet." *Johns Hopkins Hospital Bulletin* 7 (1896): 11–16.

———. "John Keats—the Apothecary Poet." In his *An Alabama Student and Other Biographical Essays*. New York: Oxford University Press, 1908.

Paget, James. *Memoirs and Letters*. Edited by Stephen Paget. London: Longmans, Green, 1902.

Pettet, E. C. *On the Poetry of Keats*. Cambridge: Cambridge University Press, 1957.

Pettit, Henry. "Scientific Correlatives of Keats' *Ode to Psyche*." *Studies in Philology* 40 (1943): 560–67.

Piper, H. W. *The Active Universe: Pantheism and the Concept of the Imagination in the English Romantic Poets*. London: Athlone, 1962.

Pitfield, R. L. "John Keats: The Reactions of a Genius to Tuberculosis and Other Adversities." *Annals of Medical History* 2 (1930): 530–46.

Plato. *Timaeus and Critias*. Translated by Desmond Lee. Harmondsworth: Penguin, 1971.

———. *The Timaeus and The Critias or Atlanticus*. Translated by Thomas Taylor. New York: Pantheon, 1944. First published 1804.

Pope, Alexander. *The Poems of Alexander Pope*. Vol. 2, *The Rape of the Lock and Other Poems*. Edited by Geoffrey Tillotson. London: Methuen, 1972.

Poynter, F. N. L., ed. *The Evolution of Medical Education in Britain*. London: Pitman, 1966.

———. "The Wellcome Historical Medical Library." *Book Collector* 4 (1955): 285–90.

Bibliography

Priestley, Joseph. *Heads of Lectures on a Course of Experimental Philosophy, Particularly Including Chemistry Delivered at the New College in Hackney.* New York: Kraus Reprint, 1970. Facsimile of 1794 edition.

"A Report from the Court of Examiners to the Court of Assistants of the Society of Apothecaries." *London Medical Repository* 6 (1816): 341–42.

[Reynolds], John Hamilton. *The Garden of Florence and Other Poems.* London: John Warren, 1821.

Richardson, Benjamin Ward. "An Aesculapian Poet—John Keats." In volume 1 of *Disciples of Aesculapius.* London: Hutchinson, 1900.

Ricks, Christopher. *Keats and Embarrassment.* Oxford: Oxford University Press, 1974.

Ritterbush, Philip C. *The Art of Organic Forms.* Washington, D.C.: Smithsonian Institution Press, 1968.

———. *Overtures to Biology: The Speculations of Eighteenth-Century Naturalists.* New Haven, Conn.: Yale University Press, 1964.

Roberts, John H. "Poetry of Sensation or of Thought?" *PMLA* 65 (December 1930): 1124–39.

Rollins, Hyder Edward, ed. *The Keats Circle: Letters and Papers and More Letters and Poems of the Keats Circle.* 2 vols. 2nd ed. Cambridge, Mass.: Harvard University Press, 1965.

Rossetti, William Michael. *Life of John Keats.* London: Walter Scott, 1887.

"St. Thomas's and Guy's Hospitals." *The London Medical and Physical Journal* 32 (1814): 258.

Salisbury, William. *The Botanist's Companion.* 2 vols. London: Longman, 1816.

———. "Mr. Salisbury's Botanical Excursions and Calendar of Flora for May 1816." *The London Medical and Physical Journal* 35 (1816): 516–17.

———. "To the Editors." *The London Medical and Physical Journal* 35 (1816): 430.

———. "To the Editors." *The London Medical and Physical Journal* 37 (1817): 425–26.

Sallé, J. C. "Hazlitt the Associationist." *Review of English Studies* 15 (February 1964): 38–51.

Sandys, George. *Ovid's Metamorphosis Englished, Mythologized, and Represented in Figures.* Edited by Karl K. Hulley and Stanley T. Vandersall. Foreword by Douglas Bush. Lincoln: University of Nebraska Press, 1970.

Saunders, William. *Elements of the Practice of Physic, for the Use of Gentlemen Who Attend Lectures on that Subject. Read at Guy's Hospital.* London: Cox, 1780. MS. notes by Jane Sutton.

Scarlett, E. P. "John Keats: Medical Student." *Archives of Internal Medicine* 110 (October 1962): 535–41.

Severs, J. Burke. "Keats's 'Mansion of Many Apartments,' *Sleep and Poetry,* and *Tintern Abbey.*" *Modern Language Quarterly* 20 (June 1959): 128–32.

Sewell, Elizabeth. *The Orphic Voice: Poetry and Natural History.* New Haven, Conn.: Yale University Press, 1960.

Sherwood, Margaret. "Keats' Imaginative Approach to Myth." In her *Undercurrents of Influence in English Romantic Poetry.* Cambridge, Mass.: Harvard University Press, 1934.

Bibliography

Sickels, Eleanor M. *The Gloomy Egotist: Moods and Themes of Melancholy from Gray to Keats*. New York: Columbia University Press, 1932.

Sinson, Janice C. *John Keats and The Anatomy of Melancholy*. London: Keats-Shelley Memorial Association, 1971.

Smith, H. R. "Matthew Green, 1696–1737." *Notes & Queries* 199 (June–July 1954): 250–53, 284–87.

Sontag, Susan. *Illness as Metaphor*. New York: Farrar, Straus & Giroux, 1978.

South, John Flint. *Memorials of John Flint South*. Edited by C. L. Feltoe. Introduction by Robert Gittings. Fontwell: Centaur, 1970. Facsimile of 1884 edition.

Sperry, Stuart M. "Isabella Jane Towers, John Towers, and Keats." *Keats-Shelley Journal* 28 (1979): 35–58.

———. "Keats and the Chemistry of Poetic Creation." *PMLA* 85 (1970): 268–77.

———. *Keats the Poet*. Princeton, N.J.: Princeton University Press, 1973.

Spurgeon, Caroline F. E. *Keats's Shakespeare: A Descriptive Study*. Oxford: Clarendon Press, 1966.

Stillinger, Jack. "Another Biographical Sketch of 'Young Keats.'" *English Language Notes* 18 (June 1981): 276–81.

Stocker, Richard, trans. *Pharmacopoeia Officinalis Britannica: Being a New and Correct Translation of the Late Edition of the London Pharmacopoeia*. London: Cox, 1810.

Tatchell, Molly. "Elizabeth Kent and *Flora Domestica*." *Keats Shelley Memorial Bulletin* 27 (1976): 15–18.

Taylor, Thomas, trans. *The Works of Plato*. Vol. 2. London: T. Taylor, 1804.

"Third Report of the London Committee of Apothecaries and Surgeon-Apothecaries of England and Wales." *The London Medical and Physical Journal* 31 (1814): 259–61.

Thornton, Robert John. *A Family Herbal: Or Familiar Account of the Medical Properties of British and Foreign Plants, Also their Uses in Dying, and the Various Arts, Arranged According to the Linnaean System*. London: Crosby, 1814.

———. *New Illustration of the Sexual System of Carolus Von Linnaeus: and the Temple of Flora, or Garden of Nature*. London: T. Bensley, 1807.

———. *Practical Botany. Being a New Illustration of the Genera of Plants*. London: Symonds, White & Stockdale, 1807.

Thorpe, Clarence Dewitt. *The Mind of John Keats*. New York: Russell & Russell, 1964.

Unger, Leonard. "Keats and the Music of Autumn." In *John Keats: Odes*, edited by G. S. Fraser. London: Macmillan, 1971.

Van Ghent, Dorothy. "Keats's Myth of the Hero." *Keats-Shelley Journal* 3 (1954): 7–25.

Vickers, K. M. "Keats." *Guy's Hospital Gazette* 85 (1971): 37.

Vincent, Esther H. "A Medical Truant." *Surgery, Gynaecology and Obstetrics* (Chicago) 101 (November 1955): 647–52.

Waddington, Joshua. "Lectures on Anatomy and the Principal Operations of Surgery. Delivered at the Theatre, St. Thomas's Hospital; Between the 1st of January, and the 1st of June 1816; by Astley Cooper Esq." 2 vols. MS. Wills Library.

Bibliography

Wall, Cecil. *The London Apothecaries, Their Society and Their Hall.* London: Apothecaries Hall, 1932.

Ward, Aileen. *John Keats: The Making of a Poet.* New York: Viking, 1963.

_____. "Keats and Burton: A Reappraisal." *Philological Quarterly* 40 (October 1961): 535–52.

Wasserman, Earl R. "The English Romantics: The Grounds of Knowledge." *Studies in Romanticism* 4 (Autumn 1964): 17–34.

_____. *The Finer Tone: Keats' Major Poems.* Baltimore: Johns Hopkins Press, 1953.

Watson, John R. "Keats and the Pursuit of the Sublime." *Philosophical Journal* 6 (July 1969): 112–26.

Weiskel, Thomas. *The Romantic Sublime: Studies in the Structure and Psychology of Transcendence.* Baltimore: Johns Hopkins University Press, 1976.

Wells, Walter. *A Doctor's Life of John Keats.* New York: Vantage, 1959.

Whittaker, Sir Edmund. *A History of the Theories of Aether and Electricity.* 2 vols. 2nd ed. London: Thomas Nelson, 1951.

Wigod, Jacob. *The Darkening Chamber: The Growth of Tragic Consciousness in Keats.* Salzburg: Universität Salzburg, 1972.

Wilks, S., and G. T. Bettany. *A Biographical History of Guy's Hospital.* London: Ward, Lock, Bowden, 1892.

Williams, W. Hyatt. "Keats' 'La Belle Dame sans Merci': The Bad-Breast Mother." *American Imago,* 23 (Spring 1966): 63–81.

Wingent, R. M. *Historical Notes on the Borough and the Borough Hospitals.* London: Ash, 1913.

Withering, William. *A Systematic Arrangement of British Plants.* 4th ed. London: T. Cadell, 1801.

Wordsworth, William. *Poetical Works.* Edited by Thomas Hutchinson. Revised by Ernest de Selincourt. London: Oxford University Press, 1936.

_____. *The Prose Works of William Wordsworth.* Edited by A. B. Grosart. London: E. Moxon, 1876.

Wordsworth, William, and Samuel T. Coleridge. *Lyrical Ballads 1798.* Edited by W. J. B. Owen. London: Oxford University Press, 1967.

Wycherley, H. Alan. "Keats: The Terminal Disease and Some Major Poems." *American Notes and Queries* 7 (April 1969): 118–19.

Zwerdling, Alex. "The Mythographers and the Romantic Revival of Greek Myth." *PMLA* 79 (1964): 447–56.

Index

Index

Index

Index

Index

Novalis, 203
Nurse, female figures as: Cynthia, 183–84, 186; Indian Maid, 185–86; Peona, 178–80, 183, 214; Thea, 214; Venus, 183

Ober, William B., 205, 226
Obstetrics. *See* Midwifery
Ollier, Charles and James, 43
Opium, 20, 59–60, 204–05, 226, 227
Ovid, 108, 178
Oxford, 53, 69, 101, 201

Pain and suffering: Keats's reaction to while training, 20–21, 39; in Keats's understanding of life, 116, 132, 140, 164, 166–67, 182–86, 190–91, 212, 216, 218, 220–22, 225, 230–32, 238
Palsy, 184, 213, 227, 230
Passivity, 71–72, 96, 99–101, 106–08, 110, 118, 140, 204. *See also* Indolence; Negative capability
Pathology, 28, 45, 46; affected by emotions and imagination, 161, 173–75, 177, 179, 181–82, 189, 192, 194–95, 198–99, 207, 209, 210–12, 215, 217–18, 230, 234; affected by weather, 169–72, 175, 196–97; defined, 125, 162–63; state of, 160–62. *See also* Cancer; Fever; Melancholia; Palsy; Tuberculosis; Venereal disease
Pettet, E. C., 78
Pettit, Henry, 10, 135–36, 143
Pharmacopoeia Officinalis Brittanica, 32, 59–60
Philosophy, 5–6, 10, 51–52, 63–64, 71, 124, 188–89, 211–12, 220–22, 223, 225, 233, 237. *See also* Knowledge
Phrenology, 143–44
Phthisis. *See* Tuberculosis
Physician: Fanny Brawne as, 208–09; poet as, 11, 52, 148, 163–69, 179, 183–88, 189, 212, 216, 220–22,

224–25, 231–33, 235, 238; sympathy of, 182–86, 232, 237–38
Physicians: Colleges of, 17–18, 22, 86; Guy's, 30, 37, 167; Keats's, 46, 162, 202, 207, 210, 234; training for, 15, 17–18, 19. *See also* Apprenticeship, Keats's
Physiology, 20, 42, 46, 67, 109, 184, 192, 217, 237; and botany and chemistry, 121–22; defined, 125; Keats's courses in, 23, 27–30; as taught at Guy's, 24, 34. *See also* Brain; Hand; Nerves; Nervous system; Sensation
Plato, 100–01, 181
"Pleasure Thermometer," 56–57, 77–80
Poet, 164, 177, 223–25; Endymion as, 182–88, 216; in *The Fall of Hyperion*, 216–19, 228–33. *See also* Apollo; Knight; Physician
Poetic creativity. *See* Botany; Chemistry; Fever; Health; Passivity; Sensation; Weather
Poetical character, 154, 156
Poetry: axioms on, 69, 75, 106–07, 108; escapist, 165–66, 188, 212, 222–23, 228–29; as healing force, 164–70, 175–77, 188, 210, 228, 233; versus medicine, 21, 34–36, 42–45, 164–66, 232
Pope, Alexander, 186
Pre-Raphaelites, 8, 14
Priestley, Joseph, 12, 48, 56, 68, 119

Rasori, Giovanni, 193
Reason: "consequitive reasoning," 3, 11, 70–71, 134; and negative capability, 100, 111, 153, 214–15
Refinement (chem.), 56, 60–65, 67, 69, 70, 79
Reynolds, John Hamilton, 17, 74, 107, 134, 143, 196, 203, 208; Keats's letters to, 5, 71–72, 94, 99–100, 101, 107, 111, 124, 132, 133, 175, 189, 190, 196–97, 200, 211, 221, 232

289

Index